Occasions

Eudora Welty

Occasions

Selected Writings

Edited by Pearl Amelia McHaney

UNIVERSITY PRESS OF MISSISSIPPI ◆ JACKSON

www.upress.state.ms.us

Designed by Peter D. Halverson

The University Press of Mississippi is a member of the Association of American University Presses.

Library of Congress Cataloging-in-Publication Data

Welty, Eudora, 1909–2001.
  Occasions : selected writings / Eudora Welty ; edited by Pearl Amelia McHaney.
    p. cm.
  ISBN 978-1-60473-264-1 (alk. paper)
  I. McHaney, Pearl Amelia. II. Title.
  PS3545.E6A6 2009
  813'.52—dc22   2008049815

British Library Cataloging-in-Publication Data available

For John Bayne, Noel Polk, and Tim Seldes

Books by Eudora Welty

A Curtain of Green and Other Stories, 1941
The Robber Bridegroom, 1942
The Wide Net and Other Stories, 1943
Delta Wedding, 1946
Music From Spain, 1948
The Golden Apples, 1949
The Ponder Heart, 1954
The Bride of the Innisfallen and Other Stories, 1955
The Shoe Bird, 1964
Losing Battles, 1970
One Time, One Place, 1971
The Optimist's Daughter, 1972
The Eye of the Story: Selected Essays and Reviews, 1978
The Collected Stories, 1980
One Writer's Beginnings, 1984
Morgana: Two Stories from The Golden Apples, 1988
Photographs, 1989
A Writer's Eye: Collected Book Reviews, 1994
Country Churchyards, 2000
On William Hollingsworth, Jr., 2002
On William Faulkner, 2003
Some Notes on River Country, 2003
Early Escapades, 2005
Eudora Welty as Photographer, 2009
Occasions: Selected Writings, 2009

Contents

Biographical Note

Eudora Alice Welty (April 13, 1909–July 23, 2001) was born in Jackson, Mississippi, where she lived all her life save for studies at Mississippi State College for Women, University of Wisconsin, and Columbia University; sojourns of one to six months in New York and San Francisco; travels to Mexico, Italy, France, England, and Ireland; and writing residencies at Bread Loaf, Yaddo, and Byrn Mawr and Smith colleges. Her father, Christian, founding president of the Lamar Life Insurance Company, and her mother, Chestina, a teacher from the mountains of West Virginia, raised Welty and her two brothers Edward and Walter to think progressively and to learn by reading and from experience.

Beginning in her youth, Welty studied and practiced art, imagining herself to be a painter, and then a photographer, and finally a writer. She gives meaning and shape to her childhood, education, reading, and family relationships in "Personal and Occasional Pieces" in *The Eye of the Story: Essays and Reviews*, her memoir *One Writer's Beginnings*, and in her Pulitzer Prize autobiographical novel *The Optimist's Daughter*.

In the summer of 1936, Welty traveled throughout Mississippi for her job as a junior publicity agent for the Works Progress

Administration during which time she also took photographs. She did not succeed in publishing *Black Saturday*, a collection of photographs and stories, but she did have two exhibits of photographs in New York. Primarily of Mississippi places and people, the pictures were first collected in *One Time, One Place: Mississippi in the Depression: A Snapshot Album* in 1971. The subsequent collections, *Photographs*, *Country Churchyards*, and *Eudora Welty as Photographer*, demonstrate the breadth and range of her visual art.

Welty published her first story, "Death of a Traveling Salesman," in 1936. Four collections of stories and five novels followed. Her dozens of essays, book reviews, tributes, and comments published in national or local magazines carry the delightful, and sometimes exacting, often humorous, tone of her fiction. Twelve of Welty's forty-one collected stories garnered individual prizes, and she won numerous awards for individual works and for lifetime achievement including a Guggenheim, a National Institute of Arts and Letters Gold Medal for Fiction, and a Légion d'Honneur. Her work has been translated into more than fifteen languages, and in 1998, Welty was the first living writer to be recognized by the publication of her canon by the Library of America (*Complete Novels* and *Stories, Essays & Memoir*). Her subjects are the unremitting power of the past understood through memory and the complex mysteries of human relationships approached with honesty and imagination.

Throughout her lifetime, Welty was an active local and national citizen and a champion for education, for the arts, and for the writers she believed in. She campaigned for causes she found just and contributed her critical perspective to aid young writers just as successful writers had encouraged her. In her essays and reviews on creative writers, Welty steers readers back to the power of fiction—there, she wrote, is where you can find truth, if it is to be found at all.

Foreword

Occasions brings together more than sixty informal essays, stories, recipes, salutes, and tributes. As a volume of previously uncollected writing, *Occasions* supplements *The Eye of the Story: Selected Essays and Reviews* and contains highly relevant expressions of Eudora Welty's commitments, passions, wit, and self-revelations as an artist. Her keen evaluations of her first published story, "Death of a Traveling Salesman," of her Pulitzer novel, *The Optimist's Daughter*, and of her Morgana stories "June Recital" and "Moon Lake" from *The Golden Apples* came about after *The Eye of the Story* was published. Now included here in *Occasions*, they illustrate the kind of extended analysis that the author rarely shared about her own work.

Also included in *Occasions: Selected Writings* are the personal essays that she frequently wrote at the behest of social and civic groups such as the local New Stage Theatre and the Junior League and her journalistic essays promoting reading, education, and the arts. Her opinions appeared both locally and in national media: letters to editors of the Jackson [Mississippi] *Clarion Ledger*, *New Yorker*, *New Republic* (following the defeat of Adlai Stevenson for president), and the *New York Times Book Review*. In *Harper's Bazaar*, *New Yorker*, and *Vogue*, she published wise and witty pieces about Mississippi's summer heat, February's snow, and the difficulties and pleasures of photographing.

Writing of "Acrobats in a Park" (considered her earliest fiction), Welty realized that in this first story, she was "finding" her "true subject"—human relationships. Although this story "never made a book" as she says, it has elements found in the majority of her fiction: a "family fortress . . . narrowly besieged," a gesture, a still moment, a journey, an outsider, mystery, love, and passion. *Occasions* reprints six stories that "never made a book" to be read and pondered. "The Doll," "Magic," and "Retreat" are no less interesting than the stories Welty gathered for her first collection, *A Curtain of Green and Other Stories*, which for its time was incredibly full (seventeen stories). "A Sketching Trip" and "Hello and Good-Bye" from the 1940s came between two volumes of stories organized in ways that perhaps made these two pieces of short fiction outsiders of sorts.

Among the surprises in *Occasions* ("cause for fireworks" said one reader) are "Women!! Make Turban in Own Home" (inspired by Welty's adolescent reading of *Popular Mechanics*, this essay is a *tour de force* of wit), a foreword to Virginia Woolf's *To the Lighthouse*, and tributes to Flannery O'Connor and Isak Dinesen. Also here are a letter to the editor of the *New York Times Book Review* excoriating Richard Gilman for his page-one review of Reynolds Price's novel *The Surface of Earth* and an introduction to a sculpture exhibit by John Rood, her first publisher. Of another artist, José de Creeft, whom she first befriended in 1941 at Yaddo, a writing colony outside Saratoga Springs, New York, Welty noted that his "material is making the sculpture as he, simultaneously, is learning and working from it," a comment one could make of Welty's work also.

Welty was interested in arts of all kinds—painting, music, photography, and drama—even as she was writing. *Occasions* includes her 1948 skit *Bye-Bye Brevoort* that was to be part of a musical revue intended for Broadway, a review of a Jackson production of *Cat on a Hot Tin Roof*, and an unused press release that she wrote for Jerome Chodorov and Joseph Fields's 1956 Broadway adaptation of her novel

The Ponder Heart. As Welty tells us in her afterword to *Morgana*, when through her open windows she heard Belhaven College music students practicing, she heard "longings so expressed, so insistent, so repeated" that they "called up still more longings *un*expressed. I began to hear, in what kept coming across the street in the room where I typed, the recurring dreams of youth, inescapable, never to be renounced only naming themselves over and over again." This experience not only gave her the opening chords of her marvelous story "June Recital" and the themes of *The Golden Apples*, in which this story appears, it also reveals a method behind her work.

In her foreword to mystery writer Ross Macdonald's *Self-Portrait: Ceaselessly into the Past*, a project similar to *Occasions*, Welty observes that "Reading the succeeding pieces, you are really allowed to see the author not in time stages but all at once." In *Occasions*, we find Welty's inimitable cosmos "all at once." Here we find much evidence of Eudora Welty's involvement in the political world—locally and nationally, admiration for writers and friends, details of her real and imagined world, and we find everywhere—in her writing about painting, fairy tales, dance, and especially in her fiction—the "indelible human element."

Pearl Amelia McHaney
September 23, 2008

Acknowledgments

My most grateful thanks are due to Mary Alice White and Elizabeth Thompson, executrixes of the estate of Eudora Welty, for their enthusiasm, permissions, and encouragement. Without John Bayne's verve for collecting and Noel Polk's bibliographic research, and their years of generous friendship, *Occasions* would never have been realized. I thank Tim Seldes, Welty's agent who always answered my questions with a smile, and Judy Long, who thinks all good things possible, for their assistance in this as well as in other endeavors. And to Tom, thanks for the encouragement and love.

I. STORIES AND SKITS

Acrobats in a Park

The Zarros, a family of acrobats, are eating their lunch in a little park in the center of town. It is a day late in October when
the wind suddenly falls and the sun makes still objects warm to the
touch.

The Zarros belong to a circus which performed in Jackson the
night before but left at dawn without them. The van in which the
Zarros live and travel can be seen from here if one stands tall enough,
down the hill below the town, solitary on the circus grounds near
the river bridge, a worn red van painted in tall letters with the name
Zarro.

In the brilliant light and the almost-blue shade of mid-morning,
five of the six Zarros lie flatly in something of a square about the red
silk cloth and the paper bags. A chinaberry tree, turned the color of a
lemon, casts a round shadow, and the old man is sitting erectly against
its black trunk. Further away are tall straight trees just turning gray or
pink, and around the entire park is a screen of thick magnolias, all of

the same height, which are dark green like olive trees. Around behind the closed trees lies the horizontal plane of the city, with a dome and a steeple and far away on a hill an observatory with the lid raised. It is very still in the heart of the park. This is an old park, with pedestals bearing small concrete dancers on whose heads birds alight, a deeply shaded band pavilion, a fountain basin planted over with streaked banana plants. The leaves are falling slowly everywhere.

The family is very quiet in the park. There is Beppo, the old father; Nedda, the mother; the two young men who look nearly alike, Bird and Ricky; the child, Betty; and the outsider, a young woman. This is Tina. Her hair is blonde: she is most plainly a member of another acrobatic family who has married into this one. Bird is her husband.

Their bodies are all smaller and more long-waisted, darker, more hairy, more specifically outlined and developed than is becoming to the noncommittal "street clothes" they are wearing now. Their anatomical structure is both obvious and strange in such subduement. Ricky looks strangest of all, for his right arm is in a sling. It is only the old father who has dressed himself like an acrobat.

Beppo is old. Over the chinaberry roots, he draws his short legs up in their dusty dark-red velvet trousers, his silk-sleeved arms enclose them, his brown skimming fingers lock together. He has no words to say, and today he has no rest. Betty, his little girl, buttering her bread, watches him jump up again in the very next moment, to take another of his looks around. She cannot help observing that her father is really a little pigeon-toed, tipped too far forward in his posture, as if something flicks him from behind. She has noticed it for the first time this morning.

Nedda has spread a lunch upon two of Beppo's large silk handkerchiefs on the ground. It is everything they accumulated in walking through the town from the circus-grounds—sausages, fruits, buns, ice cream in cartons with little wire handles, hot tamales sold by a Mexican. They have brought along several unlabeled bottles of a dark wine. Near them in a tree are growing persimmons which Beppo has noticed.

At first they eat busily, with none of the confusion of most large families, and then none of them can eat any longer. From the town a clock is striking only eleven. Traffic rolls around the park behind the trees, a heavy fire truck passes, blowing its siren, and one of the wine bottles trembles and tips over on the ground, spilling. No one hurries to stand it up again, until Nedda gives a belated, sharp cry.

Bird feels Tina's stockinged foot touch his upper arm. He opens his eyes enough to look down the round surfaces of her body to her eager face.

"Look," she says smiling, the hint of malice in the protuberance of her tongue between her white teeth. She notices everything. "There."

She points with her foot beyond the statue to the little round, columned pavilion. It is not empty after all.

"In that merry-go-round?" asks Betty.

They all rise on their elbows and discover a shabby young man with his back to them standing alone inside. He makes a gesture, and they can hear his voice. He seems to be delivering a lecture to the empty park.

"People!" they hear him cry beseechingly. He throws out his arm in the loose sleeve.

Tina's eyes shine. They all look back at her and sink again under the tree. Bird watches Tina's head turn slowly as her eyes find all that may be seen through the trees—a clock tower, part of a white wall, a square with reflecting windows and electric lights burning behind them, the pale garden back of the governor's mansion where convicts, Negro men in stripes, rake the leaves almost motionlessly, and opposite, the tall dark Catholic church with its cross.

"A nice place," says Tina, and they all look at her again, as if to them all she has become simply unbelievable.

Now and then someone enters the park, but no one has stopped except a boyish girl who came early and read on a bench. At intervals she would sniff very loudly, but she never lifted her eyes from her page. Before long she got up and went away, with the purposeful stride of someone with no friends.

A very pale man strolls through the park and looks at them almost angrily. The park, his prominent eyes seem to say, is not an undesecrated retreat: everyone seeks it, everyone—even, at last, acrobats. In the next moment he tells them that he is on his way to the cemetery to lay the chrysanthemum he carries on the grave of a friend. But he has obviously never spoken to anyone else of this. He walks on in shame.

Another man who comes down the walk stares at the acrobats and says disgustedly to his little fat spaniel which hurries to keep up with him, "Now what would those carnival people be doing in this park? In *this* park?" After he has led the dog to a tree, he turns and looks back at them again from a distance, as if, thinks Beppo nervously, some disintegration had scattered them there upon the public property, and he expects to see things even worse when he looks again.

A little girl bounds into the park and stops dead-still. She remarks, "I'm going to play on the Maypole while Mania goes to confession."

The Maypole is an iron staff with small rusty handles on iron chains dangling from a wheel on top. After one long, absorbing look at the Zarros, who say nothing, the little girl walks up to the Maypole and begins to swing and turn around it, winding herself up.

Betty rises and takes a step toward her.

"Perlino," cries her mother.

Betty stops almost before she is called. She is big enough to realize for herself that this day is some unusual, in-between time, that they should all only wait quietly and not play or be rough, although they have never been inside a park before. She contents herself with watching the little girl, who wears a red dress, a blue hat, and glasses.

Perlino is a baby-name which Nedda sometimes calls her youngest child, after a little prince in a fairy tale who was manufactured of almond paste. They had hoped Betty would be a boy. Nedda smiles. She has a very short upper lip, although enough to show a narrow mustache. She lies back without waiting to see if the child obeys. Nedda is indifferent now. Her physical pleasure is over: the rest is nothing. Sometimes in the van at night she wakes all the others and cries, to see whether she has not lost their attention forever. They stop and get her something good to drink. But in the daytime she is silent and uncontemplative, and in the performance she now stands beside the formations or beneath the trapezes, her arm fatly curved, her forefinger out, in a permanent gesture of assumed wonder and helpfulness, and of course she takes the final bow.

Ricky's allowing his arm to break during last night's performance, Beppo's sudden-coming old age, Bird's impotency which she has so often lamented, Tina's contempt, her literal obedience to her, poverty and the stranded days to come—and now today—all these things are alike facts, like her own weight. Perhaps after a while it will all come out all right.

"Bring Mama a plum," she mutters to little Betty.

Bird, who lies listening to the shabby man in the pavilion, lays the paper of plums under his mother's tiny-nailed hand.

He has to reach across Ricky. And suddenly Ricky feels tears in his eyes. He loves his family. He has always been aware of the difference between Bird and himself. Pity, modesty, horror, reactions against the unwelcome spectacle of hope and penalty, and even an unwilling secret exaltation have been steadfastly dormant in his love for his brother. Now he feels like crying.

"Give me a plum too," he says.

"Do you hear him over there?" demands Tina. She looks from the pavilion to Bird.

I do not want the child, thinks Ricky angrily, in a sentence, as if he were about to speak. I will abandon him, in a town, a town like this.

"You are feeling good today, eh, Tina?" inquires old Beppo timidly. Perhaps it will be a man child, he thinks, and to the sound of a fanfare the image of the "Zarro Wall" rises again on the shoulders of a third stately, unsmiling boy.

Ricky props himself against the hard, ribbed trunk of the chinaberry tree. He holds his sling across his chest and watches the clumsy child tangle herself in the playground trapeze.

Ricky's is a perception of the physical world that is constantly betrayed by changes. In the world of Zarro, performing under a dome, he has always been aware of the contributing structure and function of every person and every movement, the pattern and timing of arms, legs, ropes, and catapults, the dimensions of his allotment of performable space, the speed, the balance, the pure objective figure of his life . . . Never before has he felt at all appalled at the intimacy between his performance and his life, between the routine and the desire, having thought they were one.

The more they have added to the act, the more ardently have his energies flowed. To keep working, the Zarros have been gradually forced to adopt every form of acrobatics—trapeze, feats of strength, balancing, juggling. From the first, Ricky has been quick to do them all. There is even the moment now when, to tango music, Bird and Ricky throw Tina back and forth between them across the stage, a sequence for which Nedda has made all three of them red sashes out of silk handkerchiefs.

The little girl swings herself noisily and cheerfully, stumbling in the dusty rut that runs around the iron pole. She looks back over her shoulder at the frowning Ricky, sticking out her tongue.

From where she is lying Tina calls, "Let's see you hang by your heels."

Ricky thinks, what if this, now, were the end of Zarro? He looks up wonderingly at the black and yellow vault of the chinaberry tree, but he is aware of the bodies behind him on the ground. It is they who are the foundation and support of his world. He knows the body of each member of Zarro to its limit of potentiality and vulnerability. He knows how good an arch each body makes. He knows how far it can stretch, how small and compact it can make itself. All his life the rise or decline of these surrounding figures has gone on about him, displaying the strength with which weight is borne, the probability and extent of hesitancy, the timing of contact, the lightness of falling. Practically and demonstrably he knows the pride of each body . . .

Tina keeps calling out, "You are poor. You are no good! Let's see you hang upside down," until the child blushes darkly.

Ricky hears old Beppo sighing, and he knows that the integrity of the Zarros took the form of an occurrence of a certain time each night: the "Zarro Wall," when all motion and relationship was lifted and directed toward one critical moment, built in the rigid time-worn combinations, in profile, and borne onward in routine to its finish with the flags of all nations.

Last night, when his arm did not hold, he saw old Beppo walk from the toppled structure blinking his eyes, all his features dim and diminished, as if he had been discovered in a hiding-place hitherto impregnable.

"Let's see you hang from your knees, you," says Tina to the child.

It is easy to see now that she is pregnant. In this plain dress she is far too solid and round. Last night, it was a difference in the weight, the moisture, and temperature of her body when she stepped into his hand that drove catastrophe into his very center. Forcing his eyes to the side and upward he saw her where she straddled the space between him and Bird, with little Betty just rising upon her back, and knew instantly. It burst in his brain, rebounded to his muscles—a sudden release, and an overwhelming sense of bliss.

Without warning the formation collapsed. All of them fell lightly in one beat of music. The band played on. So inexplicable had it been that for an instant little Betty stood straight, with her mouth drawn down in open dismay. Then she bowed in her brief, awkward dip. Old Beppo came walking out like a little, hunched man. Bird took a step back and waited away from them. Tina's face shone . . . And Nedda's fat arm still gracefully drew attention to the spot where the formation had stood. Applause broke from the audience, the louder because an attempt had failed.

In the next moment, when they began again, Ricky discovered that his arm was broken. Bowing, he had run lightly off the stage, wildly applauded.

Now it is next day. Still Tina's pregnancy is not an open thing. Altogether without words, the troupe has watched the broken arm set, and stayed behind the rest of the circus, walking through the streets and into the park. Beppo now and then touches Ricky on the bad arm, as if to comfort him for the inward violence which has been destroying him with its secrecy.

But Ricky is staring at Tina in the sun until his eyes literally hurt him. She is sitting untidily in the yellow leaves; she picks one leaf up and brushes her face and lips with it.

He is disturbed even now by any small careless deviation which she allows to touch her. This morning, the first one up, with her red comb she parted her hair an inch higher on her forehead. This too has altered her for him. A pattern over which his vision had begun another journey of recognition has shifted again before his eyes. His looking is a maze. In his incessant care, he can never quite find his way through a world which is being made so endlessly known to him.

The little girl's mother appears in the park. But she finds it useless to beg her child to leave the Maypole, the acrobats. With a calm, devoted expression she sits down on a bench to wait.

Tina smiles at Ricky, and so intense was his preoccupation with her lowered head that the change in her expression, the sudden approach, makes her seem a stranger.

"What is it?" he growls.

They all listen to hear what Tina will have to say to Ricky.

But still she will say nothing, and they remain wide apart.

All at once Nedda cries, "Why don't you go to confession? . . . Only across the street."

Whereupon the mother of the little girl gives Tina a challenging, fighting look from the bench.

Tina turns her eyes from Ricky's stiff lips, and stands up. She puts on her shoes. They see her walk away from them, off under the trees and lightly down the embankment out of the park. Glancing all about but never looking behind her, she crosses the windy street and walks up the steps of the church.

As she goes inside, Ricky closes his eyes and lies still. He hears no sound except the persistent screech of the chains and the short panting breaths of the little girl who will never stop playing.

Once there are footsteps marching. Loudly, in an almost military fashion, a pair of lovers walks toward them. Keeping in step, with their arms around each other, their faces blank in double profile, they are completely absorbed. They walk past the silent acrobats, who look up at them. Like tightrope walkers, they look nowhere; their balance is maintained from another source as they walk in a straight line directly through the park.

Bird turns from the sight of the lovers, rolls over on the ground and sinks his broad head in his folded arms.

Bird in his childhood was called "The Little Bird" because he could be tossed through the air across the platform, back and forth, from his father to his mother, so lightly, with his arms obediently held out like wings. Then he wore small blue or yellow silk dresses. Beppo would swing him about his head (a terrible smile directed from his younger face) until the sleeves would fill with wind, his body felt nothing, and his ears stopped up with a kind of thunder. Nedda would always catch him at the end and laugh.

. . . How fleeting it is! Bird lifts his head. Yet the lovers are still walking down the narrow walk, their arms clinging. He closes his eyes again, and the image of his wife which he always seeks comes tiredly to his mind.

She is through with her performance at last, under the great white beam . . . His thoughts of her are never directed upon that moment filled with the roll of drums, but hastily upon the moment after. To think of her in the very balance and center of her danger (and to think of her now in the church) would be impossible.

She is taking so long . . .

A little boy runs with a ball bat through the park and screams, "What's the time, Freddie?" And when the shabby man in the pavilion, giving a short, assertive nod, replies, "Long after six," he turns an eager face toward them, while the boy shouts with gratification. This must be a town joke, Bird supposes, to ask the afflicted man the time.

He digs his fists into his eyes to drive out the glare, and persists . . . There is Tina . . . a microscopic figure of acute vision, held compressed between his fist and his brain, no larger than a being in a teardrop. She moves, is still. The performance is over. Abruptly, her legs crossed, her weight lightly on the left foot, the red round mouth opened, she holds out her arm, and stands briefly in a sort of minute expansion, like something in bloom. There is a fleeting chord of brass—he can hear it—soft applause descends upon his wife, safety is hers, she bows her head and runs away, her hand lifted in farewell and promise: next time!

Betty wakes up restlessly, and turns her head. She has been sleeping against Bird's shoulder.

"There's a fly crawling on you, Mama."

Her mother does not answer.

Betty frowns. "Doesn't it tickle?" she asks.

But her mother does not answer. The fly crawls over her motionless hand and up her arm, and flies away.

What a long time Tina is having with the Priest!

By now, the sky has clouded over, and soon it will rain.

Nedda, risen a little unsteadily to her feet, looks up at the moving trees and waits until the rain, after the waiting above the city, reaches down. A gentle drizzle falls. Careful, like a finger, the steeple remains lifted . . . She stands under the trees. The touched mysterious shapes of watertanks endure, and the finished bridge. At the top of a street the full dome is closed—so small, thinks Nedda, lifting her palm,— like a pigeon. The light softly lets go the swelling trees like women beside the startling clocked towers.

"Look," says Betty, taking her hand.

Far off, the small observatory casement where stars are seen draws inward soundlessly. At that moment the statue beside her, pockmarked like a beggar and bitten by the sun, turns black.

"It's raining in this town," says Betty. "That little girl went home with her mother."

"Come on," says Bird, starting toward the pavilion, where the shabby man looks out.

But no one moves.

They look at the dark symmetrical church door under the arch. Ricky sprawls motionless, looking out over his bandaged arm, remembering with incomprehension and slow, unwilling deprecation his virtuosity in solo performances during the secret time.

Beppo has a persimmon. Squatting like a monkey, he bites into it. He crinkles his eyes and nods at his wife.

"All this—it has happened before," he says, and his face draws up from the taste of the persimmon.

A spasm crosses Nedda's dreaming face and all of a sudden she turns all the way round and laughs, clearly and thrillingly, like a young girl. It can be heard all over the park. Betty runs to her and climbs upon her breast.

The black door divides, the lighted side shows the pearly interior of the church, and Tina comes out. She has made her confession. She stands on the steps and reaches her hand into the rain. Ricky watches her: how she seems always to float down a stair! Then, looking over at them, she walks with her easy manner across the street to the park where they are waiting for her, standing, ready to go—Beppo at the head, Nedda at the foot of the little procession.

Welty dates this story 1935. It was first published in the French journal *Delta*, November 1977, pages 3–11, edited by Kenneth Graham.

Introduction to *Acrobats in a Park*

Written in, or about, the year 1935, and certainly one of the first stories I ever wrote, "Acrobats in a Park" was not published until 1977, in the November issue of *Delta*, a magazine issuing from the Université Paul Valéry in Montpellier, France, and interestingly devoting itself to Southern writing in America. The story reached its publisher, Claude Richard, through the kind auspices of Kenneth Graham, of the University of Sheffield in England. Mr. Graham had come across it in 1967 among papers of mine deposited in the Mississippi Department of Archives and History. When he wrote to me about the possibility of its appearance in *Delta*, I had all but forgotten there was such a story. But along with my surprise was an author's never-to-be-quenched hope fulfilled: accepted, after all. It appeared with an interesting and deeply sympathetic introduction by Mr. Graham.

A year later, in the November 1978 issue of the *South Carolina Review* published at Clemson University by Richard J. Calhoun, the story was given publication in my own country with an introduction by Jan Nordby Gretlund, a Danish scholar also interested in American writers of the South, who too had come upon the Acrobats in the Archives. A cosmopolitan history for a little story of eleven pages and forty years in a file box! I am happy to know that it is now making an appearance all to itself. Here is its turn, for it never made a book.

I recognize in "Acrobats in a Park" some risky things about my writing self as a beginner. It can hardly have occurred to me to ask myself first what I knew about acrobats; the answer would have been, as little as I knew about incest, Europeans, or the Catholic Church, also elements in the story. What *did* I know about, that urged me to write it anyway?

I knew very well, had known since early childhood, the experience of coming under the spell of travelling performers who appeared from time to time in my town—then a small town—of Jackson, Mississippi. It would be the event of the year to be taken by my parents to our Century Theatre, the Chautauqua, the Ringling Brothers Circus. I was exposed to the trusting wonder of seeing and hearing the visiting artists perform, the agonizing knowledge that they were not with us to stay. Galli-Curci, Blackstone the Magician, troupes of acrobats and clowns, were all as fleeting as dreams. How much more vivid were their appearances to me than those of visiting aunts and uncles, and how much more poignant. Aunts and uncles returned, but hardly, it seemed to a child, the troupe of Living Butterflies, wings unfurled, slowly ascending by their teeth while the band played them to the top of the tent.

Transient artists appear as characters in more than one early story of mine—"The Winds" and, in particular, "Powerhouse"—and in a later and longer story, "Music from Spain." These characters grew out of performances I'd seen of real artists; in their fictional roles they were something like marvelous messengers arriving from the greater outside world of life or art. But the earlier "Acrobats in a Park" centered on characters that were pure invention. (I don't know what benefit they got from my having seen Picasso's *saltimbanques* at about that time, my feeling for their isolation and their homeless intimacy.)

If the story earned a right to survive, I think it was because under the guidance of instinct, I made the acrobats into a *family*, and set them down on the ground in Smith Park in Jackson, in the shade of the tree I played under: a father, a mother, and their children. In performance, their act had been the feat of erecting a structure of their bodies that held together and stood like a wall. When I was writing about the family act, I was writing about the family itself, its strength as a unit and its frailty under stress. From family solidity to the Zarro Wall was only a step, and the test of its vulnerability was one step more.

What strikes me now, and what I was unaware of then, was that these acrobats were prophesying for the subject that would concern me most in all my work lying ahead. From points of view within and without, I've been writing about this Wall ever since and what happens to it. Indeed, in this story are the beginnings of the subject in its double form: the solid unity of the family thinking itself unassailable, and the outsiders who would give much to enter it—most often out of love and with the effect, sometimes, of liberation. The family fortress was variously beseiged in novels I later wrote, *Delta Wedding*, *The Ponder Heart*, *Losing Battles*, *The Optimist's Daughter*. Beyond the acrobats' figure of the bodies' interlocking, the subject of human relationships was what mattered to me. Before I was through with "Acrobats in a Park," I must have learned this for always.

Along with finding my true subject, something of my own obligation in learning my craft must have come clear to me too, with this story: there could be no source of honest writing that has been unable to make itself known, in the last analysis, from within.

Acrobats in a Park, limited edition, Northridge: California, Lord John Press, 1980.

The Doll

She did not drive away immediately. She thought dreamily, if Charles looks down from his office window he will certainly recognize my leghorn hat with the red cloth apple on it; and more obscurely, my hat will stand for me and for the words I said last night. Wondering if indeed he might not look down, she took off her glove and let the diamond flash in the sun, momentarily faint at the sudden accusing charge of light into her eyes: this was love. Quickly she hid her hand again. Charles had given her the ring the night before. She used her hand gently, as though it had been hurt, to touch the rag doll in the white dress which she had just bought at the church bazaar. She thought of Charles sitting leanly at his desk above, answering one at a time the questions of other people, his long hand to his head, thinking about problems of law: a chained myth when he was not with her.

It had been very warm inside the shop, very dark. Large groups of ladies talked at the tops of their voices. Her happiness, as though it were a scented flower, had in that crowded place become almost suffocating, and it seemed now to have put out queer shoots, like a disturbing tropical plant. Resentment, a queer sort of envy turned inside out, returned to her as she thought, lifting her chin, what do ladies shopping know of my love that has me bound so close to it that I am prostrate with its nearness. She was safer in feeling defensive; then she was not frightened.

When she had lifted a cloth to examine it, she had felt that she moved with secrecy, that her flesh was packed snugly to her bones, that the very apple on her hat was shrinking into an enigma. By being a secret from other people, she might be more known to Charles . . . but she shut her eyes tightly, in a sort of modest numbness toward this other side of the secrecy. She considered helplessly going to his office now. She was tempting the fear, that new tendril on the tropical plant, to clutch at her again. The sensation of faintness and nausea was becoming rhythmically gratifying. She would show him the doll. She laid her finger on its red crayon mouth; it had a strange, crooked smile, one undoubtedly drawn by a sewing lady, an amateur. Charles might tell her what it meant.

She looked up hurriedly and gazed at the stream of shoppers in the sun.

Slowly she realized that her eyes had found someone in the crowded street and were threading with him in and out among the other people. It was Charles.

He was alone. He was across the street, walking slowly north in her direction. She was half-smiling at once, forming her lips to say his name. Yesterday she would have called him. But how could it be Charles, who was sitting at his desk above her head, coming to the window to look down and recognize her leghorn hat? Was it Charles?

He did not wear his hat, if it were. His face looked darker, with the dark hair blowing over it in the late summer breeze that floated dreamily up the street.

She looked down at the doll, as if to adjust the image in her eyes, and then looked back. This could not be Charles. She reassured herself. This man was fatter. His stomach above his white summer trou-

sers looked almost plump. If it were he, it looked like him in another
time, in another place, which was not to be borne.

But it was Charles; impossibly, it was.

It was the way he was holding himself, the way he was walking, that
made the mystery. In the hot afternoon sun he seemed utterly relaxed,
even a little tired. He moved up the street in long, slow steps, carrying
his coat slung over his shoulder in a way she had never seen in him,
placing his legs out before him in an unhurried easy manner that was
somehow proud and inscrutable. He walked more slowly than anyone
else in the street. She noticed suddenly how graceful he was.

But she had never thought of Charles as being graceful! When she
was walking with him she thought of his nearness; she held with her
hand the sinews of his arm running under the cloth of his coat. She was
certain that together they walked much faster than Charles was now
walking alone; compared with Charles now, they appeared in retrospect
almost to have run; and she knew that Charles did not bend his head
down attentively and yet with superiority, as he did now, and look into
every shop window that he passed. Filled with panic, she saw that he
was then observing a window full of automobile tires which were round
and staring, undulating his head to them as he passed. She looked at
the window too, but as at something she could not comprehend.

He was almost across the street from her. She knew that he could
not see her; he was nearsighted: and he never saw me from his office
window, she thought falteringly, and yet gladly and ashamedly. She
smoothed the doll's dress. He was so calm. He spoke to no one. He
was there, he was bared to her eyes, he was displayed, he had taken off
his coat and lost his hat; she stared at him, but it was impossible not
to know that he was wrapped in a cloak of himself which he thought
unobserved, and from which the touch of her hand would roll like a
drop of rain, if, indeed, she should dare to touch him. Tears coming
into her eyes suddenly angered her, that she should be crying on Main
Street.

With an imperious gesture, one of her habits before she had become engaged, she laid her hand on the automobile horn. She would

sound it, and call him to her. The ring sparkled in the bare sunlight. Fear stopped her. Where was he going? What was he doing, so slowly, unhurriedly and alone? She saw him stop and look attentively into a window displaying flashlights, his shoulders broadened and relaxed into a downcurved line. She could see that across his shoulders his shirt was wet; the line of his underwear showed through. The back of his head, dark and angular, familiar, always touched her deeply. She clutched the doll, wanting to jump from the car, run across the street to him and touch his arm. "I saw you," she would say. But she could not.

He stood there only a moment. At last she leaned back in the car. Who was the more hidden, the more hiding, she thought, pressed against the cushion. Again he walked in his slow, obscure way up the street: she was watching him in the driving mirror. He crossed at an intersection and moved on, other people walked near him and around him, meeting him and passing him, and she lost sight of him.

Charles had been there. She looked at the little stores, their false fronts waving under the dense sky, and at the people. Charles? He was another person. He was not herself, and yet neither was he any of the others in the street. The slowness of his step remained with her. It seemed to tramp softly and heavily within her blood. She was sickened with some perception of mystery.

Dumbly she laid the doll in the seat beside her, where it lay with its arms outstretched, and drove away.

That night she took particular pains with her hair. She wore as many of the things he had given her as she could, the gold chain, the little pin from London. She was careful to lock the other things in the case. Fastening the pin, feeling its slender point at her trembling fingertips, she remembered her terror on the night of their first dance together, when she had just met him, when she had just come back from her boarding school in the north.

She heard his car door, his step on the walk, quick and eager.

Even while she was greeting him, she was leading him to the dark porch. She felt his footstep beating in the veins at her temples, the way it had been in the afternoon, in counterpoint against his faster step on the tile beside her. She was confused and shy, and drew back into the swing. He talked. Finally she leaned in a rush against his coat and shut her eyes, putting her fright against the smell of starched linen and the lotion he used on his face.

"What have you been doing today?" he asked her after a while.

"Oh, I did a little shopping. Nothing much."

She turned her head and looked into the magnolia tree. She heard him tearing open a cigarette package and striking a match. She could not ask him what he had been doing. In dread she looked up at his face. She saw his mouth, in the oblique matchlight, made of curves and bulges and its dark canyons, its size uncertain. Strange, often-kissed mouth. She remembered wonderingly, he has even been in the War, and a scratchy black and white landscape in a moving picture she had seen stood still in her head.

"You haven't given me a kiss," he said, turning his face down to hers.

She swept herself instantly free from his look and flung her shoulders against a pillow in the corner of the swing. She began to sob convulsively.

"Marie!"

It was her name in his voice, but she heard herself answering childishly, "That's my name!"

He stood over her pulling gently at her arms.

She did not know whether she said it or not. "I can't kiss you."

He turned her by the shoulders so that she was looking up at him. His face was in the dark, part of the still leaves. His body in white was like a shaft being sunk into her stupid brain. She stopped crying finally. Stretching her arms up to his head she pulled herself up and caught her lips to his in a kiss the end of which she dreaded more than she could bear.

"Now!" he said gently. He seemed a little shocked by her behavior. He sat down beside her. She raised her head and looked up at him but he said nothing else. She jumped up.

"Look, dear, what I bought today."

She led him in tumult into the lighted room. Her eyes throbbed with pain. The doll lay on its face on a table. She picked it up. Under the lamp her ring blazed into her eyes.

"What is it? What's it for?" he asked.

"It's just a doll. Just a funny doll. I bought it while you were busy today. I was going to surprise you."

"I thought you would be at home all afternoon sleeping," he said.

They stood apart, at a loss. She touched her engagement ring, with a gesture strangely like wringing her hands. Then quickly holding the doll by its un-elbowed arms, she made it glide in its long dress over the tabletop. He began to smile, but did not offer to take the doll and look at it.

"It was just something I decided I wanted."

"You're so strange tonight," he said. "My darling."

"What's she smiling for?" continued Marie. She pouted like a little girl, and listened askance for his reply.

Suddenly, as if signalling from the uncurious outside world to their dilemma, came the sound of the fire-siren, and the close-coming, penetrating roar of firetrucks. They laughed suddenly, suddenly snatched from their aloneness and projected into the world.

"Let's go to the fire!" they cried together.

In the car they saw where the sky was red and went in that direction.

It was a house on the other side of town. They left the car and walked closer. Leaves of the trees they stood under framed the red spectacle, which crowds of people stood silently watching; they were the new-comers.

Black, round clouds of smoke rose rhythmically from the yellow box the fire made, and floated away to the south. The burning made a vibration, a trembling, invisible curtain in the air, and now and then leaves from the trees over their heads would suddenly ignite and quickly perish in dying triangles of blaze.

They stood side by side watching. Separately, and then slowly to-gether as if hypnotized they saw the long, red scarves of flame part and disclose a little square window, and there, standing with stick arms raised like a doll, a woman waiting to be rescued; then, lowering their gazes, which were twisted together into one strand, they saw the lad-der and the fireman in his helmet ascending. It was like the crude ac-tion of opera, they felt, and then, their arms tightly touching, believed gradually, as the man climbed, that indeed they were the ennoblers as well as the helpless projectors of this fiery danger, this cheap res-cue pantomime: they were the music of the opera, the reason for this compulsion and crudity; and in tumultuous peace and self-worship at last they threw themselves with haste into each other's arms, hiding their eyes from the glare of the burning house in the shadows of each other.

In their throbbing pride they walked to the car and drove for a while over the little square blocks of the city, feeling like precious jew-els, not like people who might be afraid again. They were in horror of speaking.

Finally Marie lay in sudden exhaustion against Charles, her whole body relaxing and feeling dead and tender toward him.

He was saying something softly. "I wonder how we can be so sweet to each other—what makes us be so sweet to each other—and some-times we seem a thousand miles apart—until—do you know—?"

"No." Her whole flesh began to rally about her surfeited heart, and she was glad at last to hear him, to desert her fear for his own. "No," she said, comfort and contrition deepening her voice until it was round in her throat like fruit. "Don't wonder. Just—*now*—"

The Tanager 11, June 1936, pages 11–14, a bimonthly journal published at Grinnell College in Iowa from 1925–1948. "The Doll" was reprinted in the *Georgia Review* 53, Spring 1999, where editor Stanley W. Lindberg noted this praise by H. L. Menken: "*The Tanager* seems to me to be the best thing of its sort coming out of American colleges. I always read it with great pleasure."

Magic

One foot curled around and hooked the other legging; his round boy's hip, curved like a hard green apple, swayed green-khaki against Capitol Street as he bent over and marked negligently on the lamppost with his dead cigarette. His elbows jutted with unconcealed intentness from the short sleeves of the Western Union shirt. He drew a circle and filled it with more and more spokes, and did not smile. He heard her stop and clear her throat, but he was not going to look up.

"Did I keep you waiting?" She had a voice lightly shrill and pleading.

"Naw, you're like as not early."

Her eyes were as big in her face as a cat's, and she began looking at him slowly, the way a cat does. It was a day between winter and spring. She held her coat in tightly with her folded arms, the shorthand notebook hanging yellow over them against her brownness. She wore a new hat.

"Well, ain'tcha gonna say hello?"

She waited, but she could not stand still. Just ahead, a few yards away, her girl friend waited too, but she was waiting for the interview to end so they could walk on home. She stood stock still, only her eyes and jaw moving, hand on hip, holding her notebook in her crooked arm, looking out and away over the street, first here, then there, then back again, without moving her head. For a minute she would seem to be listening to the oracle in her chewing gum, and then she would go on looking some more, batting her lashes, the chewing a disparaging accompaniment to her eyes. Two black horns of short hair had been folded down and sheared with sibyllic sternness into her ruddy cheek. Her fat feet were in a V.

"Hello," said the Western Union boy finally, looking beyond the post at the girl in brown. He still stood bent over, drawing. It would be hard to know, such was their confusion and desire, the distinction between what had been their past and what would be their future. The girl friend alone patted her foot in distant impatience.

Still hugging herself and her notebook, the girl in the brown coat came a few steps nearer, and began to smile. Then it seemed as if she could not stop smiling. She had a few pale freckles on her chin, which probably could not be seen at night, but only in the daytime like this. She looked at the boy, but his eyes ran around the wheel he was drawing over again with his dead cigarette, and back and forth across the smutty spokes. Watching everything he did, though she could not from where she was see what he was drawing, but bending and moving her head as though at some inner distraction, her eyes followed him as he turned and spat between his teeth into the street.

"Whatchu doin' up town?"

"Why, I come to meet you here."

"Yeah, but whatchu been doin'?"

"We been up at shorthand."

"What you laughin' about?"

"Nothin'. Not a thing."

"Anything funny about me?"

"Aw! No!"

He tossed the cigarette stub into the air, caught it on the back of his hand, and dropped it gently into the street.

"Well, when I gonna see you?"

"In church."

"Before that."

"I'm scared."

"Where we go tonight?"

"Maybe Mary Agnes. But I 'o' know."

"How's that gonna be—Mary Agnes?"

They both looked at the girl who was chewing gum and waiting.

"I 'o' know."

"Your ma'll think you just spent the night."

"We could go walkin', just . . ."

"Where, up on West Street?"

"Uh-huh."

"Naw. I 'o' wanta go walkin' up on West Street. See you in church."

"All right." She was still smiling, although her eyes faltered.

He said, "I tell you. You gimme phone."

"I did, this mornin.'"

"I' be there."

"Reckon sure you will be?"

"You gimme phone call 'bout four, four-thirty."

"Maybe I call you 'bout five."

"Four."

"I call you 'bout five o'clock."

"Get me four, four-thirty, quarta five."

"What you think about . . . we go to Mary Agnes?"

"Where's Mary Agnes live?"

"You know. She knows you. She lives up yonda on West Street."

"Up by the cemetery?"

"Uh-huh, on up yonda past." She looked up. "You know."

"Call me up."

"Well, I call you."

"Wipe that smile offa ya face, you always smilin', people think you crazy."

"Oh, I been laughin' all day long." She looked crestfallen. She moved back and forth on her low heels, like a child on new roller skates. Her girl friend slid her eyes toward her, but remained motionless.

"You're crazy," he said.

"Naw, I been laughin' this way all day long."

"I see you in church." He straightened up.

"Well, if we don't go to Mary Agnes."

"Aright, call me four-thirty."

He was halfway across the street, where the Western Union office was. Her girl friend had started walking on, broodingly switching the bulge in her coat behind. The younger girl in brown stood still for a minute and then ran, her shorthand book bobbing, and caught up.

It was a little before eight o'clock that night. In the room the two curtainless windows were stretched over by pinpricked green paper shades, ragged like banana leaves in winter, against which the un-shielded electric bulb, pendant from the cracking center of the ceiling by a knotted cord, threw clear shadows when the girl moved back and forth dressing. On the blue iron bed lay her shorthand book. There were no pictures on the wall; the roses on the wallpaper by the bed were outlined and shaded with pencil. The girl's school dress hung, still warm and round at the sleeves, on top of the brown coat over a cane chair.

The girl, whose name was Myrtle Cross, was walking back and forth before the mirror which hung on a bent nail above the wash-stand. In its narrow blurred surface she got an unfaithful picture of how she looked. The light splashed in the mirror like the moon on waves, and sometimes she would see behind her her own shadow on the window-shade grow enormous when she crossed the floor, waving at her like a hungry tramp.

She stood in her stocking feet looking steadfastly at herself, as best she could, in the rose-colored crepe-de-chine dress. It had cost $3.98.

It had a fancy light blue crocheted bertha and blue corded laces down the bodice, against which she breathed now with difficulty. The pulsing contrast of the two colors, which had made it seem impossible that the dress in the store window should ever belong to her, filled her with excitement, and the pupils of her eyes, watching now the application of round brick-pink spots of rouge to her cheeks, were immense and almost blank of light. Her mouth gaping black under the beating light with complete suspension of breath, she rubbed on lipstick with her finger in pushing movements, deeply and energetically, as insistently as she would ring a doorbell. Her lips, released, trembled slightly and bulged into fulness.

She wished she could afford to have her permanent set, like some of the girls up at shorthand. She imagined her hair, which was now flying out under strokes of the pink comb, crusted close in even ridges down both sides of her head, with a stiffened froth of circled curls over each ear. She sighed. Her breath spread over the glass and obscured the disappointments; and smiling like Marlene Dietrich she slowly disclosed, by drawing her finger through the film, her close image in the mirror, eyelids falling, mouth stiffly and ambiguously smiling. "I love you," she said.

She licked her fingers and slowly plastered her eyebrows into shape.

She had to put on the same shoes she had worn all day. They were still warm at the toes against the cool stiff foot of her Sheer-O-Sheer stockings. Sitting on the bed, she looked up into the mirror, for she must observe herself every minute, all along, and saw herself lacing her shoes. Even in this abject posture she was satisfied that she did not look at all the way she looked when she did not have a date, or in the daytime.

The clock in the living room struck eight rapid strokes.

Myrtle jumped a little, tied the knot, and hurried to a shelf under the window where a Kewpie Doll stood. Her trembling fingers reached under its dusty braid-trimmed sateen skirt and brought out a small, lustreless phial with a gilt sticker hanging by one corner to its surface. She did not want to lose the sticker. It said "Magic Love Philtre." She had sent a dime with a coupon cut from a movie magazine to Kansas City. Her girl friend had shown her the coupon and laughed and winked, and then looked strangely solemn.

She pulled out the black-crusted cork stopper and with her forefinger placed a drop of the liquid behind each ear, one on her collarbone, and one on her lips. She added another under her nose where she could smell it. The odor was stinging and strong, her heart beat loudly, and she thought of the smell of red plush seats on a slowly starting train.

She really heard a whistle blow across a field. In a sudden sadness, a fit of saying goodbye to she did not know what, she clutched the Kewpie Doll, talking to it roughly and sweetly, in a hushed monotone. "Honey baby little old thing we run away won't we we go hide us out in field play all day, nobody get us, nobody find us, we go, won't we baby baby baby—" She drew the dusty face with its sweet bisque-smell and its unshut eyes against her cheek as though to console it against some immeasurable sacrifice and sorrow it would have to bear. But her face was soon puzzled and forgetting in anticipation of the door; she was not saying goodbye to anything she had known very well.

There was a materializing whine of the screen door and a rap on the glass pane. Myrtle heard the scrape of her mother's rocking chair and the hurried knock of her shoe against the floor in the back hall.

"I got my shoes off, Myrtle!" whispered her mother through the passage. "You go to the door."

Her father was on the cot in the back, asleep. He was a policeman.

"That's all right, Ma," said Myrtle evenly, looking in the mirror and fixing an expression of anticipation on her face. "It's only Ralph. It's for me."

Then picking up her coat and not moving a muscle of her smile she walked into the front room.

"Why, hello, Ralph!"

"Hi."

They were both different from the way they were on Capitol Street in the daytime; their eyes shone in acknowledgment.

Ralph had scrubbed his red bumpy face into complete sullenness. He wore a pair of dark green trousers with darker green bulges below the knees, and a brown coat and shirt, with a grey bow tie on an elastic at his collar. His raked hair was wet. He stood with his hands fumbling over the knots in the weakened coil-spring on the screen door, and he looked from Myrtle's smile to the wall where there was nailed a tin Coca Cola sign in the shape of a bottle with a thermometer in it.

"You all be good, Myrtle. You're holding the door open!" called her mother from the back hall. Her voice was soft; she had been reading "Dream World."

"Yes'm!" She looked at the wet strands of Ralph's hair and then down at his eyes. They looked as though the blood rushed into them when he spoke.

"Wanta let's go walkin'?"

"I'm goin' walkin', Ma!" she called.

Mrs. Cross cooed absently.

Ralph was already out on the porch. She shut the front door behind her, bidding goodbye again, but weakly with a glance, as if to arrange and harden the already well-moulded scene of the upright piano with its inflamed maple varnish, the sheet music of "Girl of My Dreams" on the rack, and on top her photograph taken a year ago and a blue glazed flower pot over which sagged in abandon a geranium plant with dusty leaves.

A streetlight hung beyond the branches of an elm tree. As they walked nearer, it made the small new leaves swell and gleam like bubbles.

Myrtle walked beside Ralph, struggling by genteel degrees into her coat. Ralph stepped away for a minute and balanced with one foot on a small water-hydrant in someone's yard, and then caught up.

"Where we goin'?" he muttered.

"Well, you said let's go walkin'," she countered.

They trudged in silence.

"Reckon will the moon come up?" she asked in her shrill voice. She stretched her tightened throat, looking up at the misted sky.

"Good night, not over there, anyway," said Ralph. "Ain't you got any sense of direction? Look over yonda where the Enterprise Market is, maybe you'll see it come up over yonda sooner or later."

She looked at this close dark triangle of roof. From an open window of the house on the corner came a sudden flood of Hawaiian music from a static-pricked radio. Their heads turned together toward the grovelling sweetness of the guitars.

"Oh!" She backed up and caught Ralph by the arm. He took his hand out of his pocket and laid his wet palm against hers.

"Listen!" she whispered as they stood still. "Ain't that beautiful!"

Listening, they began to move aimlessly around under the open window, their arms about each other. The chorus was played over and over. In the room they could see a family sitting under a fringed lamp, their heads sunk as though all their necks had been broken.

Ralph stood with one foot on a For Rent sign in the yard. Myrtle clasped his thumb tighter in her fingers.

"We can go over to the cemetery and walk around," he said, still balancing, and jumping down added, "I bet you're scared."

"Uh-uh." She continued to hold his thumb. "I reckon I know there ain't any such things as ghosts."

"If you don't like it, shut up," said Ralph. He was talking to himself and she was not listening. "I know plenty women that do." He turned over on his back and then over again on his stomach and began to cry. His cheeks were like big swelling knots that would close up his eyes.

Myrtle looked straight up at the sky. The moon had come up but she did not look at it. She felt no need to turn her head and look at the moon. It was over her left hand. Beyond her foot was the statue of the little lamb in curly dirty stone. By her other foot was the tall bush with the red scalloped flower blooming on it. It was a japonica bush but Myrtle did not know that; she had never seen one before.

Behind her was the big stone angel standing up with its arm pointed straight into the sky. It had looked so big and close at first.

Myrtle began to move her fingers. She felt a blade of grass, wet and thin with dew, that clung to her thumb, and then, with her fingers, the round ground, round and hard.

"We've been layin' here on a grave," she said, but her lips were so stiff she could not hear what her words were.

Ralph had been crying for a long time. His voice went chug-chug, chug-chug, over and over, like an owl at night when people are listening all alone. She was content to lie still and keep looking at the japonica flower turned to the moonlight. Its scallops led people around and around it, the way a song did, played over and over again late at night by the calliope at the Fair below the hill, that could be heard by people in their beds lying in the dark.

She would never have remembered to go home, or to change from lying there, listening and looking, and empty.

But then she saw a man looking at her over the hedge on the back street. He was a man with a black felt hat and he was laughing without making a sound, thrusting his black hole of a mouth outward at her like a funnel.

That had been it. It was over. That had been the thing.

The man lifted his head and shoulders up and laughed and then went on.

She screamed again and again. Her arms and legs struggled, she pushed herself onto her knees, shocked, as if it had thundered somewhere in the outside world; she pulled at Ralph, who sat up and looked at her, and then rushed from him, running ahead, knocking in silence against the resisting tombstones, catching her breath and screaming again. She never looked behind her. She heard her footsteps pounding on the spongy ground and then louder on the sidewalk under the dark window where the music had played to them, up her walk, up her front steps, into the front room which opened like a box, to the sight of the geranium.

In her room she tore off the dew-stained dress and laid it carefully on the chair over her dark school-dress. In her nightgown, tiptoeing, she found the little phial and dropped it hastily out the window into the flower-bed. She looked down and saw it. It was there, all right, but it was not broken. It had stuck on end, and stood in the flower-bed like another stem, rising up to grow.

She closed the window. In bed she caught up the Kewpie Doll. She muttered and moaned as if to console it, and whispered and pleaded with it until she was very sleepy. She could not forget the man in the big black hat who had laughed without any noise.

Ralph walked home by way of Capitol Street. At first, on leaving the cemetery, he had stumbled a little, but by the time he reached the lighted street he had thrust his wet hands, with the bits of grass sticking to them, confidently into his pockets, and now strode along with broad steps, shifting his shoulders from side to side.

I knew it would scare her, he said to himself. I knew she would get scared and run off like a jackrabbit.

He looked at the clock in front of the jewelry store. It was the first time he could not have guessed within five minutes what time it was. He stopped and leaned against a wall, and stood with his weight on one foot, his other foot thrown across his toe knocking rhythmically against the sidewalk. He started to whistle, but his breath had not come yet. He looked into the interior of the hall, lighted and full of smoke, as though a gun had been fired off, and watched the men shooting pool. After a minute or two he grasped the slick iron door handle, pulled it with a quick wrench, and went inside.

Manuscript 3, September–October 1936, pages 3–7. Welty's first story to be published, "Death of a Traveling Salesman," was accepted with "Magic" on 19 March 1936, by *Manuscript* editor John Rood. See also "Looking Back at the First Story" and "John Rood" elsewhere in *Occasions*.

Retreat

All of a sudden Norris had left Granville, Indiana, and caught rides south until he reached Vicksburg. He stood empty-handed where he had gotten out of the car, at the foot of the town by the canal. Three days ago, after he had almost been taken up for loitering by a Granville policeman and Elsa had walked out on him two nights in one week, he had cried on the bed, out loud, with his mouth pushed down into the pillow. He knew he had felt then that his mother would take care of him. Vicksburg was where she lived. He could see the house, a box in the higher distance, on the edge of the naked hill. He had not seen it in twelve years.

He looked furtively behind him toward the river, where the sun, striking the sides of thick jungly trees, made a green fruitlike vision, trembling in glassy waves of heat. As though his skin had turned sensitive to light, he flinched, and stood suddenly full of memory, off to himself in the sunset on the riveredge like a child hiding from school, with his mother's house there in the corner of his eye. As a little boy

he had walked in his sleep. Now, in a passion as relentless and mean-
ingless, he had stolen money and shot two men, for a woman like Elsa.
Of course his mother, who in his mind had no face and no words, only
warmth, would not hear this or believe it, and it would not be real in
Vicksburg. His mother had never spoken to him of the complications
which opened dark sacks over one's life with a loosening drawstring,
permitting unfamiliar and terrible things to fall upon one's head. She
had never said one word of the need to endure betrayal, to steal and
make violence; or predicted the unsupportable drag of the heart or the
way a hurt could spread wider and wider over one's life until it was as
shapeless as life itself. He heard a child kick a stone into the canal, and
watched the ripple spread. He felt very helpless, almost wounded. The
thought that his mother was there in Vicksburg would spring up like
a wind filled with forgotten odors. A sudden simplicity fell over him,
and with an impulse which like a string in a toy involved and short-
ened his whole tired body, he began to run over the cobblestones, up
the steep hill, toward his mother's house.

The house was dark. It looked secret and safe there at the dead-
end of a street, so far back that it jutted partly over the edge of a bluff.
There were the dark lilies growing high across the front of the house,
with spear-shaped leaves, black in the twilight. He looked again behind him and went up the path, which was familiar, leading straight to
the low door which rested level with the ground. Under the lowered
shade he could see a dim light in the back of the house. There were no
sounds. He knocked. When he heard the heavy footsteps he remembered his mother's size, her moist embraces. He opened the door and
walked into the dark hall saying "It's Norris, mother, I've come back,
I'm sick . . . " and almost fell.

Her gasps, her hasty soft arms, drew him in. He let her hug him
and kiss him, wrap him in questioning tears, lead him through familiar rooms, feed him, cover him up in bed. He went to sleep obediently
like a child.

But in the middle of the night he woke up. He did not know where
he was. The walking and uncertainty frightened him. Cowering, he

looked out the window. He saw nothing. Everything was diffused with moonlight which churned through the air like smoke. He realized that he was actually standing at the window, looking down unprotected into emptiness. As though it were some sort of hellish destination he had reached through Elsa and the pursuit of those who wanted to punish him, he stared down with an acceptance of finality. Sighing, he let his hand fall from its grip on the curtain. When he heard his mother groan in her sleep in the next room, he remembered where he was. Childlike trust returned and he sank back into bed, drawing himself into a knot, covering his head with the sheet, although the night was stifling. He went back to sleep almost hurriedly.

The days in Vicksburg began. The mother and son lived on a small pension and on the proceeds from the mother's baking. Norris went for a walk every day, at first. He made no attempt to find work: that would have meant thinking of the future. Besides, his mother said she would not have him try to work, for he must rest and regain his health. She wanted to support him. Norris did as she told him; he was unable not to obey her. She talked to him constantly, comforting and silencing him like a vague dream. Norris gradually occupied himself to a lesser and lesser degree. He did not read the papers, and he stopped his walks down to the river. He did not even go into any rooms except his own and the kitchen, which was on a small back porch adjoining it.

The summer was long and desperately hot. White banners of heat floated each day over the river, dust scattered down the hills. Norris did not seem to suffer. There were violent thunderstorms which bent the thick trees and pushed the water into a tangle of currents. But Norris did not see the trees or the water. Once he stood on the small kitchen porch during a storm. While he could hear his mother moving about in the other room, he felt no longer a part of anything that happened. When the lightning struck a tree next door, he was unconcerned, as if he wore a long invisible garment of protection.

He only gradually recognized in the place of his faceless and wordless protector a heavy and untidy woman, with large asymmetrical features—one eye was larger than the other, the mouth was slanted.

In her monotony and constant presence, his mother seemed part of the pressure of summer. Her movements were slow and cumbersome, she never dressed completely because of the heat. Her body gave off an oversweet odor. While she worked her big breasts were shoved out like steaming covered dishes. Most of her talk was about her beliefs, hopes, and fears for Norris, as though his life had not yet begun. Constantly walking into the back room where he lay on the bed, dragging a flowered wrapper over the matting behind her heels, telling him that whatever happened she would take care of him, she approached as easily as if all this were years ago the wishes of his heart.

From recognition of her appearance, he presently became aware of the violence of his mother's personal traits. Any sound she might make reached him magnified to deafening proportions. He was startled by her whistling speech and panting sighs, her heavy groaning yawns, her explosive sneezes which she followed with a sort of cry, her sniffling and swallowing, the slap of her feet when she went barefooted early in the morning, and even the extreme splashing with which she washed her face and arms before she went to bed at night. Every night she would walk with assured clumsiness into his dark room to kiss him goodnight. Her size seemed enormous. She would bend over him, heaving great wind-sighs of tenderness. "Your mother loves you," she would say, and, while he drew himself even smaller to receive it, give him a noisy kiss on the mouth. In the night he would almost listen through the wall for the inner sounds of her body when she lay asleep. He would feel quiet and separated from her only when she asked questions about his life in Indiana. He could tell her nothing, feeling dumb and forgetful. Gradually his memory had become his only privacy. His mother had folded him once more to her breast.

When summer ended it was as if a lid had finally been lifted from a steaming kettle. The sky retreated from the river, the heat escaped. Norris wore his coat in the house. He had a sort of fever that made him tremble with cold.

One day he went outdoors. He noticed the torn tree lying on the ground next door and felt a belated and frantic shock at its destruction. He could hear his mother walking heavily inside the house, just beyond the wall. Some paradox of her great oversweet bulk and its function of envelopment made him start to attention: she made him remember Elsa.

He walked up and down the sidewalk in front of the house. Each trip displayed the fallen tree. A chill wind swept his back. Nothing about Elsa had ever enveloped him. How well he remembered that she was flat, small, rigid, mocking. Abruptly he stopped and allowed past time to catch up with him. It stared at him, like a stranger—no, like a neighbor he rarely saw—pointing to the love he had given Elsa, tortured by her derision. It narrated that she allowed him a completely lonely pleasure of her body, and that often if he woke up later in the night he found her gone. It implied bitterly to him that she had destroyed his child. He remembered. She could walk noiselessly and quickly, slip through the door, take him unawares, spy upon him, laugh at him. She laughed at him for holding up the filling station after she told him to, and shooting the two men so ineffectually that they still lived to identify him when he was found; and she seemed to harbor him in her room only for the pleasure of a threat of betrayal. Yes, he remembered when he was reminded, how if she happened to wear the ring he bought for her with the stolen money, he would be filled with humiliating happiness.

He walked up and down. Past time was inside him now. In Indiana he had been a prisoner, confined by his own desire until he should wish to run away. Now, the ever-approaching figure of his mother stood beside the leering one of Elsa. Indiana was in Vicksburg. There was now no place that he could trust. All were faithless.

While his mother cooked many little sweets for him and coaxed him to eat, he felt suspicious. She might betray him, poison him . . . He watched closely his secretly recovered misery, his desire for Elsa, his hiding from pursuit, his crimes and mistakes which his mother waited to smother away. He hardly ever left his back room. He stayed in bed until dinner time. When he remembered how the earth fell away beneath the window he was even afraid there.

One day, out of a clear sky, his mother told him he must go to the circus. She pretended that it would be good for him. He laughed. She pulled him out of bed and scolded him and gave him a dollar.

He pleaded with her; he had not even had a haircut: he looked too funny. He walked out trembling and untidy, filled with distrust. People stared at him on the street. He heard them all talking about him.

By the time he reached the circus grounds he was burning with fever. He had not been in a crowd of people for a long time. He felt safer inside the tent, but he was minutely apprehensive, looking carefully into the face of everyone who came near him. He sat on the front row, with the children, so that he could run away quickly in case of emergency. The people in the circus were letting the noise of the band and the smells penetrate through the holes in his skin. He was terrified at the trapeze performances, that such things should be attempted, and the animals filled him with dread, their roars vibrating through his very hair. All this was done to torment him. He burned with complete hatred for his mother, who had sent him out. In terror he tried to think of a place to hide. Here he would only be eaten by lions or suffocate under the falling tent. He looked all around him and up above. A girl was walking a wire backwards. He felt horrified at the concerted roar of the crowd which had discovered his own teetering danger. The girl on the wire, with a knowing smile at him, suddenly threw something which fell into his lap. It was a dead pink rose. All faces turned inward toward him. He felt as if he would faint. He summoned the strength to throw the rose far from him. He stumbled out of the tent and up the hill, with the rattling drums in pursuit.

That night as he lay in bed, burning from his exposure to danger, he dreamed that he rode to Indiana, to Mississippi, in a circle, backwards along the roads he had come. The policeman took pity and stopped him and bore him far away to jail. It was after long wearying years. At last he was within sight of the cell that was to be his. It was small and dark, warm, sweet and square. There was no door. This cell was within another cell, which was in the bottom of the Mississippi river, underground and under water. Speculatively, he walked around it once in his mind—that was its measurement. The window was only rudimentary, too high and too well barred to allow sights and sounds to enter. But that was the way he would enter.

Somehow he was there just outside, and with no effort at all he pushed his body through. He tore only a thin curtain of lace. The wind let him by.

He dreamed that from now on he would lie leisurely, stretched out freely, on the cot in his own cell. He was safe. Even his mother could not get in.

River: A Magazine of the Deep South 1.1, March 1937, pages 10–12. Other writers in *River*'s inaugural issue included George Marion O'Donnell, Nash Burger, and Peter Taylor. Publication of a portfolio of Welty's photographs was planned, but *River*, edited by Dale Mullen, Oxford, Mississippi, went out of business in June 1937 after three issues.

From "Song of the Times"

The New York Times, Duet, with Dancing Chorus
Man, Wife, Egbert (reliable newsboy)

1.
The New York Times
Is the paper for me,
And the reason why
Is plain to see—
The New York Times is always

    The New York Times
2.
It never printed news
Unfit to print.
Others did,
But the Times di'nt.

    O the Times.

6.
The New York Times
Is as thick as the Bible,
And not a word on
Love or libel.

    O the Times.

7.
Better than a hoot owl
Loves his hootsburger
I love Cyrus
H. Sulzberger.

    O the Times.

8.
Better than a dog
Loves his bone
I love Mr. Brooks
Atkinson.

    O the Times.

11.
The Book Review
I love better than books,
But Literature's lovely,
From the way it looks.

    O the Times.

15.
And a reader's interest
Never fails
As long as there's
A Bloomingdale's

O the Times.

16.
Sak's! Stern's Sloane's for the house!
With a hey nonny nonn and Arabian Strauss!
Wanamaker, Wanamaker,
Peck and Peck!
Here's a great big hug and a mail order check!

O the Times!

The Welty Collection, Mississippi Department of Archives and History, Jackson, Mississippi, 1949.

In the summer of 1948, Welty and her friend Hildegarde Dolson (*We Shook the Family Tree*, stories, 1947) wrote *What Year Is This?*, a little revue intended to be a musical. As reported in the Memphis *Commercial Appeal* a year later, the authors said that "the current Broadway offerings are so mediocre, it seems that anybody could write a musical without even trying hard" (17 July 1949: V4). See the one-act play *Bye-Bye Brevoort* in this collection for another sampling from *What Year Is This?*

Bye-Bye Brevoort

CHARACTERS

MILLICENT FORTESCUE
VIOLET WHICHAWAY
AGATHA CHROME
EVANS *Miss Fortescue's maid.*
DESMOND DUPREE
FIRST WRECKER
SECOND WRECKER
THIRD WRECKER

*M*ISS FORTESCUE'S *sitting room in the Brevoort, a room not yet reached by wreckers dismantling the building and obliviously occupied by her.*

Set marked off perhaps by one collapsible wall and one folding screen. A window, heavily looped with curtains. A large dark oil painting of a lady ancestor in ornate frame, which can fall. Crowded and abundant

Victorian furnishings, two scrolled wicker high-backed chairs and a wicker settee, a tea table down front big enough to load with china and service and fixed so as to shudder or shimmy with every crash outside as the Brevoort is being torn down, so that some dishes and a flower vase eventually fall off. Right, a stand with old-fashioned telephone on it, a big sea shell, and a large silver dish with a mountain of calling cards in it. In rear, a dumb-waiter. Other things might be stacked albums, a fishnet full of postcards and Valentines, at least one musical instrument. Plant stands with luxuriant growth appropriately placed. Door, down left.

Curtain rises to show FORTESCUE, WHICHAWAY, *and* CHROME, *three old Brevoort relics, in* FORTESCUE'S *sitting room, each playing her own game of solitaire—one on the as yet unlaid tea table, the other two perhaps on checkerboards on their knees.*

The old ladies are dressed de rigueur. *Suggest* FORTESCUE *in lace,* CHROME *in velvet or in floral silk,* WHICHAWAY *in tweeds with white shoes and stockings. A lace parasol will be available for* FORTESCUE. *All wear hearing aids, though* WHICHAWAY *may prefer the trumpet.* CHROME *and* WHICHAWAY, *who come from across the hall, may wear their hats throughout.* EVANS *will wear an elaborate maid's uniform, starched and winged, with frilled cotton drawers as seen.* DESMOND DUPREE, *for whom the extra chair waits, is an old sport in a chesterfield, with a furled umbrella (as he goes out to the park) and yellow gloves.*

The moment before curtain rise, a few bangs and a dull thud. The wreckers dismantling the building are coming closer and closer as skit proceeds. Noises come intermittently, sometimes a hoarse shout. The ladies do not hear, or else they ignore these crude sounds. But a moment after curtain rise: A faint tinkle. Ladies all hear that. They sit bolt upright in polite, pleased anticipation. All speak up in high, carrying voices.

FORTESCUE (*Waving her battery gaily.*) Tea time! Tea time! Four o'clock! Did you notice I'd had an alarm put in my hearing aid? Tiffany's sent a man down. To work by the *hour,* my dears.

WHICHAWAY *Et tu,* Tiffany.

FORTESCUE (*Calling out.*) Tea, Evans! Isn't Evans back?

CHROME (*As crash, off, dies away. Without flinching.*) I haven't heard even a little mouse.

FORTESCUE I sent her to Charles's for petit fours. Desmond's coming, with his appetite.

CHROME Our Thursday Tiger!

WHICHAWAY Desmond! Shall we go back to our rooms for our hats?

FORTESCUE You have on *something*, dear.

WHICHAWAY (*Touching up top.*) Chances are it hasn't been removed since *yesterday's* tea. Simpler. (*Tinkle again, from hearing aid.*)

FORTESCUE There goes the second bell. If Evans isn't back soon, I'll telephone down and have the Brevoort search Sixth Avenue.

(*Enter EVANS, from door left, in cape, parcel in both hands and purse swinging from teeth. She is riding a bicycle. They don't turn to see her.*)

EVANS (*Speaking through teeth.*) The cheese straws from Charles's, mum.

FORTESCUE Evans: don't—hiss.

(*EVANS dismounts. With faint clicking sound as she walks, goes with burdens behind screen, comes out in her elaborate apron, and begins business of setting the tea table for high tea. Brings from behind screen a linen cloth and napkins, elaborate tea service, which seems to overflow the whole set, covered dishes, several pots, silver and china, cake stand with half a tiered cake. Whenever the pounding or a crash occurs off, all this shakes.*)

CHROME (*Sharply clapping her hand to her back as if shot by an arrow.*) Oh! There's a draft! It struck me!

WHICHAWAY For thirty-nine years I've said the Brevoort had a draft. And have mentioned it Downstairs. (*Meaningly.*) They know it.

FORTESCUE We should simply *avoid* the *corridors*.

EVANS (*In normal voice, since they won't hear. As she bends over to set a bud vase with rose and fern on tea table, as final touch.*) Draft, they call it. We're living in a fool's Swiss cheese.

FORTESCUE *Evans!*

EVANS (*Bending Over, arrested motion.*) Mum?

FORTESCUE You've come in with your bicycle clips on. *How* did you come through the lobby?

EVANS (*Proudly.*) Sidesaddle.

FORTESCUE (*To others.*) And *yesterday*, she came in on skates!

EVANS *One* skate.

CHROME Millicent—is *Evans* slipping—or the *Brevoort?* (*A large crash, off.*)

EVANS (*Sitting down hard, with the rose.*) We'll go down together.

FORTESCUE And as you came scorching through the lobby, Evans, tell me—did anyone budge?

EVANS No one saw me downstairs, mum, except some persons with axes and the persons with dynamite to blow up the building.

FORTESCUE No one with lorgnettes? Then thank your lucky stars.

CHROME Must we wait for Desmond?

FORTESCUE Dear Desmond! So dashing! Such a wreck!

CHROME Mr. Knickerbocker says, nothing keeps Desmond in one piece but penicillin and *passe-partout.*

WHICHAWAY Nonsense, he's always looked that way. It's only from wincing.

CHROME He insists on going *out*, you know.

FORTESCUE There's something gallant about him. Shine or shine, he goes forth and strolls in the park. (*They all shake their heads over it.*) And I understand the elevator isn't running past our floor. Some sort of obstruction in the passage!

EVANS It's got the hiccups. (*Knock at door.*)

EVANS (*Going to door and opening.*) Hold that tiger.

DUPREE (*Entering, with EVANS behind.*) Hullo, old things.

LADIES (*All together, gladly. All kissing.*) Desmond dear! Desmond, you're looking *shattered!*

DUPREE (*EVANS trying to take his coat. Does so.*) Difficult time getting through again. Odd thing in the corridor: persons all about sawing the walls. Didn't look too savory. Can't help noticing—thing like that during *Lent.*

CHROME (*Gives him a pat of comfort.*) Riff-raff. Best *not* to notice them.

DUPREE (*Sinking into chair, offhand.*) They must be looking for treasure.

WHICHAWAY Yes. Millicent, didn't you once lose an old Carolina moonstone?

FORTESCUE (*Coldly.*) *Not* in the corridor.

(*EVANS, busy with tea, now brings it in. As she bends over tea table, DUPREE stares.*)

DUPREE Aluminum garters? Daresay it was bound to come.

FORTESCUE Dear Desmond. You're looking frightfully crepey.

DUPREE Thanks, old thing. Shall we feed?

FORTESCUE Evans!

(*EVANS skips, dropping napkins in everybody's lap and DUPREE'S on the floor, as in drop-the-handkerchief. Goes to FORTESCUE'S side.*)

Telephone down, Evans. Ask rooom service for an earthen jug of *hotter and fresher water. Pouring, dears!* (*FORTESCUE begins to pour. All the dishes start to hobble and shake as bangs and thuds begin coming louder. They bravely ignore. They call a little more loudly and at higher pitch to one another to make themselves heard. Drink tea, eat cake.*)

CHROME Modern times! The noise of the city is frightful. The vehicles!

WHICHAWAY Yes. Rat-a-tat—rat-a-tat.

FORTESCUE I cawn't think why they don't make vehicles go *around* the island!

DUPREE This cake has a marvelous texture—marvelous crumb, Millicent. Wherever did you get it?

EVANS (*Over her shoulder. She is still at the phone, which doesn't answer.*) Hearn's, and I didn't say Hicks's.

FORTESCUE No answer below, Evans?

EVANS No, mum. The last we was in communication with the out-side world was a week ago Saturday. A copy of the *Villager* was thrown through the window.

CHROME *(As crash comes.)* I think they're trying it again.

(All shudder.)

FORTESCUE Keep listening, Evans. I cawn't think they'd have given *me* a telephone without the other end. Thirty-nine years in the Brevoort—why, the phone should ring incessantly by this time. *(Decides.)* Hang up, and let them call *us*.

EVANS *(Hanging up.)* I'd rather skate across the street and fill my earthen jug at the King Cole Room.

FORTESCUE *(Offering chocolates out of enormous satin-lined candy box, requiring both hands to handle. Ladies choose, cooing.)* Desmond? The liquid cherries are in the fourteenth row—balcony.

DUPREE *(Cramming.)* Teddibly good of you. Any quail sandwiches, or do I presume?

EVANS *(Carrying long, old-fashioned flintlock across stage and standing it in corner.)* You presume. It's Lent—remember?

CHROME *(Gaily.)* That last time we had a bird! Do you recall, Millicent?

FORTESCUE *(A short scream.)* Oh! Indelibly. That was the afternoon Raymond Duncan came to tea.

WHICHAWAY Threading his way down from the Waldorf.

CHROME Bringing his weaving.

FORTESCUE Saint Valentine's Day! . . . And he took the bones home in his pocket.—He *had* pockets, hadn't he?

CHROME For the goats. The Brevoort, of course, doesn't sanction goats.

WHICHAWAY *(Calling over noises off.)* Sanction who?

ALL THE OTHERS, WITH EVANS Goats!

(The portrait falls off the wall at this extra clamor.)

EVANS (*Gesture of announcement.*) E-o-leven! (*Then rehangs portrait. On second thought, turns it face to the wall.*)

FORTESCUE (*Explaining to DUPREE.*) Evans is keeping count of the times Aunt Emmeline falls—*excellent* count. (*Fuller explanation.*) This was *her* home, you know.

WHICHAWAY (*Broodingly.*) There are moments when I seem to notice something over and beyond the noise of traffic and falling portraits.

FORTESCUE You hear the seashell, dear. Evans, hold up the seashell for Miss Whichaway.

(*EVANS holds it up, and it vibrates and jerks in her hands as the noises sound. She shudders.*)

FORTESCUE See, dear? It makes Evans shudder.—That will *do*, Evans.

EVANS (*Gesturing with seashell aloft, reciting.*)
    "It was the schooner Hesperus
    That sailed the wintry sea—"

FORTESCUE More tea? Let's all have more hot *tea.* (*She begins to pour.*)

EVANS (*Reciting with shell.*)
    "We are lost, the Captain shouted
    as he staggered down the stair."

(*This makes DESMOND'S hand shake; his cup falls and breaks.*)

DUPREE Seems to me at times *china* isn't lasting much better than *we* are.

(*EVANS is immediately bringing him another cup.*)

EVANS Ooh, don't talk that way—Mr. Wedgewood!

FIRST WRECKER (*Off.*) That's it! Hook a chain around her middle and drag her down!

CHROME Did you speak, Desmond?

FORTESCUE I think that was someone in the corridor, dealing with a maid.

EVANS Doing it with chains now, are they? (*A large crash, off.*)

SECOND WRECKER (*Off.*) Crack her open—ah! Chock full of termites!

WHICHAWAY Do you feel that life's quite the same, since traffic? I say, a disrespectful element is creeping in.

CHROME The Brevoort should do away with the taxi stand.

DUPREE It's worse than that. I'd meant to keep it from you—but the skaters in Washington Square of late are heavily bearded.

FORTESCUE I *do* think we should alarm the Brevoort. Evans, will you telephone below? Inform the desk that out there *bullies* are *skating*.

(*EVANS goes to phone, jiggles it. A pounding right at door.*)

CHROME (*Crossing to EVANS, graciously.*) Here, Evans. Let me try. I'm awfully good with a telephone. My father played chess for years with Mr. Bell. (*Takes phone, jiggles.*) Hello? Hello? . . . There seem to be *mice* at the other end. (*She hangs up.*) (*Pounding at the door.*)

FORTESCUE Often I console myself by pretending the traffic noises are simply pistol shots—the riffraff *murdering* one another.

DUPREE (*Touched. Kissing her ear.*) Dear Millicent!

FIRST WRECKER (*Just outside door.*) This door's locked! My God, whose *bicycle*?

(*Crash and bicycle bell ringing.*)

CHROME The traffic seems curiously active for St. Swithin's Day.

EVANS I'm holding out for St. Vitus's Day. (*The WRECKERS break down the door and enter. EVANS steps to the door as it falls. To the WRECKERS:*) You knocked?

FORTESCUE Evans, we are not at home.

FIRST WRECKER Anudder nest of 'em. You can't smoke 'em out.

SECOND WRECKER Want to use the block and tackle on these, boss?

FIRST WRECKER Foist we'll see if dey won't come out nice.

(*Pounding outside keeps on.* WRECKERS *galvanized at sight of the tea table shimmying.* WRECKER *speaks in wheedling voice.*)

Folks—how about coming outside in de nice . . . *sunshine?*

(*They all rise, reel, give little cries, and cling together.*)

THIRD WRECKER (*Unwinding ropes and chains and creeping up at* DUPREE.) Ya see? Ya never loin, Leonard.

FIRST WRECKER (*Trying again. Smiling.*) Would youse boys and goils like to come out and see my great, big, shiny—*bulldozer?*

(*They cry out again.*)

CHROME Bulldozers, or any other kind, are not mentioned in the Brevoort Hotel.

(*THIRD WRECKER holds up a square rule.*)

FORTESCUE I *beg* your pardon. I think you people are looking for Klein's on the Square.

(*A carrier pigeon flies in window, bringing a note to* FORTESCUE.)

FORTESCUE (*Explaining brightly to* WRECKERS.) Oh, the mail. There you are, my pretty. (*Pokes cake crumb at pigeon, which flies back out window. Prettily, to* WRECKERS.) We much prefer pigeons to the government. Always on time—and in the end, of course, they can be eaten.

WHICHAWAY Open your letter. Maybe it's from the Metropolitan Museum again—insisting that we take care of ourselves.

FORTESCUE (*Opens note, reads, gasps.*) Oh! Listen to this! (*Reads aloud.*) "The management-in-exile of the Hotel Brevoort hereby notifies you that Wreckers are on their way to your suite. You will please receive them and carry out their wishes."

(*Horrified pause.*)

DUPREE *(Manfully.) Where's* that pigeon?

EVANS *(Pensively.)* Their wishes?

FIRST WRECKER Okay, boys.

(They begin moving stuff out of the room, the plant stands, musical instruments, etc. But leave the group at tea table for moment.)

FORTESCUE *(Brightly.)* Tea's what we need, my dears. Fresh tea! Do sit down. *(Flutters at tea table.)*

(WHICHAWAY sits, extends cup.)

CHROME *(Sitting.)* One must be impervious to the riffraff. Two lumps.

DUPREE *(Remains standing, thoughtfully.)* Yes. But still, I cawn't think too highly of those old women knitting on the roof of Wanamaker's.

FORTESCUE Desmond, dear—room service! *You* can get them. Tell them *fresh hot tea* on the dumbwaiter instantly.

(Dumbwaiter signals.)

Why, here it is! Evans—tea!

(WRECKERS still carrying out. EVANS goes through them to dumbwaiter. Lifts tray and turns to room, showing it loaded with lighted dynamite sticks.)

EVANS *(Taking dashing position, with crossed feet.)* TNT is served, mum.

FORTESCUE *(Grandly.)* Bring it on!

(EVANS brings tray forward and sets it down on the tea table, DESMOND absentmindedly tucking in his napkin, and they all sit there grandly. FIRST and SECOND WRECKERS swoop down on WHICHAWAY in her wicker chair and carry her off. She snatches her solitaire pack and deliberately plays the first card, up in the air.)

WHICHAWAY I *insist* there's a draft. *(WRECKERS return and pick up CHROME in her chair.)*

CHROME Will you dip in Suite Two for my tippet?

(They bear her away. Return for FORTESCUE, who is on the settee. She takes up her lace parasol and opens it over her head. Rides out with it over her, as in a howdah.)

MILLICENT *(Aloft.)* Shall I tell you what I think about Life, all? I think there's something of *elegance* gone.

(She is borne off. EVANS jumps up on the back of the remaining WRECKER and rides out piggyback, showing her bicycle clips attached to her long drawers. She prods him in the back.)

EVANS *What* wishes?

(WRECKERS return and surround DUPREE. A fusillade of crashes, off.)

DUPREE *(Stiffly.)* I can go unaided, thank you.

(He opens his collar and bares his throat, as one going to the guillotine. Suffers the WRECKERS to light his cigarette, or a long cheroot, for him with a dynamite stick. To sounds of wrecking, mingled with a strain of the "Marseillaise," he goes nobly out ahead of WRECKERS. Last WRECKER out lifts Aunt Emmeline's portrait and carries it under his arm. Aunt Emmeline's fingers are in her ears. Explosion and walls collapse as curtain falls.)

From *What Year Is This?*, a musical revue written in 1948 with Hildegarde Dolson. The Welty Collection, Mississippi Department of Archives and History. It was performed in *The Littlest Revue* starring Tammy Grimes, Charlotte Rae, Beverley Bozeman, Tommy Morton, George Marcy, and Larry Storch, and ran for thirty-two performances, 22 May to 17 June 1956, at the Phoenix Theatre in New York.

II. WIT AND WISDOM

Women!! Make Turban
in Own Home!

I haven't read *Popular Mechanics* in years, but when I was a child it was the only magazine I ever would read. I used to keep it in the bottom of my desk, and read it at night.

How I ever got on to the magazine to begin with is a little puzzling. Ours was never a mechanically inclined family. It is more the musical type. Stringed instruments lie around on the sofas, but never tools. The nearest to being handy our men come is in playing golf, although one brother does take a pencil and fix up candidates' campaign photographs in the newspapers—he can make them look like chickens. As for my mother, she would no more have read *Popular Mechanics* than she would *Lady Chatterly's Lover*, and for the same reason. It is safe to say that the knee from which I got my first copy of this magazine was not hers, but our colored cook's. She was a laugher, and probably enjoyed looking at the pictures while she was working. I must have begged the magazine away from her, or even stolen it, because I craved paper-dolls. There are men paper-dolls in *Popular Mechanics*.

True, they are all busy; many of them are suspended or submerged, or strapped into something with only the eyes showing—hard to fold at the waist and pass for human on a chair. But any child with a shoe-box full of nothing but mothers and children can get desperate. The only men in the mail-order catalogue wore long underwear, smiled, and carried another pair. I think they still do. My choice was the man under water. In *Popular Mechanics*, besides these undersea men at 45-degree angles, and frowning inventors with spangled headlights on their foreheads, you could get standing-up men like Lionel Strongfort and Charles Atlas for fathers of your families. They had their measurements, with fractions, printed on dotted lines across them, I remember. They very nicely matched the mothers with pricemarks on their upper arms.

Once I had found out about *Popular Mechanics*, I went on and read it. I can remember turning the fragmentary pages, where I'd already cut out all the fathers, reading in a tense, disturbed way, generally during a thunderstorm. How well I remember the page, "Once It Was an Old Wash-Stand!!" What was? Don't ask me—but there was a change. Everything either was, or was going to be, something else. That was the thrill and the lure of *Popular Mechanics*. What would be made out of what next month? I couldn't wait. It really was a terrifying, rather Yankee philosophy I was being exposed to, there in secret. Nothing was ever let alone in *Popular Mechanics*. Nothing ever got old in the course of time or fell to pieces. The grim wits were always at work. You waited around with an auger. I read on and on, and acquired *Popular Mechanics* month after month, by whatever means was necessary.

Of course, all that time I never made a thing. As a matter of fact, I am singularly inept at all mechanical tasks. To me, all *things* are motivated and active enemies, and a stuck table drawer will always be more cunning than I am. But throughout my childhood, I was a constant mental handy man. I could have fixed anything and if I had ever wanted to, I could have made anything. I could have changed everything in the household into something else if I had wanted to, just like a witch. But I never did.

Maybe I had an instinct of what would happen to me, the very first time. If I were to make a ten passenger pleasure boat out of our old china closet I'd get hell, even today. That word "spare time" (the condition attached to all the stunts) worried me, too. It meant you would have to get busy doing something else first, as a ruse to throw the family off; and I did not think I could fool them.

Maybe, too, I instinctively wondered if I would be happy in the end, after the transformation was all done. At about this same time, my grandfather sent me a very thick book: if I remember correctly the title was *101 Things Any Bright Girl Can Do*. I shied off from it until it was summer and I got poison ivy and was put to bed bandaged from head to toe. Then I told them to bring it to me. I read the book straight through, and mentally accomplished the 101 transformations with both rapidity and distaste. I told them to take it away and bring me *101 Things Any Bright Boy Can Do*, the companion volume, which had come to my brother, and I read that, in a sort of cold horror. That made 202 things done mentally during one day in bed with mittens on.

However, I was definitely haunted by *Popular Mechanics*, and I still am. Only a year ago, when I was ill and in a sulfanilamide dream, I sat up in bed and declared: "Nobody Lifts Anything—Nobody Sweats." That was another legend out of old *Popular Mechanics*—not a set of directions, of course, for, editorially, they wanted you to lift things and sweat, but an advertisement for something. How such a restful message ever crept into the magazine we'll never know: but I caught it. The true message of *Popular Mechanics* is: "You want something? You've got it." And that's like having a finger pointed at you. There's a feeling of guilt there somewhere; I still don't think it's a good idea to read things like that unless you have poison ivy. You haven't got this thing you want, such as a high dive for that home-made pool of yours, in its ultimate form, of course: it's your old fireless cooker. But in its lesser state, that high dive is right there looking at you, staring at you. In one more minute you are going to open a box of as horrible a set of tools as I have ever seen outside "The Return of Frankenstein," and work your head off.

It is to this lifelong haunt of *Popular Mechanics* that I lay my sudden decision of last winter to make a Hedy Lamarr turban. I was going to make it out of something in a trunk, and I was going to make it the hard way.

There was no reason for making a Hedy Lamarr turban, except that my hair had gotten too long and instead of getting it cut I wondered if I couldn't just hide it. As for making it the hard way, that is because I am Southern. We Southern women would not think of having a washing machine installed in the home, but we may at any moment descend (or ascend) to some form of heinous physical drudgery, emerging only to declare our prowess before falling flat. I don't know what causes this. We all do it. We are so proud of being able to do anything you might name. A prominent lifelong resident of my town once papered a room in one of these high-flown moods. It came to me to make a turban, and, because of *Popular Mechanics*, to make it out of something else.

When I opened the first trunk, looking for an old washstand cover or something, I came upon a little rabbit-fur muff I'd worn as a child, the kind that hung from a chain around the neck. It could have been turned into a Daniel Boone hat, but that was too easy. Here came a Spanish shawl, but it seemed to be all fringe—just like my hair. I kept going, through Hallowe'en costumes and organdie dresses, until I found exactly the right thing, just as is supposed to happen to you in *Popular Mechanics*.

This was the front panel of a dress I bought in Lord & Taylor's Budget Shop. It was a maroon silk print with a design of little keys. It came off a navy-blue dress—the girls who bought the rest like it on the rack and who read this, will remember. It was about 1935. Everybody who saw you said, "Look at the keys." I wonder if all these girls made turbans. Lord & Taylor had better read no further, but I will say here that the dress did not last through the trip to Mexico for which it was bought; nothing was left but the panel.

I was now ready to make a Hedy Lamarr turban from an old Lord & Taylor Budget Shop dress panel that came out of Mexico whole. But, how?

Talent, of course, is considered purely hereditary in these parts, and it was only too believable that none of my forbears had ever made a turban, or ever worn one except to show off and act funny. Without being a speck of kin to Hedy Lamarr, I therefore saw no use in the method of sitting down and just thinking up how a turban should be made. No telling what would happen. Besides, I wanted to do it the hard way. So the next time I was down town I dashed into a department store and went to the turban department.

I would never have known them. Without heads inside, turbans look utterly unconvincing, rather spurious. The clerk let me handle several, laid them across the palm of my hand, and watched my face, but all to no good. She could see that nothing came to me. The turban, as Hedy Lamarr wore it, remained an abstraction to me. With the clerk's sympathy, I finally had to buy one to take home and study by myself. She explained that she was wrapping up a blouse with the turban, made of the same material and attached to it. I had thought it part of the turban's tail, and that had added to my confusion.

"Comes with it, hon," said the clerk. "It's an inducement." She pointed to where you could break a thread and separate the things; but she said that I would have to be the one to do it. With that complication, a Javanese turban and its Siamese blouse, I almost quit. If only spring would come, I thought, I would call the whole morbid thing off.

Before taking the bought turban to pieces to see how it was made, I wore it awhile. It was not my real turban, of course, but it was a grand concealment for my hair, which was growing longer and longer. I had now, approaching the subject through some other angle, begun the Ogilvie Sisters' Home Treatment, with much brushing, extended through absentmindedness and brooding, and I daresay the back hair was growing about an inch every other day during all this period.

I would look at the turban each time I put it on or took it off, and all I could safely say about it was that it was made either of two pieces of cloth partly sewed together, or of one piece of cloth partly split. It was completely impossible to tell what made it a turban. Then one day I took the panel and the bought turban and threw them together into a drawer, banged it shut, and left them awhile. Perhaps I thought the panel would turn into a turban by itself.

It was not until the night we had a real snow here, for the first time since I don't know when, and everybody was running around outdoors in a kind of madness and exhilaration, that I actually started construction. I had come in from playing in the street, and wanted something to do before I went to bed. I'll make that turban, I thought with flashing eyes. After being out in a ten-inch snowfall, making a turban seemed one of the least far-fetched things I would ever do in my life. I snatched up the bought turban and took one squint at it, and it all came to me like a flash. I didn't even have to take it to pieces to see how it was done. Any fool could make a turban, out of anything. I woke my mother up and asked her for the scissors.

"What on earth for, at this time of night?" she asked. "Are you going to cut your hair?" and she pressed them into my hand.

So in one instant, I whacked into the panel and cut out a turban. I must be kin to Lilly Daché. After that, all I had to do was sew on it a little. There was nothing to be dreaded about the process, no soldering or clamping in a vise, or standing and looking out of mounds of sawdust, as there always used to be in *Popular Mechanics*. You didn't even have to make it in a basement; you could make it in bed. I even thought of writing a little article to send *Popular Mechanics* on how to make a turban; but this is it.

Not that I finished the thing that night. It takes a good while to make a turban, at least working under a bed lamp and trying to keep quiet.

My brother noticed me late one night as I was hemming away in my spare time.

"What are you making?" he asked testily.

"Hedy Lamarr turban," I replied.

"Why don't you make a Dotty Lamour sarong?" he countered.

That could be made out of the bought turban, but I've put it away in a trunk. I put my handwork away too. When I got through with it, it was tacky. It had ears. When I brushed my hair and put it on, I looked like a lady in *Popular Mechanics*, ready for goggles and a rocket ship. It served me right, I suppose. But what with the snow melting and all, and the birds singing, I went down the next day and got a haircut and have been taking life easy ever since.

Junior League Magazine, November 1941, pages 20–21 and 62.

Letters to Charles Shattuck
Regarding Ida M'Toy

1119 Pinehurst St.
Jackson, Mississippi
March 28, 1942

Dear Mr. Shattuck,

Thanks for your letter and I am glad you like the little piece on Ida and are going to use it. I told Mr. Russell when I wrote him just now, so that's all right about letting him know.

As to the points you mention, I am in complete agreement that the title is a bad one, and if you can think of anything, use it—I can never write a title to anything. In my own mind I had changed this to the simple name, "Ida M'Toy," but seem capable of no more. (1) I don't think the first sentence would be affected to amount to anything by a change in the title, and can be left as is. (2) The dates could be made to connect by changing, on page 3, 53 to 56. I am outdone that I left something wrong about the date for I had had a terrible time with the ones Ida gave me, and had to write the whole first page over taking them every one out, because they threw the entire thing into hopeless confusion and would have made her begin midwifery at the age of 3—I am poor at figures but I did catch that. (3) I think leaving the "however" to modify "hiding information" is all right as it is. (4) That sentence does go on, and if it would be clarified by enclosing "and he will kneel . . . mural figure" in a parenthesis, enclose it; Mark Twain of course said that anybody who will wilfully use a parenthesis would steal. (5) Yes, change the "very slowly moving" to "moving very slowly," much better. (6) It's all right to cut the two last sentences in the second paragraph.

Since you seem to like Ida as much as I could hope a reader would, I feel cheered and you will be interested to learn that she is waiting as impatiently as possible for this to appear in print. I told her that it is no reflection on her, but only on me, that it is not printed yet—I wrote it Christmas, and I think it will do to take her for an Easter present, a little late. She hasn't read it, but will of course think it only the faithful writing down of her own words and will scarcely bother to read it. I hope you will send me two copies so that I can take her one, for she will frame it and hang it on the wall during her lifetime and it will, I am afraid, be buried with her if and when she dies. She is really a remarkable person and I wish I might have done her better justice, but it is easy to see how the task can stop you almost before you begin.

I'm glad you like "Powerhouse" and thanks for the kind words about my book.

Sincerely yours,
Eudora Welty

✦ ✦ ✦

Jackson, Miss.
Aug. 25, 1942

Dear Mr. Shattuck—

Thanks for the extra copy of the magazine, which I took out to Ida right away. She shut off all the musical things going and regally took hold of the magazine and kissed it. She set it on her bed up against her pillow where her head goes, took me by the hand and put a kiss on it, and said, "Here's where I get out my glasses." She said "That's my Christmas present."

She didn't say she was going to nail it to the wall but she did announce that it was going to the very bottom of her trunk and the trunk would be locked. "Then I'll get it out when I'm ninety, darling." She said only an angel would have got all that written down. And she was glad the task finally got done. Then she led me to the front room where she had set up a big glass china closet full of jelly and told me to pick out a glass for Christmas. Just thought you'd like to hear how it went. She said she would read that book on her till she died, she supposed a thousand times, because it *couldn't* be read enough. —I'm enjoying the magazine too.

Yours sincerely,
Eudora Welty

✦ ✦ ✦

Jackson, Miss.
September 1, 1942

Dear Mr. Shattuck:

Do not be surprised at what follows. The other morning at crack of dawn Ida M'Toy telephoned me to for God's sake come straight out there, as she had read the book on her life. When I got there she greeted me with three fingers stuck up in the air—I had three things wrong. First, I had said her watch was silver, when it was gold—how could I have done a thing like that to her? and she took it out of its hiding place and put it under my eyes. Second, I had left out Sudie, who had helped her in the store for six years and Sudie felt so bad about it—"Sudie, Sudie! Come stand here and let Miss Wealthy see how bad you feel—that's right—that's all, Sudie, get on back." Third, why did I think that one copy of her life was going to be enough for her and all her friends? Two hundred would be more like it. I then apologized for 1 and 2, and said it was unlikely that I could get 200 copies and besides the price of each was 30¢. "Thirty cents! My God, there are people would be glad to pay thirty dollars cash on the barrel head to have a copy right at their hand of Ida's life." In the end I said I would write and see if there were about ten copies you could send me. I'd of course pay you, and let Ida do the grand distribution, I think she wants to take orders and force it on her customers. She says she wants a copy in Camp Shelby for sure, to teach those soldiers to live right. She had pride in the article, but was dismayed that I had come without a pencil, for she assumed that immediately on finishing and printing that much up, I would go on and write up all that was left out. "It wrote what it could remember," she said compassionately, "there's just so *much*." She calls this copy of *Accent* "The Book of Ida" so you can see I would hate to deprive her of spreading it to her world. When you have time, do let me know if you can spare me ten or twelve copies, and thanks a lot. Ida is really beside herself and has guaranteed that you and I both will go to heaven and see the angels.

Yours sincerely,
Eudora Welty

♦ ♦ ♦

1119 Pinehurst St.
Jackson, Miss.
September 14, 1942

Dear Mr. Shattuck,

Thanks ever so much for the letter and for the magazines, which arrived safely. I'm touched that Ida and her story have been received so wholeheartedly by everybody at *Accent*. Ida would be gratified and I guess I'd better tell her, that the Book of Ida will be at at least *some* soldiers' camps where it will be of such value. I enclose check for the magazines and the other dollar is for subscription—it's good that *Accent* is to go forward and I wish you luck. Ida received the 10 copies and hid them right away, and now to pick out the ten people who most deserve to buy first. If you have some flawed copies it would be wonderful to let her have them, and it's generous of you but I fear a lot of trouble. I doubt if any magazine ever pleased anybody so by printing an article than *Accent* has done by printing this—Ida refers to you all as "those precious people up near Chicago that has my life." Thanks again, and my best wishes.

Sincerely,
Eudora Welty

P.S. It was perfectly OK about any omissions etc. This was *enough*.

+ + +

1119 Pinehurst
Jackson, Miss.
September 23

Dear Mr. Shattuck,

Your nice letter came and so did the stack of books, so I went straight out to Ida with the present—and it was her only thought to write you a letter on the spot. Here it is, and I only hope you can put your imagination to bear on it, because (of course I had to sit there all the time, never to take part but just to be a witness) for every sentence she got written, ten were being simultaneously said, and acted out. I doubt if Ida has written many letters and it wouldn't occur to her that you would only receive the written down words, not the augmentations or the physical accompaniments of shouts and groans—when she was writing about Mama's Dinner and wrote "in sulted" she jumped up out of the chair and yelled MAD! then sank down and added "mad" but you would have to imagine such things. She would have gone on forever with the letter, because she wanted to set you straight on some things I got wrong or left out, taking your desire to hear from her perfectly seriously in that way, but her tablet gave out. She is so overcome by your printing this much of the life that her mind really wanders and staggers under the load more than is good for her! She will never rest, maybe, until the account is perfect & complete. The copies I first took her she went and sold as if they were dresses and as you see from the enclosed envelope has given me the money—I declined to take out her commission—this in spite of the fact that the books were a present to her. She is also going to sell the ones you sent, in spite of all, and turn the money over to me for the army or navy. I'll get it to the U.S.O., I guess, to make things right and just so. I'm sending two pictures I took of her, and asked her to write on them for you. She declared writing would spoil their perfect beauty but consented to write on the "darling one"—she doesn't like the other one because it shows old freckles. They don't do her total justice but here they are. She has changed the spelling of her name to Torry, for unknown reasons, but it's on her husband's tombstone M'Toy, she used to have a photo of her on the wall that showed her kneeling at the grave with a sheaf of lilies, which she pointed out as "Me Mournin."

I'm doubly pleased to have *Accent* for two years, and thanks for fixing it that way. With many good wishes to it and good luck to you.

Sincerely,
Eudora Welty

The letters were published in *Ida M'Toy*, Urbana: University of Illinois, 1979, with a facsimile reproduction of Ida M'Toy's letter to Shattuck. Welty's essay on Ida M'Toy was first published in *Accent* (Urbana, Illinois), March–September 1942, edited by Charles Shattuck.

Literature and the Lens

1. I took this snapshot in New Orleans on Royal Street one day, and the next minute a chorus of three old ladies on a balcony muttered— the same as asked me why. It is hard to guess why the act of taking a picture with a camera is always suspect. You can do all kinds of other things in public without a question of being asked—but if you click your camera at something people from nowhere run up and ask "Why did you take that?"

Perhaps it goes back to atavistic beliefs that to carry off an image of something, or its picture, means you want to steal its soul. In Mexico a woman forbade me to photograph her baby because he had not yet been christened, and an eccentric old lady in Louisiana threatened to shoot me with her gun if I dared photograph a beautiful statue in her garden. It is clear that the fascination of a photograph of anything is that it imprisons a moment in time—and is that really different from stealing its spirit, its soul? Perhaps one does right to protest.

Yet this must be in a sense, the purpose of nearly everything we do—certainly in the arts, painting, and writing, we steal spirits and souls if we can, and in love and devotion, what do we do but pray: Keep this as it is, hold this moment safe? So in the lowly photograph we can do this to anything—a little boy walking fast in a shuttered street—with a little machine and the slightest motion of the finger. Photography is crude in itself, but the act of photographing is kin to something better when we look at the little prints that come of it, we get a fine, unproportional satisfaction, as if we had netted a prize.

2. This photograph was made at first sight of this house. A descendant of the original owner had gone looking for the place, taking me along, and we had seen the chimneys just at first-dark, after following a cedar avenue that curved up out of a dark ravine where the Natchez Trace once went by.

It was an evening in November or December, with a wind smelling of night-rain filling the air with blowing leaves and the clouds coming over the sky. It seemed haunted and beautiful at the same time—indeed much had happened in it. I expect it was haunted with that early happiness of houses built in its time, before 1810—a plain, Georgian, very hospitably designed house that would always hold a quality of vitality and of vivid happenings. The bricks, baked of the red clay of the place, were of a glowing rose that seemed to hold light on that first dark day we saw it, and in sunlight shone very splendidly on that quiet hill.

Spring would come and a fruit orchard would suddenly come to life down an overgrown slope, and the thick irises would show where a garden was, with roses gone to the wild blooming in countless tiny flowers in the tangle. Always the dark cedars were standing there, dark in every season, unchanging and tragically shaped by storm and years and very beautiful in their placement and significance, guarding the approach and the ruin. At last, with it all to the ground, I took some of the fiery bricks home and put them in my garden around a bed of spring bulbs.

3. In my town, other religious groups among the Negroes looked down on the Church of God in Christ Holiness, and I suspect with just a grain of envy, for that congregation surely had the best time. They not only danced, sang, prayed in the unknown tongue, and got raided, but they met oftener—four or five nights a week—and Holiness members were more sanctimonious out of church than anybody. They had signs all around their church saying: "Be Prompt," "Be On Time," "God Is On Time," but time had very little to do with their meetings, which were drop-in affairs of no settled procedure.

The preacher, shown here at the top, was a little man, jet black, with monkey features and antics. He played the banjo, both solo and as accompaniment, and as a sort of gong—with single, abrupt twangs when he wanted attention or appreciation. He preached strolling around, up and down the aisle. He was nimble and nimble-witted, he never let his flock get bored, and when he saw it getting restless, he would interrupt himself in the middle of a sentence to suddenly click his heel down sharply on the floor, call a word or a name—"Lazarus! Holy Lamb!"—and start a dance. He could also do a dance himself with the cymbals, and handle a tambourine, rap it behind him with a neat kick of the heel. It was said he had two wives, one for sorrow and one for joy. His congregation was divided between the Sanctified (in white) and the Willing Workers, or W.W.'s (red and white).

The overlay of religion, or business procedure, over these rites, was intermittent. The minutes were more fascinating than any I have ever heard read, for they extended from the time the secretary sat down from reading them last time till the moment she got up to read them this time, beginning: "The secretary responded sweetly." Then she primly sat down and began writing again, until dancing took her.

The members always applauded the collection and announced the total, and all went to the preacher. They admired him for amassing wealth at their expense. He would brag and they would clap. He seemed, by his dancing and his random references to the fertility of the women and the fine fettle of the men, the abundance of rain or the threat of drought, to attribute to himself some of the oracular properties of the impudent medicine man of the country of his origin, and in this he was ever enthusiastically encouraged.

Vogue, 1 August 1944, pages 102–3. The photographs printed with Welty's text may be viewed in *Photographs* (1989), numbers 144, 117, and 107, respectively.

The Abode of Summer

In Mississippi, at least, we sometimes wonder what vacationers who come South in Winter see. What do we look like then—our trees gone bare, and we with coats on? That is an obscure time. I know my vision of where I live is a Summer one; and Summer is the vision I keep year-round. Summer is the time when Southerners are South, where they live; and South is where it is summertime most.

Our South is the abode of heat—and the source of what's good for it: the high ceilings, the cross halls, the porches, the frosty drink with mint coming out the top; the cotton dress, the cotton nightgown; those precious and cooling summer fruits, small blue fig and great big watermelon; parties moved out to the porch and yard, where the moonlight, in patterns of leaf and flower, descends along with the possible breezes to our skin and clothes, and music sounds sweet when it is played outdoors or steals out through a window to us.

The South's Summer is the heart of Summer. Those ribbony afternoons of childhood (it is the children who stir in afternoons) live in our memory; I think the memory of every Southerner lies fixed in summertime. From the beginning of our lives, it seems, we knew the big, slow month-after-month turning of sights and sounds and scents, the kaleidoscope of pleasures in the duress of heat—the swimming of ice in china pitchers of tea or lemonade, ceiling fans wheeling on porches, punkahs in the oldest houses in stately back-and-forth above the long table, fans in the hand, church fans, party fans, silk and feather and ivory fans, old ladies' black fans, children's fans, on chains that went around the neck. And the evenings of childhood Summers, where in companies we used to play out, pulling by strings those homemade toys, tiny steamboats, candles inside alight, blinking out from crescent moon and star windows as night came down.

Southern Summer is nostalgic, because even when it happens it's dreamlike. Find the shade of the biggest tree; in it your hammock is dreaming already, like a boat on the stream. We return to Summer each year like the swooning nosegay we loved so well: magnolia fuscata flowers (which look like inch-long bananas and smell the same) tied in a corner of a cambric handkerchief. There are the Summer nights of the waterfall-sound of the ice-cream freezer being turned somewhere on the back porch; the rifle crack of another watermelon being split open on the grass at the picnic; the band concerts sounding from the park, the parties sending up Roman candles from the river; the hay rides down country roads where people sang themselves nearly to sleep in the gently jogging dark. And—like dancing at night—there was swimming at night—in water not much cooler still than the skin, but delicious because wet, because no longer reflecting that sun.

We are one of the natural homes of the parasol. In the little southern towns all of us used to prance about under parasols to fit our moods and years, though now only the most old-fashioned of family retainers are likely to go carrying their own shade, in the form of large black cotton umbrellas. Afternoon "teas" and receptions were sometimes held on shady lawns, late on, and dances in pavilions at night with paper lanterns, and picnics in places we used never to find again. Sitting outside on the steps in the moonlight talking has remained, thank Heaven, an uninterrupted way, as well as the finest way, to keep happy and cool.

Galleries are where we live best—front and back, upstairs and downstairs, on the blessed sleeping porch. We court the cool like shameless lovers; dream about it noon and night. Shade trees, shade hats and somebody (who?) to keep fanning us with a fan—that's ideal; and air conditioning cannot be the same thing at all. O pavilions, gazebos and summerhouses, where are you now?

Yet Summer animates our spirits and brings us new ideas, if only because Summer is a challenge as well as a condition of life. We do not fight Summer, we persuade it; it is our own, we have learned measures, little ways to accommodate it, from which we take virtue. If on hot days we appear for the first moment cool and fresh as a daisy, we are likely to be complimented on living right.

In Summer we live at night, come to life then. We live indoors in the daytime, outdoors in the nighttime, as much as we can. From now on, the day is too bright and blinding. When heat dances like a dervish in the garden, the grass lies down and dies, the flowers blaze, nothing seems to move but hummingbirds. All is brighter than it has any business being; and what led old John Law, who in early times organized the Compagnie d'Occident, to display diamonds in the shop windows of Paris, saying they were produced in the Summer wildflowers along the banks of the Lower Mississippi, may be questionable, but it's easy to see how he was inspired—he went out in the midday sun.

We seek the shade. We love trees, those live oaks especially, vast and majestic and venerable roofs that they are. Lately torn by the storms of the equinoxes as they have been, in Summer they spread impervious again in blessed new layers of green. They are beautiful. Spanish moss that hangs from their branches is a species of pineapple, and swings in the Summer air taking life from no other element—like a dream in the tree. These live oaks line the old roads, old Academy grounds, the river banks in towns, and speak of an outdoor society— the shade-loving, promenade-loving kind. Aaron Burr was tried under the oak trees in Washington, Mississippi, in an outdoor trial that was a sort of social and theatrical event as well, with ladies and gentlemen arriving in their finest, with cooling refreshments going around during the speeches.

And under these trees, too, the first English-speaking theatre in this part of the world began, in 1806 in Natchez. A regular season of the drama was held on the Esplanade, with a backdrop of river and wilderness behind (Burr's dream itself), and the river breezes blowing on actors and audience. Elizabethan and Restoration comedy and tragedy were the fare on this frontier stage, being followed by afterpieces of bird mimicry and ventriloquism, recitations of *Alexander's Feast* and the singing of Irish songs. After that, nothing could displace *She Stoops to Conquer* under the trees but the Show Boat on the River itself—and there under the wet warm stars, on the decks of those boats, true floating palaces, there were whole French Zouave troops for instance—and delicious refreshments, and breezes.

Our farthest-back predecessors that we know of, in this particular part of the world, were Sun worshipers: they are extinct now. In that long ago, when Summer arrived, those Natchez Indians—who dressed gloriously in every season if accounts are true—threw off their swan-feather mantles of Winter ("made as carefully as wigs") and draped themselves in single garments from waist to knee decorated in thin, geometric vermilion lines drawn with porcupine quills, with puffs of down on their heads, round feather fans in each hand and a string of pearls.

In the home of Summer, fashion might well spring up, find favor, when based on mere hope of amelioration from the heat; but we dote on style. And what will always be the style for Summer but lightness? "Summer," in the *Faerie Queene*, though then she was going in a cooler land, in Ireland, was wearing "a thin silken cassock, coloured greene, that was unlyned all, to be more light." And Summer's child—what could come lovelier into her life than the dress that is "unlyned"—a leaf, a cloud, a drift of stars to her?

Harper's Bazaar, June 1952, pages 51 and 115.

A Flock of Guinea Hens
Seen from a Car

The lute and the pear are your half sisters,
The mackerel moon a full first cousin,
And you were born to appear seemly, even when running on
guinea legs,
As maiden-formed, as single-minded as raindrops,
Ellipses, small homebodies of great orbits (little knots at the
back like apron strings),
Perfected, sealed off, engraved like a dozen perfect consciences,
As egglike as the eggs you know best, triumphantly speckled . . .
But fast!
Side-eyed with emancipation, no more lost than a string of pearls
are lost from one another,
You cross the road in the teeth of Pontiacs
As over a threshold, into waving, gregarious grasses,
Welcome wherever you go—the Guinea Sisters.

Bobbins with the threads of innumerable visits behind you,
As light on your feet
As the daughters of Mr. Barrett of Wimpole Street,
Do you ever wonder where Africa has fled?
Is the strangeness of your origins packed tight in those little
    nutmeg heads, so ceremonious, partly naked?
Is there time to ask each other what became of the family wings?

Do you dream?
Princess of Dapple,
Princess of Moonlight.
Princess of Conch,
Princess of Guinealand.
Though you roost in the care of S. Thomas Truly, Rt. 1
(There went his mailbox flying by),
The whole world knows you've never yet given up the secret of
    where you've hidden your nests.

New Yorker, 20 April 1957, page 35. Welty sent this poem as a December 1970 holiday
greeting printed by William Ferguson for Albondocani Press. Poems that Welty
wrote as a youth and as a college student may be read in *Early Escapades*, edited by
Patti Carr Black.

Weddings and Funerals

THE EASIEST WAY

Weddings and funerals have been called "the easiest way to get people together" in a piece of fiction. It's a Southern mode, but it's more than that. It's a crisis, a climactic moment when everyone is keyed up, a moment more dramatic than others. Such a moment might even be a picnic, perhaps the characters themselves are not fully conscious of the crisis, but it is a moment different to every person, and I use it frequently in my work as a means of keeping up the dramatic intensity of my story. I find it a great help.

Of course, we're human beings first, Southerners second. The wish to write supercedes the accidents of birth or time, or place. The Southern writer, I'm sure, will continue to write about his South, and when he does it very well, it will mirror mankind as a whole. My hometown is about twenty worlds in itself. The variety of any particular place is tremendous. It's very important to know *your* country, whether by birthright or adoption. That was something Faulkner knew well, and that knowledge was reflected in several ways, for instance, the names he gave to his characters. Faulkner was the master of the name. Katherine Anne Porter once told me that her names are born with the character—not mine. I have to work real hard at it. Phoenix (Phoenix Jackson), for instance, suggests very strongly in my mind the idea of persistence, of trying something over and over again. At the root of her persistence is love. Even when she forgets the reason for her journey, her *love* remembers. The path, the journey, and the taking of the journey become, in fact, the only thing that matters.

In a short story like Phoenix, the situation dictates the characters, the circumstances predicate character. On the other hand, with a novel, the work grows from characters and I augment them with detail from various sources, including the newspaper. A writer is a magnet, not a random observer. The writer is looking for something and the imagination directs him.

What I've gotten off on now is structure. The structure of a thing often comes by accident. The creative process usually only surfaces after a long period of personal involvement with a thing. It's important to know the implications of what you feel—that gives you the structure. I'm not talking about social commentary here. Of course, most of my work does make a social comment, although I've never made specific comment with it. I don't think an author would make those kind of specific statements unless it serves the story. The story should speak for itself. I don't want to be preached at and I have no wish to preach to other people. Justice and injustice—these are basic to human life, and my characters best state my themes.

ON WRITING

While he's at it, the writer studies his story intensely. But when the story or novel is finished, he probably couldn't tell you how he did it, how he proceeded—which is probably best for what he will write sometime in the future. Each work is new, and if you're dedicated to it, it's very hard work. I think in terms of stories and for me writing has become a tool. I love the short story as a form. It has an identity of its own. Like a table or chair, it's objective.

THE FUTURE OF LITERATURE

Whenever anyone asks me about the future of literature, I have to reply that I don't really think much about it while I'm writing. As a reader, I think about the future of the novel. Right now, literature is in an eclipse. But I have faith that if we're readers we'll be writers. Writing in any time reflects its time, and the best writing from any period reflects honesty and communication.

The New, Non-Fiction novel is hardly new. People like Norman Mailer are dealing in little tricks and paste-up jobs. Real life isn't consistent—works of fiction are. You make it fit if you're a fiction writer, you make your material conform to the ideas and what you want to say. The new novel is not a congenial voice to me yet. I like the human touch, the common ground. The current New Novel is nothing near as old as Homer, and it hasn't taken over yet. I think we can last this out.

CRITICISM AND WRITING

They operate in opposite directions. In life, criticism can be thought of as the ocean's reflection of the sky. It's in opposite, in reverse. The thought process isn't adverse to the creative process. One simply builds while one takes apart. I don't mean that to sound derogatory. It's just a shift in the mind. The *New York Times Book Review* is, at times, though, very reckless. I don't like hatchet jobs on books. If I don't like a book, I don't write a criticism of it. I don't think it would be fair to the writer if I did. When you look at a novel and realize that it's probably taken someone a year to write it, then I believe you're a little more appreciative of what they're offering, and a little less likely to condemn what you might personally view as a shortcoming.

Writing fiction is, after all, an internal, an interior affair. The best writing comes from intense personal feeling and convictions. The way life is experienced is individual and unique, and so my only advice to young writers would just be to read—to read, and by reading see what others have done. You have to be honest with yourself—that's what matters.

Silhouette (Virginia Polytechnic Institute and State University's Literary Magazine) 2, Spring 1979, pages 2–4.

Charles Dickens's Eggnog

This is the eggnog we always started Christmas Day off with. I have the recipe my mother used, though she always referred to it as "Charles Dickens's Recipe."

6 egg yolks, well beaten
3 Tbs. powdered sugar, sifted
1 cup Bourbon
1 pt. whipped cream
6 egg whites, whipped into peaks but not dry
nutmeg if desired

Add the powdered sugar gradually to the beaten egg yolks. Add the Bourbon a little at a time to the mixture. Add the whipped cream and the beaten egg whites, folding gently in. Chill. Serve in silver cups with a little grated nutmeg on top if desired.

✦ ✦ ✦

In our home while I was growing up, I don't remember that hard liquor was served at all except on one day in the year. Early on Christmas morning, we woke up to the sound of the eggbeater: Mother in the kitchen was whipping up eggnog. All in our bathrobes, we began our Christmas before breakfast. Throughout the day Mother made batches afresh. All our callers expected her eggnog.

It was ladled from the punch bowl into punch cups and silver goblets, and had to be eaten with a spoon. It stood up in peaks. It was rich, creamy and strong. Mother gave full credit for the recipe to Charles Dickens.

But its taste was simply, and absolutely, the taste of Christmas Day, as palpably as the smell of the big cedar my father had cut in the woods was the smell of Christmas. The bells all ringing and the firecrackers set off by little boys were Christmas to our ears. We were partaking of all the jubilation; the eggbeater was just keeping up with us.

The Great American Writers' Cookbook, edited by Dean Faulkner Wells and published in Oxford, Mississippi: Yoknapatawpha Press, 1981, page 16. Welty's comments appeared in the *New York Times*, "Writers Savor Christmas Memories," 24 December 1986, page C1.

III. THE ARTS

José de Creeft

In its way it is typical of José de Creeft and his *taille directe* that, when asked to name someone to write an article about him, he named me. I had been invited to do work at Yaddo the same summer he had been, and my designation was "writer." This is outside de Creeft's world—both words (except as purely functional or graceful, as in exchange, and then it does not matter from which language any consecutive ones spring up) and words about himself. De Creeft does not talk about himself, or his life—though talking, the pleasure, is a delight to him. He works, and in every way that signifies anything to him, his work is his life. Most biographical facts in this little article come out of *Current Biography* and the notes to exhibitions of his work.

The formalities of life, the conventions of education, were shed from the first by de Creeft. He evidently ran through them like a boy through a shower of rain. It is wholly probable that instinct has always led him surely by the hand, and warned him never to assume such burdens of thought and habit as would only have to be shaken off before he could go freely in his own right way of working. He was born in 1884 of Catalan parents, with some Flemish ancestry, in Guadalajara, Spain, "time Valley of the Stones." (His sculptor friend, Alexander Calder, has suggested that "he must have carved his way out.") He probably first opened his eyes in the outer world upon stones, and perhaps he saw from even a child's glance some spirit in them which he had a desire, that some might call atavistic, to release. He didn't like school. The family was poor. He became an apprentice in a bronze foundry when he was twelve, and by the time he was fourteen, with the family living in Madrid, he had an idea that he would be a sculptor. He lived, almost literally, in the Prado, that being the best teacher available to him then. He was recommended by the Minister of Art and put to apprenticeship under the kind of old, dogmatic, fussy, spiteful teacher who seems destined to confront eager spirits and turn them lightning-like to mischief. Bound to such a one, who forced learning by the copy-this-cast method, he found the random hands and feet of plaster, the shrouded, uncompleted, ridiculous statues, the tipsy scaffoldings fine props for playing impish tricks, and with a final comment of a foot let fall within an inch of the master's bending body from the top of an old statue where he perched, de Creeft departed from formal learning for good.

He met a painter almost right away, set up a studio with him, and when the painter won the Prix de Rome and went off, de Creeft gaily made a date to meet him in Paris in three years, though his pockets were turned-out empty at the time. As a matter of fact the date was kept, for by that time de Creeft was living in a rather famous studio on the Left Bank, the other inhabitants of it being Juan Gris and Picasso. Here he labored in a stoneyard as a craftsman, where he learned a great deal of practical things, and had his first actual art training at the Académie Julien. The World War brought poverty to him, and he made a thin living as a caricaturist and sometimes as a house painter, but once the armistice was signed there was great demand for statues for war memorials. He was given a commission for an eighteen-foot granite statue of a poilu for Puy-du-Dome. He carved this statue directly, and has never worked in any other way since that day. He knew without question that this direct method was the true way for him.

After living the long-haired years of the twenties in Paris, the dazzling and bedazzled art groups and cliques may have grown a little too much for de Creeft. At any rate, in 1925 he entered, in the newly founded Salon des Tuileries, the life-sized Picador made of stove-pipe, a wondrous and hilarious compilation, which looked too much like a comment on the rest of the salon to give people comfort. By 1926 he was in Majorca, in a garden, making all the fountains and big and little seasonal and animal statues that came into his head—a famous and rich estate had given him carte blanche to decorate the grounds with his work. With the money from this, he sailed for America, with three tons of sculpture on the same boat.

It was in Seattle that he had his first American showing. The director of the museum there, Richard Fuller, had an Oriental collection, and when he looked at the work of this Spanish sculptor, he saw something in it that held his same admiration. Then, East, the Ferargil Galleries took up de Creeft's work. But illness intervened, caused by the Majorcan stone dust, and it was not until 1936 that he was able to work and exhibit again. This was at the Georgette Passedoit Gallery which since then has given annual exhibitions of his work.

So great is de Creeft's energy and imagination that a year always brings a whole new room-full of work—which would take the ordinary sculptor about a lifetime to bring the hard way out of metal and stone, granting that he could. De Creeft also teaches regularly at the New School for Social Research, and has time to paint an occasional watercolor show. His studio on Greene Street is a work room. It opens off the sidewalk and is about the same size as a country store, and as tightly packed with ungainly and mysterious things piled, crowded, standing, hanging, crated and uncrated. Furthermore, de Creeft likes cats. The studio has been called "cat-haunted." It has upper quarters with a ladder disappearing upward, for de Creeft lives there.

The simplicity (it is really abstract concentration) with which he sees his work problems, he sees daily life with too. He needs a nail, he has none, so he makes one—it takes time, of course, but this is part of his work, whereas leaving his work for the wild jungles of the dime store is outer distraction and would not occur to him as allowable during the intense concentration and meditation of his labor. Early hard times gave him the knowledge of how to make nearly every small needed thing, which was luck in one way. He never goes far away from his work, for it is his life.

If I were describing de Creeft's appearance, I would think first of all that it is fully eloquent. His face (lined, tanned, with light eyes) in animation is mobile and alight, in repose meditative. His hands look both gentle and strong, above all, vital. Their power seems quite visible. You can imagine them easily in the tirelessness and the delicateness and the energy of his hard work. There is no bluntness in the fingers, no heaviness from the tons of matter that have been held in them. His talk (made up of Spanish, French, and English with onomatopoeic words and some spectacular pauses and frequent delighted laughter) carries a pantomime as agile and explicit and sometimes, for his and your amusement, as exaggerated as an acrobat's or dancer's. Once when I saw Massine (whom in some way, not too literal, he resembles) dancing the Gay Peruvian in "Gaité Parisienne," his unbounded high spirits reminded me of de Creeft at Yaddo before lunchtime—indeed, de Creeft says his energies are too exuberant in the morning for him to fully control and concentrate his direction of work; he waits until they have been expended somewhat. At Saratoga Springs he would leap on a bicycle of English racer design, and, wearing a striped sweatshirt, brief shorts, and a cap on backwards, he would tear off, waving to everybody—actually to spot stones lying on the hillsides that he might dream of some day carrying off. The most wonderful of these stones, he would say regretfully, were parts of gateways, or holding up some house. He coveted them from his bicycle. Materials used by de Creeft have been things found in a field as well as things acquired at great cost and sacrifice. Material is important to him for its own sake in a very deep sense; fundamentally it directs what he does with it. It has taught him the great craftsmanship which is implicit in his work—it

is an inspirer itself, a piece out of the earth, with the whole of life implicit in it, and its earthy shape, grain, color, weight, warmth, and the
undefinable qualities, which he, by study, calls forth, are brought into
full spirit and life by his physical work upon it. He therefore never has
seen an uninteresting stone in a field or bit of driftwood on a beach.

In the spontaneity of conversation, the way de Creeft begins some
tale and tells it with words agilely plucked from any and all languages,
with his wiry gesture, forms it, as it were, and then with delicacy and
humor suddenly abandons it at just a certain moment to let it stand
before you. You can understand that he is a creator even in his freest
moments—that every act, every little joke even (which he seems to be
performing under his nickname, Pepe), is a using of the material of the
moment and a bringing it to form.

De Creeft is a kind man, he listens to others with the patience
of a tried understanding (how often he responds, *"Est possible!"*) and
from him—though he can be logically brief and ironical—comes the
unmistakable spark that shows real interest in other people and in-
vites their best ideas. He seems seldom surprised: he is the one who
surprises others. With artists able to understand talk of work and its
meaning, and with pupils learning from him, de Creeft must certainly
be at his most eloquent and at his most explicit. I would guess this in-
struction to sound quite simple, essential, and yet, as always, four-di-
mensional, with that other, bolstering dimension of expression which
is his conception (and certainly the right one) of communication.

He loves every small life. He would watch the fat Yaddo squirrels
with what I can only call a very Spanish amusement, slightly imita-
tive. He was always hoping a telegraph boy would walk in the great
hall with some news about the condition of his mother cat, who was
expecting kittens in New York. He seemed the kind of man who could
feel rather far from daily things and would miss being sure of them,
though he had luxurious isolation for his work. He did no sculpturing
that summer. He had arthritis somewhat in his hands. Then, too, it is
possible that he had an apprehension that the appeal of such institutions as Yaddo, however well meant, is to the artist's vanity, and de

Creeft had no vanity to receive it. He did some rapid red and yellow watercolors in his studio there, frieze-like, imaginary, bacchanalian-looking figures, though he did not paint much of the dark and park-like landscape around him. Looking at it he nodded, "Is for oils."

He also occupied himself with a whole colony of two- and three-inch-high clay figures which he brought with him. A marvelous and sympathetic sense of the absurd in man could account for the playful but astonishing and keen distortions in these figures, which are a kind of thinking in clay. A godlike affection as well as a devastating devil-glance has perpetrated these. Caricature can be the sign of the whole of tolerance—and limitless delight in the unending possibilities of form. And the absurd is often the last gate before the most unexplored fields of the imagination—where any undreamed of beauty might be.

The extreme variety of de Creeft's work has never ceased to astonish people. Sometimes colossal and elephantine, it has been called Asiatic. Much of it has a subtle, flowing, smiling energy like the sculpture of India. Again it will have the galloping, mocking quality that comes straight from Spain. *Semite Head* is more like an Assyrian seasonal god. There is one common factor in each piece—something lives. In *Maturity*, English stone turns as ripe as a plum and yet is still stone—a warm life comes out of it. His working on garden images and fountains might be thought symbolic in de Creeft's life—for out of his stone he has always seen and released forces of nature, and jets of living life. He is not so much imposing a dauntless will on the rock as giving to the rock his creative labor and his imagination, and allowing it to release a form. Creation is, in its practising sense, taking one thing and making another thing out of it—which yet shows its origin and gives to that origin greater glory. Its greatest strength would seem to imply the most intimate as well as the most abstract (in that it is humble and the self disappears into work) way of using material—the *taille directe*. By *taille directe*, de Creeft's imagination, abundant and profound, generous, daring, ardent, yet always coherent, above all utilizes the material at his hand. This is almost to say that the material is making the sculpture as he, simultaneously, is learning and working from it. If this is extreme, I believe it could be said that it is not far from de Creeft's belief. His is a noble conception of work, which fills the sculptor with dignity, and endlessly leads him to experiment.

Another variety exists in de Creeft's work—variety in mood. *Group of Women*, in English limestone, whose embracing figures make a cluster of ripe swelling curves, is as delicious to the sight as a Hindu carving, with a lulling, joyous quality. And *Cloud*, of similar composition, is complete abstraction. *Seguidillas—Spanish Gypsy Dance* is a sculptural examination of what happens in four beats of gypsy music. De Creeft knows not only the majestic moods of the spirit, exemplified most purely, perhaps, in *Himalaya*, but the gentle, passing moods, the humorous, the gay, and the mood of the child. This is because de Creeft knows the timelessness of the most momentary, the most fragile aspects of the human being and the human form, when they are seen in the illumination of the spirit. If only de Creeft would work a playful expression, *a moue*, into pink quartz for eternity, it would be perfect proof of his delight in life itself, his evaluation of its most fleeting moments. All of life is as real and enduring as basic rock—nothing in life can be lost—and the most playful moments, equally with the most serious, endure and have their place.

In all truly great works of art we find ourselves looking at many faces upon it; many ideas out of other times and countries crowd upon us, as when we look in the vastest pools, a world of reflections strikes our eyes. This need not be the same as thinking the pool is "influenced" by what is seen in its depths. Mayan and Oriental things are seen in de Creeft's work—in the fruitful curves and fullness and subtlety and twining of forms—likewise an ascetic beauty, a purity and loftiness that speak out of work like *Himalaya*. But does it not all spring out of one profundity? Profundity does not know how to be influenced, for in its own being is its own secret of learning. Time alone is its influence.

Magazine of Art 37, February 1944, pages 42–47.

Chodorov and Fields in Mississippi

Mr. Chodorov and Mr. Fields, known to be a warm-hearted team, felt so kindly inclined toward their newly acquired "Ponder Heart" as to be willing to leave the environs of Broadway and enter the environs of Mississippi early last year, in order to see what their property had to do with and where Uncle Daniel had sprung from. Without having any experience to draw on, I still somehow doubt it's every playwright who would go so far.

As author of the original story I hadn't yet had the opportunity to meet the gentlemen. Things had been settled by remote control, and with my old friend and schoolmate, Lehman Engel, acting as advisor throughout. He has been of long and patient help to me, and as a penalty for his kind deeds he has had to write the music for the play, in the middle of all the other things he's doing—for which I'm most proud and grateful.

It seems Mr. Chodorov and Mr. Fields alighted from their plane about at Atlanta, thinking to drive to Jackson, Miss., in a U-Drive-It car, the better to get a look at the setting. They saw a great deal of it, for the South, like the rest of the country, is a lot roomier than the Easterner ever dreams, and we are about as far from Georgia here in Mississippi as New York once was from Michigan, where I understand that David Wayne came from.

The minute the playwrights were over the Mississippi line, they parked and got out—they were in the small town of Meridian—and before they were even both altogether clear of the thing, the wretched U-Drive-It, like one of Chodorov's and Fields' own Frankenstein props, drove itself unaided up over the curb, across the sidewalk, and into the plate glass window of a jewelry store.

It was siesta time in Meridian—matinee time in New York. An immediate crowd, though, materialized from nowhere, and the playwrights were surrounded, not knowing exactly what to expect. What they got was a great, big, general, aspiring sigh going up from everybody, expressing all the gratification in the world. They were met not with restraint but with acclaim. Chodorov and Fields were a smash hit. The jeweler came on with a line about his being perfectly willing to have given the gentlemen whatever it was had attracted them in the window without their having to come inside after it; and a pair of policemen appeared, as charmed as the rest, to tell each other how seldom in life you could hope to see a bullseye made like that, an achievement so thorough, so complete and spectacular, all lit up with rhinestones. Entertainment had come to town. It was a wonder the boys weren't asked to do an encore.

They were too nice to tell me what they were asked for, but they made a graceful and snappy exit, and by the time they reached Jackson the U-Drive-It had been dropped from the act. But I like to think that, at whatever cost and I hope a modest one, there was born then and there a bit of insight or even rapport: Chodorov and Fields learned what to expect of Mississippi, and Mississippi learned what to expect of Chodorov and Fields: appreciation on both sides.

As it happened, I was away from Jackson, where my home is, when the playwrights arrived, unaware that they were here until next day.

When I came home there was a vase of enormous red roses on the table with a card reading "Welcome home, kid, you're gonna like it here." This was my introduction to Mr. Fields and Mr. Chodorov, and our association—mostly thereafter across the distance, with one lovely meeting in New York—has continued to be as warm and as popping with surprises as that big red bouquet.

It is scarcely worth mentioning—since I had nothing to do with the writing of the play—that we probably never could see eye to eye on the matter of "The Ponder Heart." I recognized and valued the playwrights' affection for the story, but to begin with, I could not imagine it as a play, and they could. Mr. Fields and Mr. Chodorov know all about *that* sort of misgiving—lady authors in particular are prone to it; and gaily whipping out the script—for they'd brought it along, through Meridian and everything, they would let me hear how it went.

I was later on to be better educated about play scripts and to learn that playwrights of the vast experience of Mr. F. and Mr. C. toss off at least 20 versions of their plays, the last one maybe in the aisle in New Haven. But at the time I supposed their first version to be their only one, and that unless we could set each other straight on a few things, we were all going to end up in Bedlam. (Maybe we are.)

Even if I'm not under the illusion that there's an emergency, I don't understand much that's being read aloud to me. This happened to be a play-version of a story I thought I knew better than anything, being read aloud in my own living room, on an unseasonably hot day in February, in an indulgent Southern accent assumed for the occasion by Mr. Chodorov, who had prefaced it all by saying, "Kid, this is going to be a very great shock."

And I did feel a little as if I'd been taken through a plate glass window in Times Square. But that's only how it has to feel to a lady-author who is having something of hers transformed at her ear from a story to a Broadway play, and after it is all over she will undoubtedly laugh as hard as the rest. This was only the first version. The final version I've never seen (or heard). It's all going to be one grand surprise to at least one member of the audience when the curtain goes up Tuesday night.

Of course the greatest distinction and luck that could possibly be hoped for has come to it in David Wayne's being cast as Uncle Daniel. Even before I see his performance I feel immensely happy about it. He is a lovely actor, and if I could have a wish as author it would be that some of his own spangling imagination could shed backwards forever onto the original of my story, who would accept it and bask in it in due gratification and highmindedness.

Mr. Douglas, the director, has also visited Mississippi in the course of things. An inhabitant of Beverly Hills, he seemed a trifle nervous that money had such a big role in the play, when he could look around and see there was very little of that in Mississippi at all; and I await opening night to see if he's felt compelled to devalue the Ponder largesse. But how could he dream he could get away with that, in the beaming face of David Wayne?

This essay, written 11 January 1956, was requested of Welty for potential use in promoting *The Ponder Heart* production was published in *Eudora Welty Newsletter*, April 1979, pages 4–6, transcribed from a four-page typescript in the Theatre Collection, the New York Public Library at Lincoln Center, New York.

John Rood

John Rood came out of Ohio; he was born in Luhrig, near Athens. When he was not quite school age, his father died leaving the family not well off, and he grew up with early responsibilities. He had to wait a while before luck, or affinity, had brought him friends who understood his talents and longings and gave him the help toward travel and study that he needed. It was such help as he himself gave when in publishing the stories of young unknown writers in his "little magazine" *Manuscript,* he gave the first start to many of us, among them the undersigned.

He saw the art of Europe before he found out he was a sculptor; he was already a writer and something of a musician. We can surmise from what followed that certain works and places spoke to him with great impact and clarity—the hunter—figures on the walls of the Dordogne Caves, the dreaming Gothic saints, folded like leaves, that stand in the French Cathedrals, the sportive, lively figures on the Etruscan tombs. Mr. Bruno Schneider's monograph says that John Rood met his fate when he walked up on a country craftsman carving figures for the cross of a wayside shrine in France. (And the name Rood is a word for cross.) At any rate, the experience of meeting art at first hand had happened to him.

He came home to Athens, Ohio, and after his day's work at a printing shop began his real work at night, carving in wood with carpenter's tools at his basement work bench. He worked with a growing passion and at passion's rate of speed and conviction and increase of skill. He has worked and traveled, since, in many places of the world, but he has remained, as he began, entirely self-taught.

The early pieces are spontaneous and sturdy and have great honesty and skill. They are the folk heroes, figures from the Bible, and the ballad that the boy had grown up with—as if this might be a modest way for an art to begin, from a story read or a song heard. But it was not long before he went for good to primary sources. His ideas, tapping deeper and deeper roots, have become increasingly abstract; new forms and images steadily emerge; his use of new materials has left behind his early self-limiting reliance on wood alone. Besides carving, he models, now; sometimes he welds; he constructs with glass and intractable metals; he employs color. Maturity has simply assigned him to go ahead—the better he knows, the farther to try; the more he has to risk, to risk it. In the words of the highest praise any artist can give or receive, he goes out on a limb.

Implicit in these forms is his conception of the cycle of growth, a spirit that can be called change, transformation, becoming. We respond the most fully to the beauty of motion charged with completing itself. The moments going before and after are bringing the round to the present; the spirit of continuation deeply informs them. Time flickers all over these "Salamanders." Or, in "Moth," we come on the spirit lying asleep, an embodiment—the moth changing as if internally in our presence, by way of its sleep, into the phase just next, not quite yet. The time is meanwhile; we look at and touch a dream, a spell rapt in marble.

Often, indeed, time is more than implicit—it may almost be called the subject. The two marvelously animate "Pistils" might be dramatic figures performing time, two aspects of mortality. In the "Scrolls" we seem to have time's endurance before us, time that has lasted out everything to reach the point of its very termination, and fused—time into which even mortality has burned itself. In "Exploding Star" there is nothing finite; it is all expansion, the renewal of time, its self-duplication and prophecy. We turn to the "Fountain" and are looking straight at this very moment.

As John Rood continues to exhibit we have increasing evidence that as he has studied and worked out his forms of growth, growth, like a good fairy, has attended him. Honest and forthright as it has been from the start, his work has spoken in plain sequence; it has quite open stages of development and a clear direction. It seems likely that he will always be developing forms that keep the exuberance and spontaneity of the early figures while they move into an even further liberation from confinement. More and more, his compositions in space stir with a life and fill with a presence to match the solid masses out of which they spring. The relationship is visible between them; we are aware of mutual tensions and reflections, of an orbit imposed on the whole.

Today, his imagination is seizing hold of that last point of contact between earth and air. Here is a sculptor moved to his finest work in iron and glass and steel and stone by the point of incandescence—the salamander and the burning bush, the explosion of a star.

What he has to say is still fresh as a birdcall at morning. His subjects pull their own weight, and have never given trouble to him or us by calling for the sad, loaded drapery of symbolism. Here has occurred mastery of the medium without a jot's loss in the joy and wonder the artist felt on the first day he discovered—it may have been in France, but it could have been the soonest possible moment, in Ohio—that he could make something beautiful. With the years of experiment, this happiness has never been confiscated, and will never have to be ransomed. The treasure is here.

Introduction to *Exhibition of Recent Sculpture John Rood*, New York, 1958. Rood was editor of *Manuscript* and published Welty's first and third stories: "Death of a Traveling Salesman" and "Magic" in 1936.

William Hollingsworth Show

W illiam Hollingsworth knew this world; the paintings will tell you how well. When you go back to see again the 64 examples of his work now on view at the Art Gallery, you keep thinking of what he loved: the hour of the day; the day of the week; the month of the year; water; sky; the road going over the hill. All might have been a phenomenon to his eyes—all Mississippi. He loved the violet spaces hanging beyond the last ridge, the rich red gullies, the loneliness of telephone poles marching away, the hush of snow, the warm streaming lights of city rain; and he kept going back to the festivals of life that would suddenly break out at a country crossroads, the figures that might have sprung out of our Mississippi clay in simple spontaneous combustion.

The mud in "Brown and Wet" shines in its puddles like a rainbow stirred with whatever stick came handiest in Mississippi. The Vicksburg backyards pitch downhill in cascades of olive-brown, tawny-brown, violet-brown, yellow-brown, from the silent, winter-backs of houses. The broomsedge over the field in "Cold Wet Day" looks venerable as a tapestry, weightless as gauze, and alive as a Collie dog's back. All these are winter landscapes; seeing them on this new visit, I felt that the spirit of our place stands perhaps the closest here, among the silvers, violets, browns, and sudden clear blues. It is a presence that could walk. Snow itself seems to have held the greatest magic for him. Indeed, in "The Ice-Covered Tree" there is an enchanted quality; about the tree in its dress of white we all but see the embrace of the Snow Queen.

With what knowledge, yes, but with what tenderness he painted! It was not a tenderness that stood in the way and blurred what his eye told him; rather it must have come of ever-increasing awareness. It opened some door further down the perspective, and showed him new things—those relationships he has expressed between grass and sky, between roof and roadway, between rain and the upstreaming smoke from a cabin.

We see again as we visit these paintings that his was the quietest of techniques, and the most affirmative. He knew what he saw, and here it is—not the copy of life, but his vision of it. Here are the famous antic figures skittering through the sudden shower—but what his eye took in, and his hand set down, is charged not with anecdote but with poetry. Who can ever forget the dream-circled eyes of that bemused child, as he waits his time on the porch outside the door, holding the gift of a strawberry ice cream cone—dusky and splendid as a Magi?

We here, of course, recognize with ease the material William Hollingsworth worked with, for he always began with the close-at-hand; and the accuracy of his eye turned on the home scene is as marvelously reliable as that of another Mississippi William in another line of work. Again like Faulkner he never stops there. William Hollingsworth set off on the Old Canton Road, and the painting is where the mind, spirit, and feeling carried him. There we're confronted with a territory we are not bound to recognize at all, but to which we give a response better than recognition, our own feeling about his vision of the world.

I think William Hollingsworth had, besides his other wonderful gifts, the gift of true gayety that is a paradox; for even despair never rules it out, and maybe informs it. For surely there are these things that were never gay in this world, or never can be gay, and yet look at this picture—they *are* gay. Or do I mean that the gay can be unbearably sad, like the clowns' songs in Shakespeare? At any rate, those figures peopling the rainy alleys and making the empty crossings suddenly alive in the little island of life are, when William Hollingsworth came right down to it, as gay a sight as the whole bunch of us is likely to make, whirling and jigging through space on this weather-wrapped planet, any old day in the year.

His was a most personal vision, and isn't it this, perhaps, that gives the enduring beauty to his work? In each of these paintings, what we know the surest and value the most is that nobody else could have seen the world this way, or will see it so again; that only William Hollingsworth, happening to travel the place we live, has seen *this,* and made it true.

We are grateful to have this superlative exhibition. It is good too to let it remind us that his work never loses a bit of its freshness, not an ounce of its force; that it is as original as a spring coming out of the ground, and there is no reason why its beauty will not flow on, perfectly clear and apparent, as long as there are people to look at painting.

Typescript, The Welty Collection, Mississippi Department of Archives and History, Jackson, Mississippi, three pages. Welty's review of Hollingsworth's posthumous exhibition of sixty-four paintings at the Jackson Municipal Art Gallery was published in the Jackson *Clarion Ledger/Daily News,* 14 September 1958, pages 1C and 4C.

On *Cat on a Hot Tin Roof*

M r. Williams' plays burst in on us with such extraordinary voltage that—just as after a crisis in real life—we find it hard to describe afterwards what hit us. Was it violence or excruciating tenderness, that sharpest moment? Was it unbearable crudeness or extraordinary delicacy that finally drove the point home? Have all our senses just been impaled on some hopeless reality, or are we arguing with a dream? And wasn't it beautiful when the whole Delta, surely the whole world outside, seemed to stop and listen while the mockingbird sang?

Brilliant as Tennessee Williams' technical endowment is, aren't we convinced by the time the curtain falls that an even greater power lies in something within, in his driving wish to show us something about ourselves? Behind every play he's written we seem to hear crying out a belief that as human beings we don't go so far—no matter how far we do go—as to tell each other the truth.

We see his characters living without honor, or in nothing but a dream of honor, haunted by the past, wrenched by the present, blind to the future. We hear them yell and holler and rave into each other's faces, or wait while they reach out in silence toward each other—they never crash the sound barrier of understanding.

The brutality of some of his characters, no less than the dreaming of others, must be a cloak to hide the truth from themselves and one another. The reason is (he seems to be saying) that out of ignorance, wrongheadedness, pride, desire, rage, despair, perversity, or just plain fuzziness—and often in spite of love—we don't know how to communicate.

"Mendacity?" pipes up Sister Woman, after Big Daddy's most searing speech. "Big Daddy, I'm afraid I don't know what that word means."

In the North, so we hear, they don't believe people talk like this. In the South we know people talk like this, and because we can recognize so much—of speech, place, character, life—might we run the risk of missing something else?

Not when we really look and listen at this play—that, bringing so much familiarity home, is as full of strange and wonderful and thought-provoking things as if it were written by some visitor foreign to our shores, who has come here and cast his eye upon us. Indeed it is the eye of a poet.

The Spotlight, program for *Cat on a Hot Tin Roof* by Tennessee Williams, performed at the Jackson Little Theatre, 2–10 February 1959. In 1955, while Welty's novel *The Ponder Heart* was playing in a Jerome Chodorov and Joseph Fields dramatic adaptation at the Music Box Theater at 239 West 45th Street in New York, Williams' *Cat on a Hot Tin Roof* was being performed a block away at the Morosco Theater, 217 West 45th.

On Fairy Tales

Trying to retell the story another has written can't help but make a hash of the story and a fool of the author. So much for authors. Fairy tales, on the other hand, can stand it, because retelling is what made them and what they are. Many mouths and many ears, many memories in many countries, shaped and sharpened them before the first hand wrote them down. Fairy tales are survivors. Authorless, timeless, placeless, they are also flawless. They are finished works. They have the prevalence and pertinacity, indeed the recalcitrant surface, of hard facts. And where wide-awake facts in our day go to pieces, the story of "The Sleeping Beauty" goes smoothly on.

These bits of old fiction called fairy tales are as smooth as pebbles washed up out of the sea. And yet what a character they have kept, every one. Inspired hands, like Perrault or the Brothers Grimm, who put them on paper, are only partly, and recently, responsible. There is in every fairy tale an indelible human element.

And in their character how they vary! Some have morals, some laugh in the face of morals; some are savage, some merry; some are marvelously decked out, some plain. But they survive alike because they are all good stories.

Their plots have never been surpassed and are still in service. They have action—unflinching, unremitting, sometimes circular. They appeal to the senses, they charm the memory. Their formal structure pleases the sense of order and design; their conversation is suitable, intense, pragmatic, well-timed, and makes sense for its own story alone.

Children like fairy tales also because they are wonderfully severe and uncondescending. They like the kind of finality that really slams the door. "Then the Wolf pounced upon Red Riding Hood and ate her up." And fairy tales are not innocent; they have been to the end of experience and back. Fairy tales were never in the world invented by children, and children appreciate them for that. Yet children have undoubtedly helped shape the tales by being their audience. Hundreds of years of close listening must have sifted and shamed every weakness out. What is left every time is a good, tough, hard core of a story, good for a long time yet.

Fairy tales are full of intrigue. Do you remember "The Yellow Dwarf"? Toutebelle, after a rash promise made to a fairy in the desert, wakes up wearing a ring made of a single red hair, on so tight that the skin would have to be taken off first, and at her wedding (to the King of the Mines) the Fairy of the Desert enters uninvited with two large turkey-cocks drawing a box, and its lid flies up as high as the ceiling and out of it comes the Yellow Dwarf (to whom Toutebelle's *mother* had made a rash promise), mounted with spurs, on a large Spanish cat.

Fairy tales are pitiless—there is no time for pity. (The pity in Hans Christian Andersen's stories may hurt them: it is a comedown to be asked to cry.) And they are frivolous. True frivolity is a luxury the youngest child can savor. And of course, best of all, the tales are true, in their fairy way. Their motivation is absolutely on the beam. "Let us open the door to find out, if it's true we'll be sorry."

It is interesting that children, rather noticeably, understand irony. They get it from fairy tales. When we get older we are offered reasons as to *why* we liked fairy tales—for they are cruel, often enough—but, meanwhile, we have already learned irony from "Puss in Boots."

As for the cruelty, do not ogres who enjoy eating people show children very well in fantasy what will threaten them later on? Modern children's stories, with neither fairies nor ogres, leave out unsympathetic characters and anti-social manners, presumably for fear of upsetting the moral that we are all brothers. We are all brothers, but some of us are loveless. If fairy tales stir the imagination toward benevolence with the "good" fairies, they can awaken respect for the power of the "bad" fairies. Without the old fairy tales, children today could easily think malice and ill-will are nothing but a set of miniature, sanitized, plastic toys—"giants 'n' ogres"—that come free in boxes of cereal at the supermarket. Sentimentality, which Jack can't kill, is guilty of more harm than any threats of Fe Fi Fo Fum.

Human truths, bolder and often more appalling than we know what to do with, much less what to tell children about them, do seem to get through to children, in their fairy-tale disguise, without harm to the children or too much distortion of the truth. Children can make distinctions in an order of their importance. Before they come to realize what's sad or cheerful, they learn what's false, what's true.

It is salutary also to learn, via fairy tales, that beauty, bravery, youth and such characteristics or rewards as diamonds falling from the lips with each kind word spoken, are all *gifts*—and that under difficulties laughable or horrendous, the less protected you go in life, the better it is to have wit.

And of course fairy tales don't end their power with our own fleeting childhood. Read and write—and the power is about its old business. Consider the debt poets owe to the fairy tales, and have paid, from Shakespeare to the lowest. So have the playwrights, not only the Elizabethan, those of the Irish Renaissance (and past it, into Brendan

Behan, whose Hostage jumps up to life again at curtainfall), and speaking of ogresses, look at Ibsen.

The short story is packed with fairy-tale debt. Isak Dinesen's "Gothic Tales," Kafka's "Metamorphosis," Pushkin's "Queen of Spades"—you could call up names almost at random. And for the odd writers, like Fitz-James O'Brien, Vernon Lee, Lafcadio Hearn, LeFanu, or Saki, the fairy tales were standing always right at their shoulders. In the modern novel, we can ignore the fairy tale's blatant presence in the sentimental serials to admire the purposeful and brilliant *using* of it in a piece of first-rate writing like Henry Green's "Loving." Throughout fiction runs the constant, casual reference to the fairy tale, for which the memory of the reader everywhere has laid up recognition.

The references and associations will even work both ways. "Little Red Riding Hood" reminds me in an amusing way of Ivy Compton-Burnett: it is the conversation, so succinct, so fell. "The Fisherman and His Wife" brings thoughts of D. H. Lawrence: once more the wildness of the weather and the alarming changes in the color of the sea have resulted from a wife's demanding will. In "Perlino" (the lover whom Violetta made at home in her room—as recalled, out of almond paste, sugar, rubies and pearls—then sang to. "Come, Perlino. Dance with me") there is the oddest echo of Colette's "Cheri."

It's all one fabric, all valid. All serious writers deal at bottom with the mysteriousness of human life: and the fairy tales gave that mysteriousness its first childhood language, a language like any other, a familiarity which can be always drawn on, and can always enrich.

Published as "And They All Lived Happily Ever After," *New York Times Book Review*, 10 November 1963, page 3. The author's note references Welty's "fantasy, *The Robber Bridegroom*," the novella she called her "Fairy Tale of the Natchez Trace."

Review of *Martha Graham: Portrait of the Lady as an Artist* by LeRoy Leatherman

Martha Graham, we read here, has said she learned her first danc-ing lesson from her father—a doctor. He had learned it from observing the behavior of his mental patients: *movement never lies.* From the beginning, says LeRoy Leatherman in his informative and beautifully mounted *Martha Graham: Portrait of the Lady as an Artist,* "Martha aimed for . . . ways of moving that would communicate vari-eties of human experience which the art of the dance had never before attempted . . . and ultimately for dramas that would be acted through movement alone."

An American from away back—Miles Standish is an ancestor—this bold and down-to-earth innovator is "a peculiarly American ge-nius of whom Americans know very little." Before she was grown, she had gone with the Denishawn Company, dancing as a Japanese boy. (This was her role on stage; off stage she was being their bookkeeper.) She did an Apache number with Charles Weidman in the *Greenwich Village Follies,* taught after that at the Eastman School, where, said

Rouben Mamoulian, who hired her, she came upon the scene "like John the Baptist." But when, in 1926, she gave her first performance as an independent artist, it was on the stage of a Broadway theater, the Forty-Eighth Street, and it has always been the theater, not the studio, that she has made her boundaries inside, performed in, created for.

Mr. Leatherman goes so far as to call Martha Graham not a choreographer but a dramatist. He is equipped to speak. Since for twelve years he has been variously associated with Miss Graham as her company manager, personal manager, and the director of her School, we may take this as official—or if not quite that, then as an opinion due respect. Since also Mr. Leatherman is a novelist, he is further equipped for translating story and movement onto the page without having his head go round. He has written what must have been, nevertheless, a difficult book to write: a book about the one artist from whose works *all* words, all "intellectualizations," have been specifically and warmly banned by the subject of the book. Yet he has done his job well: a sensitive portrait emerges; he has insight and wit; and where, in his world, he must be the only one who is standing still, he has kept his equilibrium as well as his firm affection.

The Graham ideas come from where all original and undeniable ideas in art come from—within; perhaps they are intense forms of human insight. She must mediate alone. But her work "begins to be cooperative the moment she hands her script to the composer and it becomes increasingly so until, by curtain time on opening night, a hundred or so people are involved."

Her script must be indescribable: "deliberately open and evocative," it is yet a working sheet; and for the composers she sends her scripts to, they do work: Aaron Copland, Henry Cowell, Norman Dello Joio, William Schuman, and others. When the music arrives, she never questions a note or asks for changes (she is not overly fond of music for its own sake); what she has to do is get "the pattern of the composition in her sinews." Once she's done that, she ties the handles of her studio doors together with a strip of red jersey, "and everyone on the premises knows what that means. From now on, no one unasked enters until the knot is untied."

Of her set designers, it is Noguchi with whom she has always worked best. He did *Appalachian Spring, Cave of the Heart, Night Journey, Seraphic Dialogue, Clytemnestra, Alcestis,* and *Phaedra,* among others. "There is a perfect understanding by each of the other's art, a perfect agreement about the use and power of symbols and about the design and use of stage space." These are of course the fundamentals of her work. Noguchi makes her a tiny model that he can bring her in a shoe box. But they neither one can foresee quite everything from this: the finished set for *Seraphic Dialogue* (the shining, abstract structure in tubes which was to suggest Joan of Arc's cathedral, and which might have been made by Merlin out of Tinker-toys) would, Noguchi thought, fit into a good big suitcase; it somehow requires five crates "and some mechanical genius to erect."

Mr. Leatherman's book, of necessity loosely organized though explicitly worded, takes us from the beginning of a Graham work, which may, or may not, start with a *script*—*Clytemnestra* (which Mr. Leatherman considers her highest achievement) was achieved without a script—up to curtain rise on opening night. He supplies an account both affectionate and touching of the final hectic weeks before an Opening, and shares with us the cries heard from the great artist through the pandemonium: "Why did I ever get myself into this? Cancel the season." "I haven't had a minute to work on myself. Clear the building. Get the company out of here, they've rehearsed enough. I've got to have some time alone." "I cannot think about that now." There's no time to eat or think about food, and besides "It is better always to eat the same thing." "Money? Money's nothing. If we *need* it, we'll have it." "Don't *push* me!" And, "I'm being nibbled to death by ducks!"

Then, on the night, the lone meditation to which she has returned for a last hour over with, she waits in the wings transformed. Before, in the weeks of work, "she was in her own eyes a drudge; now she is ready for the conquering . . . alert for the cue and the wash of light to bring her out to be Clytemnestra or Phaedra or Alcestis or Judith . . . or the comical, but most moving and understandable, artist in *Acrobats of God.*"

"She started, and her art starts," he writes, "with basic facts, on the ground; the floor, equivalent to the hard, resistant but cultivatable earth, is her element as surely as the ballet dancer's element is clear empty air." The drama she then builds he sees as essentially Greek: it must "move, purge and elevate the spirit." "Martha's best works are always models of poetic density, economy, and compression. She can convey more in twenty-five minutes than most playwrights can manage to do in three acts." I think he can say *that* again. When she works with history, myths, the ancient tragedies, "there is no guessing . . . how she will re-mold them." What is certain is the originality of her insight and of her approach. "She will . . . take full liberty with the events . . . but she never violates her source and never debases it. In fact she elevates her protagonists by bestowing upon them . . . a richer humanity." "She has never, as she says, been interested in anything small." Rather, her work is "an affirmation of man. Her art insists upon the meaningfulness of human experience, even the darkest."

"Dancing, she is an actress; 'choreographing,' she is a dramatist." This is interesting, it is descriptive, and certainly the distinction matters, but does it matter a great deal, one may wonder, by what name we call a truly original artist of the first water? The unique might just as well go free of all tags. The Graham genius is, past argument, itself. Rather than hover over its definition, let us seize the day and testify to its force.

She is an artist whose work is inseparable from her life, whose art and whose being are one, as this book well brings out. In the presence of such integrity as hers the audience feels it like a blaze. Furthermore, to those of us who have filled her theaters since the early days of what she now calls her "long woolen period," the excitement of her work has been increasing with time; it has performed its own drama of change and growth. It is as though her theater itself were a moving boat on a river, and we on the bank were running beside it to keep up with it and to celebrate with it where it is going. Not only are the performances new experiences, but the river is uncharted, no telling how deep, full of the dangers of a strong, unpredictable current; and the boat itself is homemade, as was the Ark, and like it based on a personal idea, a loyal company, and help from above. Martha Graham has acknowledged the impracticalities and impecunities and the dangers of her life's work with exhilaration, with many a joyous manoeuvre, many an astonishment clapped upon our eyes.

And in invention and in performance, she is consistently working in the line of magic and legend from which her characters spring. She calls up a spell and she uses it. We follow what she is doing on her stage because we are under enchantment; we are its subjects, or should I say its calculated objects? Circe had other plans for people, but were her working methods very different?

Martha Graham, a strong-minded genius, whose new season this spring introduced her hundred and fortieth and her hundred and forty-first new work, has no plans of leaving the stage to begin with, and no intention at all of leaving it her notations. She has had an enormous influence on the dance, but she will not pass on her secrets: this would mean putting them into abhorred words. She abhors also reviving a work; Clytemnestra can not go back to being the Bride of *Appalachian Spring*. No film has successfully recorded her. Her art belongs to us who see her now. Its indelibility is offered only to the memory of lucky people.

There is no other way. An art in which the spirit of the artist is translated into the body, the dance belongs to the living present in which it moves. In fact, isn't its transience one of its awe-inspiring properties? If the same physical law applied to all the arts, we would need to have lived after 1787 and before 1791, and to have known the right people, and then not to have had a cold on the night of the invitation, to have heard *Don Giovanni* once.

Twenty-seven pages of stunning photographs lead off this book, twenty-seven pages more parade at the close, and dozens of others appear throughout its text. They are by Martha Swope, made during performances of the last five years; they are beautiful in themselves and invaluable as records. Included also is a complete chronological list of the dances composed by Miss Graham from 1926 through 1965, along with the names of the musical composers.

Published as "Movement Never Lies," *Sewanee Review*, Summer 1967, pages 529–33. Two years later, Graham said of Welty, "Years ago my Company and I performed in Jackson. We were very nervous because we heard that Eudora Welty was in the audience. It puts you on edge knowing an eye, let alone a heart, like that is out front," *Shenandoah*, Spring 1969, page 36.

Introduction, *The Democratic Forest* by William Eggleston

The Democratic Forest, a most remarkable and beautiful book, is what is even rarer, an original one. Consisting entirely of the eloquent photographs of the American photographer William Eggleston, it begins as an autobiography might, with a setting for a life.

The opening photograph shows us a quiet and cared-for breadth of meadow, field and pastureland, set back at an easeful distance from its road, led to through a line of wide-spaced trees in the leafing spring of the year, protected on the upper side by an arm of the old forest. A sentinel shade tree stands beside the open-doored barn. The caption reads: "Early spring at Mayfair, my family plantation in Sunflower County." The place has been photographed in its tender rural colours. No one is in view.

I think with this we have received the first signal that this book of photographs—he has made it wholly his own—is a result of personal choosing, that it will proceed to form itself, as it opens out, into a personal whole. We won't expect the photographs to be fitted into the kind of sequence that would confine such a freedom; the order is, to my mind, the much more significant one of cohesion, of affinity with human values. The body of photographs before us might, with cause, be seen as the culmination of Mr. Eggleston's long and distinguished career.

All the photographs have place as their subject. From Mayfair on, places appear to have loomed large for William Eggleston. Now a resident of Memphis, he has been spending his life making exemplary photographs of the world around him and thereby recording its ways. These photographs that begin with his home place, which is in Mississippi, radiate widely over the United States, touch on Europe, go as far as the Berlin Wall. He has called his book *The Democratic Forest*, a title to embrace all he shows us.

The photographs range widely, they are highly differing, richly varying. In landscapes, cityscapes, street scenes, roadside scenes, at every sort of public converging-point, in dreaming long view and arresting close-up, through hours of dark and light, he sets forth what makes up our ordinary world. What is there, however strange, can be accepted without question; familiarity will be what overwhelms us.

The extraordinary thing is that in all these photographs, wonderfully inclusive and purposefully chosen as they are, you will look in vain for the presence of a human being. This isn't to say that the photographs deny man's existence. That is exactly what they don't do. Everywhere you find the vividness of his presence:

Here's a close-up of an outdoor cooker and a bloody hatchet laid down upon it, called "Near the River."

Here's the already stripped and de-wheeled front end of a red sports car, at rest under a tree by the Interstate; its radiator grille bites the dust. It seems a personal artifact, like an upper plate of a set of false teeth that's been lost on someone's way between one place and the next.

On a temporary hoarding at a construction site in Memphis, some hand wielding a stick dipped in soft tar has left a drawing of a big bridge spread like the wings of a bird over the chopping waves, and has tried to spell "Memphis" and succeeded, to the last touch of turning the "S" into a dollar sign.

Here is a just-vacated counter in a fast-foods road stop. It is stacked with uncleared plastic plates, all dripping red, like a police scene-of-the-crime file photo complete with its message to you ("Catch me before I kill again") written in tomato ketchup.

But the camera tells us nobody is there. The indelible exception is the young child photographed standing alone on a desolate street corner in some city: he stares back at the camera with the gravity of the homeless. He, too, is tenaciously present in other scenes while remaining invisible.

Indeed, Mr Eggleston's masterly photographs of places draw their strength and their significance from his never losing his own very acute sight of the human factor. The human being—the perpetrator or the victim or the abandonner of what we see before us—is the reason why these photographs of place have their power to move and disturb us; they always let us know that the human being is the reason they were made.

He has photographed every tell-tale thing we leave behind us, from leaking oil to spilled Coca-Cola. He has looked up and caught the emmanations of the Great Smoky Mountains, and a mist very like a ghost that appears to be drifting over a graveyard near Oxford, Mississippi. In photographing ivy crowding over a wall, in commotion as lively as a townful of Breughel peasants, he has got a picture of a country breeze. He moves his camera close upon a great worldly peony; our glimpse into that is as good as a visit: a bloom so full-open and spacious that we could all but enter it, sit down inside and be served tea. It was photographed, according to the caption, on the Boston Common across from the Ritz Hotel—which is the next thing to photographing an analogy. In effect, he can lay our own hand on texture and substance. He puts between our finger and thumb the slipperiness of a leaf only in that moment coming out on the budding tree. Indeed, this is what his skill performs: it makes what it shows *accessible*.

But one photograph includes: old tyres, Dr. Pepper machines, discarded air-conditioners, vending machines, empty and dirty Coca-Cola bottles, torn posters, power poles and power wires, street barricades, one-way signs, detour signs, No Parking signs, parking meters and palm trees crowding the same kerb. "Karco" (p. 38) reaches the saturation point of sign-occupied space.

His camera, held at weed level, shows us weeds close-to, shoving up their saw-toothed leaves through a crack in the pavement *and*, at a distance back in the same frame, Atlanta's skyscrapers on the rise too, proliferating and more rampant than weeds. Skyscrapers rear up like bullies planning to overrun the city, or *running* the city, from on high. He moves about the skylines of Miami, Atlanta, Pittsburgh. No last drop of humanity could come from what we've built as fortifications. He tests it with a view of the Texas State Book Depository in Dallas, indelible in the world's memory as the source of the gunshots that killed President John F. Kennedy.

Indeed, when Mr. Eggleston photographs the tall and darkened shafts rising, vacated, from the emptied night-time streets, he brings to mind "two vast and trunkless legs of stone" in the desert of the "antique land" and the inscription that remains on their ruined pedestal: "I am Ozymandias, king of kings. Look on my works, ye Mighty, and despair!"

These extraordinary, compelling, honest, beautiful and unsparing photographs all have to do with the quality of our lives in the ongoing world: they succeed in showing us the grain of the present, like the cross-section of a tree. The photographs have cut it straight through the center.

They focus on the mundane world. But *no* subject is fuller of implications than the mundane world! When you see what the mundane world so openly and multitudinously affirms, there is *everything* left to say. Mr. Eggleston's camera brings it forth. His fine and scrupulous photographs achieve beauty. All that they have to tell us, in all their variety, reaches us through the beauty of the work.

There is especial beauty in his sensitive and exacting use of color, its variations and intensities. We see the celestial blue of burning trash, the golden cloak of sunlight, or blight; the slip of a tree trying to push its way up one more time through one more crack in the parking-lot pavement is a lyrical green. But particularly there is red: the banner red of Coca-Cola signs a hundred strong, the Sienese red of rust, further and further intensities of red, the deeper into the city we go: red caught in the act of spreading, hectic and alarming, collecting and running at large through the intersections like a contagion. Solid reds: the interior of a Memphis Krystal Hamburger house, furnishings and all, a creation entirely in ruby red plastic. Throbbing reds, like vibrations being given off by the traffic.

Time in *The Democratic Forest* is the galvanic present, but as we were earlier made aware, the past, in its flickerings and shadowings, is also integral to this book. (I take it as the viewer's standing privilege of turning back to the book's beginning if the need is felt to re-visit it for freshly discovered reasons.) In the home place—*any* home place in the world—the long view is the one like memory's view: it shows us everything at once.

Turning again through the photographs of Mayfair, exterior and interior, we may apprehend and respond to the essential matters of human presence and human absence. Here is the Eggelston photograph of the family portraits set out on a library table top—a solid row of ancestors that's as calming as an unrocked boat. And, in the attic now, his camera lifts close-up to the roof-beam, into which the same hand that hewed it also carved—the camera lets us read them— the initials attesting to that mysterious thing, original ownership.

But this book's *our* portrait. We must see that. We should be prepared to see the portrait as a candid one, taken in a flash of inspired insight, at the psychological moment.

It is a forthright and brave book; it is made with the bravery required of an artist.

The autobiographical work, like much else that is autobiographical, can be taken as well for a set of visions. If only in this respect, the autobiographical approach to *The Democratic Forest* has engaged us all in its implication.

Our own way of seeing may have recently been in trouble. These days, not only the world that we look out upon but the human eye itself seems at times occluded, as if a cataract had thickened over it from within. We have become used to what we live with caloused (perhaps in self-protection) to what's happened to the world outside our door, and we now accept its worsening. But the Eggleston vision of his world is clear, and clarifying to our own.

In his own country, we have always valued William Eggleston's work for its clarity, veracity, strength of intention. Perhaps we couldn't have known until we'd met it in this book, seen it at work, the strength of imagination that conceived it, shaped it, and consistently informed it all.

Actually, what we have here is a set of visions. Like a magician, William Eggleston has raised them out of light, colour, smoke and an absence of people.

Visions or not, he remains a photographer who never trifles with actuality: he *works* with actuality, and within it—the self-evident and persisting world confronted by us all.

The human being, unseen, remains the reason these photographs of place carry such power to move and disturb us—and, by the end, somewhat hearten us.

A clear spring rises somewhere on the home place, for the human strain begins there for Mr. Eggleston, and we see it in what follows: it turns into a river that runs through, or underneath, every place succeeding it. Whatever is done to block it or stop its flow, it surfaces again. Pure human nature proves itself in likely or unlikely places.

New York: Doubleday, 1989, pages 9–15.

IV. UNDERFOOT LOCALLY

A Ballad: The Fight between Governor Johnson & Fred Sullens

It was on May the second in the Old Walthall
When these two men fought a fight in the hall,
They met by a pillar, they met by a post,
It was hard to tell who was whacked the most.

Old Fred Sullens he was 63,
Short & stocky and a sight to see,
Came in the lobby as the clock struck 6,
Where Old Man Johnson was hiding with a stick.

Little recked he of the fate in store
Once he took & opened that Walthall door,
Little recked he that words unkind
Would bring to him a blow from behind.

13 days behind a post
Johnson had waited for Sullens' ghost,
12 days behind the desk,
Johnson had waited without any rest.

11 days behind a chair
Johnson had waited to meet him there.
10 days beneath the rug
And all that came in was George Lemon Sugg.

9 days by the cigar stand,
With his cane held high in his strong right hand.
8 days he waited to let the blow fall,
But Old Man Sullens came not at all.

7 more days, and 6 still to go,
& still old Johnson was holding the blow.
5 more days, it began to rain,
Old Johnson's hopes they began to wane.

4 more days in the marble hall,
Don't look like he's coming at all.
3 more days standing in the gloom,
Anybody seen Sullens going to his room?

2 more days going without his food,
I'm waiting for Sullens to spill his blood.
1 more day standing at his watch,
All of a sudden came a click in the latch.

His wife came first, went up to her room,
Johnson knew Sullens was sure to come.
Sullens was out on the P.O. ground
Romping away with his little pet hound.

In came Sullens, without any fear,
He didn't know Johnson was anywhere near.
Without a word, from behind his back,
Out came Johnson, whack whack whack.

O Bonnie, O Bonnie, I'm wounded for true,
My head is all bloody & covered with grue.
Spread my bed with old newspapers,
And call right quick for Rev. Capers.

Rub my head with suet of mutton
And call out the pastor Dr. Hutton.
Send for my daughter and send for her quick,
Old Governor Johnson has hit me with a stick.

Ann was in the parlor, drinking her beer,
When the phone rang out saying loud & clear,
Oh Ann your papa is wounded for true,
His head is all bloody & covered with grue.

Bonnie said, Ann we never were friends,
But now is the time to make amends.
When your pa and my husband has been hit from the rear,
That is the time to call each other "Dear."

1940, printed in "Eudora Welty's Monsieur Boule and Other Friends: A Memoir
of Good Times" by Nash K. Burger, *Southern Quarterly* 32, Fall 1993, pages 41–48.
Welty's ballad satirizes the fisticuffs of Jackson *Daily News* editor Major Frederick
Sullens and Mississippi Governor Paul B. Johnson and the reporting of the fight
by the *New York Times*, 3 May 1940, and the *Daily News*.

From the *Mississippi Women's War Bonds News Letter*, Club Issue

Mrs. George C. Wallace, whose virtues as Vice Chairman in Charge of Organizations can not be extolled enough in this News Letter or in taller type, sent a message to you this time to write in your Club activities. What has come in is good and ought to drive others to enthusiasm, and you can read it below. However, there might have been too little time for presidents of clubs to gather all the material they wanted—at any rate, while the responses we got were good, they were a little on the small side in number. In the next issue we will print the latecomers—for this is too important a part of the Women's War Finance work in Mississippi for us not to publish its whole story in our News Letter—for our mutual benefit in exchange of ideas in the counties.

♦ ♦ ♦

There have been interesting CITATION AWARDS recently, which we always like to publish in the News Letter as special news.

The *Grenada Garden Club*, of Grenada, Miss., won the Treasury Department Citation for Patriotic Cooperation; and in the same city the *Twentieth Century Club* won the Hospital Equipment Citation. Nice going, Grenada, and Mrs. E. L. Wilkins, Special Activities Chairman, take a bow!

One of the pleasures of Mrs. Eleanor Wilson McAdoo's recent look-in at the State Committee Meeting in Jackson, was the presentation of a Citation to Mrs. W. V. Westbrook. Mrs. Westbrook, of Jackson, sold over $5,000 in bonds during the Hinds County Women's Hospital Equipment Campaign, and Captain Wasko, from Foster General Hospital, a young surgeon who has recently returned from the New Hebrides, presented her with the Citation awarded by the U.S. Surgeon General.

And this looks like a good place as any to list those clubs which have applied for and received the Merit Award—90% of their members buying bonds regularly. This list, however, will include only those clubs that have not been previously named in our News Letters. Since this is the Club issue of the News Letter, let their names be written in full array.

✦ ✦ ✦

And for conclusion—better go back and read Mrs. Crockett's and Mrs. Wallace's messages once again because it would do no harm to know it by heart for the Drive ahead. Can we repeat the Fourth War Loan performance? Need the News Letter ask? Naturally! We can repeat it and put a little trimming on it—for we set our own style and we're going to follow it. So—good going.

Eudora Welty
News Letter Editor

Excerpts from Volume 2, Number 3, 13 May 1944. The Welty Collection, Mississippi Department of Archives and History, Jackson, Mississippi.

On the Lamar Life Insurance Company: A Salute from One of the Family

Lamar Life, this year celebrating its fiftieth birthday, has been a part of my family since before I was born, my father having come among the earliest to be with the Company in 1906 and remaining with it until his death as its President in 1931, indeed giving his life to it; and on wishing it a Happy Birthday I do so out of the privilege—itself happy—of having grown up with it.

The Sunday visit to Daddy's office is among my earliest memories; we children were taken there as a treat after Sunday School. The old Lamar Life Home Office Building was of course the little Greek temple next door to the Pythian Castle, whose medieval front was flanked on its other side, a bit lower down, by the hospitable striped awning of the J. M. Black Grocery. This delicious triumvirate of buildings—set apart as a group by the still-vacant lots on both sides, and sometimes by the treacherous Town Creek in front—is an indelible image of the Jackson of my childhood, stamped with affection on the memory of everybody, I suppose, at this stage along in the century.

"Daddy's office" on the inside, strange and full of Sunday calm and mysterious equipment as it was, seemed a fascinating if airless Paradise on a Sunday morning; it must have been the typical office of its day. There was a big couch with leather cushions sewed in some sort of smocking design, an ice-cold surface for bouncing in a Sunday School dress. The unquiet water cooler had artesian water gone warm and flat since yesterday, which only made us drink the more. The dictaphone—my mother says she believes the dictaphone of my father's was the first in Jackson—when the earphones were tried on, gave back a ghostly version of my father's own voice, speaking riddles meant for the ears of Miss Josephine Wright. However my brothers might choose to swing on the mahogany gate provided in front of the safe, what I fell in love with was the typewriter; once that limp black oilcloth cover was spirited away, and the roller could be persuaded to chew in a sheet of Lamar Life stationery, there were all those polished keys which, if only hit right or long enough might write anything at all, while Daddy sat reading his mail. Hereby is my apology, some years belated, to Miss Josephine Wright for any bad effects her type-writer showed on Mondays.

When the new Lamar Life Building was going up, I remember my father, who in those years was General Manager of the company, taking the greatest pride and a daily exhilaration in the workmanship of it. No wonder he was proud of the beauty of what was happening. I think he felt its climax was the clock; but all the way up to that tower he personally loved and endorsed every stone that was laid, every gargoyle that peeped forth from the various stages. (I had to grieve a bit to see some of those embellishments go in the recent alterations.) My father led the whole family to the top for the first time, as I recall it now, by the fire-escape, a romantic climb; and it was lovely and worth every step to stand on the roof where the tar was just hard enough to receive our weight, and the clock just as close as your hand, and to look out at the wonderful and unfamiliar view of Jackson, seen for the first time as a whole, in one sweep.

When Jackson had a skyscraper, then, and the Company had moved into its offices, our town wasn't too drastically citified yet. I remember I used to go for my father at five in the afternoon, swing the car around in a U-turn in front of the Governor's Mansion, and blow the horn, a long and two shorts. My father would immediately appear at his window, on the tenth floor, and signal how soon he'd be down.

From those days how many kind people I remember with affection—many that I still can see there, some that are dead, a few gone away. I feel close today still, along with all my family, to Mr. Lutken, Mr. Babbitt, Dr. Segura, Mr. Owens, Mr. Edward Yerger, Major Calvin Wells, Miss Mamie Montgomery, Miss Wright, Mrs. Matte Chambers, Miss Annie Cranberry, Miss Mary Berry, Miss Mildred Brashear, Mrs. Berdie Runnels, Miss Mary Keith Moffat, Mrs. Helen Rowan, Mr. Roy Nelson, Mr. Ran Schlater, Mr. A. C. Cox, Mr. E. V. Cato, Mr. J. P. Woodward—there are still more. I remember them not only as figuring importantly in the Company, but in many a moment of warmer association—Dr. Segura on a Company picnic, for instance, hitting a home run . . .

I was privileged to know some of the Lamar Life family better because, as a child of the Company, I was in on some of the spectacular All Star trips. So were some of the other children. Sara Elizabeth Schlater, Lilian Cox, and I were inseparables on the Far West trip— giggling together on top of Pike's Peak, holding each other's hands through Chinatown, tripping along the rim of Grand Canyon in a little row, looking down in. Those were the days when there were lots of days to a train ride to the Golden Gate and back, when the arrival of the lunch hour each day meant the train pulled to a stop in the middle of the desert and everybody jumped off, with prairie dogs scampering underfoot, and made way to a little house just like a mirage called the Fred Harvey Restaurant. Mr. Malone, from Weir, was always the first man in.

Others in my family shared other trips—I see my mother in the Cave of the Winds, or riding the Maid-o'-the-Mist with my father, both of them wrapped in long, Shakespearean-looking raincoats; and my brothers in kneepants scowling in the sun at Morro Castle—we still have the snapshots . . .

My father's death when he was only 52 coincided with the Depression. It was at this time in my own life that the Lamar Life came to my rescue. Not only with funds from life insurance—it gave me a job. WJDX had been organized, one of the last projects of my father's day, and was humming along up on the roof of the building, right next to the clock, in a little birdcage of a studio into which Mr. Wiley Harris could scarcely fold himself. Mr. Harris out of the kindness of his heart gave me my first paying job. I must say it was the sort of job a young girl considers ideal: it was part-time, and it was vague. I edited, as one of my duties, a little newsletter, printing for our listeners the program schedule for the week, interviews with the Leake County Revelers, and so on. It was the nicest job I ever had.

On its Fiftieth Birthday I'm very grateful for all that Lamar Life has given me. It's not only the very real help I've had from the Company that I'm grateful for, indispensible though that's been. It isn't the warm memories, just as substantial, and for which I'd not take anything. It's not simply the enduring sight of the building that makes the old pride and exhilaration my father felt, and conveyed to me, start up in my heart. It is partly a sort of kinship, a blood-tie, the thing that is thicker than water. Most of all, though perhaps, it is the passionate and guiding belief my father instilled in me of the meaning of the "home company"—the integrity of a thing that springs from and lives on its own nourishing soil. And regardless of how we may grow and come to link up with a larger world, a natural process of development, it is the principle of that first "goodness," that original integrity, that must be the root of all excellence that can follow, and will always responsibly account for it and bless it.

In *Lamar Life Insurance Company, Tower of Strength in the Deep South: 50th Anniversary 1906–1956*. Montgomery, Alabama, 1956, pages 3–5. One of the All Star trips that Welty took was memorialized in a booklet titled *To the Golden Gate and Back Again* and includes six cartoon drawings by Welty.

Books for Hospitals, Institutions, and Prisons

In none of our hospitals or institutions, we in Mississippi are being told by the librarians whom it has long grieved, can you find a book. The shelves are empty. There simply aren't any books in Whitfield, in Ellisville, in Parchman.

Can't we do something?

To our friends who are ill or unfortunate in one way or another, we don't, because we are so well or lucky, stop speaking. Indeed our natural wish is to rush to communicate. And neither do books stop speaking to the unfortunate. Would they understand the books if they had them to read? It's condescending to ask: they may not understand all or even very much, and the same goes for us. Communication is a two-way process; but in reading, even if one intends to close oneself off, still—as long as there are books—communication, even at the frailest and faultiest, does go on. Only if both ends stop, and only then, is communication hopeless. If the line's open, something more and more comes through.

To the perpetual child and the limited in mind, to the sick and infirm, and to the morally wavering, reading permits pleasure still, and this may be a pleasure greater than they've so far known: hope. Books may say things to those mentally worse off than we happen to be that we wouldn't recognize and might not believe, but this is valid and not a bit against the law. The written word is the language of the imagination. In the hands of an artist it always means more than it says, not less. It can mean what we think it says, plus what they think it says, plus what the author thought it meant when he put it on paper, and then some.

In fiction, and in poetry in particular, the word embodies a great deal over and beyond what would be enough to convey facts. It has become the language of the emotions, common to us all—to the children at Ellisville, the sick at Whitfield, the imprisoned at Parchman, to ourselves sitting up in our living rooms, in front of the T.V. The great emotional truths, which fiction does not tell us, but conveys to us, are profound in their nature, multiple, complex, but they are also available, in part, in some part, in almost any guise of simplicity.

Does the Bible not speak to little children and to all those who stay children—to whom it must be read aloud—as we can remember for ourselves? Would we deprive a child of the twenty-third Psalm because he can't add two and two and has been set to peeling potatoes at Ellisville? And to the scholars, our own understanding must seem proportionately childlike. We, however, can read any book we like—or our libraries will be glad to get it for us.

Indeed, who says that we ourselves in general understand, really, any vast per cent of what, we can read if we want to? Yet nobody punishes us for this. Shakespeare is still handy.

If you were this child in Ellisville what if someone could sit beside you, reach for a book, and read

"Come unto these yellow sands
And then take hands..."

It would be hard to persuade any living ear that any other living ear would not be filled with the beauty of that, and somewhere, respond. Poetry indeed, speaking direct to the imagination, takes unbelievable short cuts, pierces right through blocks we don't even know of in our own minds to get there, to make itself eloquent not only after it's understood, but before.

Who are we, the supposed well ones and the upstanding custodians of the books, to say what poetry "means" to those to whom, for all we know, nothing else has power to speak? After all, the imagination is aware, even alert, when perhaps the rest of the mind is but half awake, or partly darkened or disturbed, or pulled towards acts we see fit not to condone.

As for bookless Parchman—is there any real reason why, if you robbed a bank, you are thereby judged unfit to enjoy "Robinson Crusoe"? Or to ponder Pilgrim's Progress—or at least the fact that it was written in jail. And so were many great books, let us not forget. For any mind anywhere can become alight with the wish, the joy of the wish, to get in touch to communicate with the world.

"Come unto these yellow sands" can speak infinitely and it can speak smaller ways. It is highly accommodating, the great poetry. And when a poem or a novel of magnitude speaks to the spirit, and it does, a door is opened. This is the case with us all. We take different joy of books, each of us taking what he can and then that little extra that can somehow be surmised, we take that.

Enrichment of the mind follows reading not as inevitably as the thirst is quenched by a glass of water going down, yet an open mind stays thirstier forever than a parched throat ever gets. Enrichment of the mind is gradual, increasing with time and practice, and remains as something we have absorbed due to the persuasion and the suggestion and the enchantment of the word, working on our whole lives, by way of our own individual pasts, our own peculiar powers, our private imaginations. But reading is its own end.

The reader who cannot grab as much as we can from books may suffer as much as we think we can, and more, from hunger and thirst of the spirit. Each of us has left in the end one same thing, that which is the first and last, privacy. And reading is for privacy. Not alone-ness—that disappears. The treasure in books belongs to privacy—to everybody's privacy.

To deprive the already deprived—of treasure!—by not giving them books seems a needless and callous waste of a chance—the best we've got, perhaps—to give what is, after all, not exactly ours to give but what lies, by its nature and intent, already in the public domain.

Don't let us punish anyone, anywhere, ever, by keeping any book at all away from him. Rather let us see that those hopeless, empty shelves fill up. From our end, we can still get in touch.

Published as "Miss Welty Urges Books for Hospitals, Institutions," Jackson *Clarion-Ledger*, 13 April 1961, page A-6, and as "The Right to Read," *Mississippi Magic*, 16 May 1961, page 15.

Preface: A Note on the Cook

Winifred Green Cheney is an old friend and near neighbor of mine in Jackson, Mississippi, and although I am not a cook, I am well equipped to testify to her cooking—from the dining room if not the kitchen. Her cooking is superb. But knowing there are further qualifications for a good cookbook, Mrs. Cheney has seen to those admirably too.

Winifred Cheney has not only collected and thoroughly tested and wisely chosen her dishes, she has learned all about them. She has traveled and tasted all over our part of the world with an alert, investigative interest in the background and provenance of the recipes she works from. The variety of Southern dishes is wide: indeed, the South is a big place—bigger than France, as has been pointed out—and it has had a long history. Its dishes, distinctively Southern as they have become, may go back in origin to the French, Spanish, English, German, Mexican, Greek, Dalmatian, African, Creole, or Caribbean comers to the land. Mrs. Cheney sets value on this ingredient of flavor. Her respect for the local dish and for the time-honored style of preparing it forms the *roux*, you might say, on which her own creations are based.

The recipes here come to us by way of long experience in the kitchen and out of the patience of the perfectionist. The zest Mrs. Cheney takes in her cooking comes through in the zest with which she writes down her recipes for us. She makes us acquainted, altogether, with the essence and character as well as the proper substance of the dish at hand.

The cook who can make a dream of a dish isn't necessarily able thereby to set down for others the exact way to prepare it. I can testify that one of the hardest things in the language to write is a set of clear directions. Mrs. Cheney has the gift, and the conscience, for doing it.

Winifred at home cooks for her family, for her friends, of course. She cooks to honor the visitor, and also she cooks for a varying but ever-present list of neighbors or friends who are convalescing from illness, who are in trouble of some kind, who are alone or confined to their homes. (And for some reason known only to her kindness, she includes in her list writers. Let me be confined to my typewriter with a deadline, and, as though it were a fate I didn't deserve, Winifred appears with something on a tray to sustain me.) The original Lady Bountiful was the invention of an Irish dramatist in 1707. Winifred exists as her own version. She makes her rounds with baskets and trays as a simple extension of her natural hospitality. In good weather but especially in bad, splashing forth in raincoat and tennis shoes, carrying a warm cake straight from her oven, she sympathizes with you or celebrates with you by sharing her table with you.

I hope Winifred does not mind my coming out in print about her character—after all, it is no secret in her hometown—for my reason is that I believe it has something positive to do with how good the food is. All of Mrs. Cheney's dishes came about through the explicit idea of giving pleasure to particular people—with real people, and a real occasion, in mind. I think that may be a very good secret of the best cooking.

When Jane Austen's Miss Bates, attending Mr. Weston's ball, is seated at the supper, she surveys the table with a cry, "How shall we ever recollect half of the dishes?" When I sit down to Sunday dinner at Winifred's I feel just like Miss Bates. What guest could not? But it now becomes possible for us to recollect the dishes we've dined on there. The cook herself has recollected—and here presented—the recipes for them. They are here to study and follow in her own cookbook.

It's a gracious cookbook. It's like another extension of Winifred Cheney's hospitality; she has added another leaf to her table.

The Southern Living Hospitality Cookbook by Winifred Green Cheney, Birmingham: Oxmoor House, 1976, page vii.

Aunt Beck's Chicken Pie

1 young chicken (about 4 lbs.)
6 small white onions
2 ounces bacon, cut in small cubes
2 1/2 tablespoons flour
1 tablespoon parsley, finely chopped
1/2 cup celery, finely chopped
3 hard-cooked eggs, sliced
Salt and pepper to taste
Pastry to cover a 9-inch pie

Boil the chicken in highly seasoned water and allow to cool in its broth. Separate the meat from skin and bones, leaving the chicken in large pieces. Boil the onions in salted water until tender, but not mushy, and drain. Fry the bacon until tender, without browning; remove from frying pan and set aside. In the remaining fat, cook the flour over very low heat for 3 minutes, then gradually stir in 2 1/2 cups of the broth in which the chicken was cooked. Add parsley, celery, salt and pepper; simmer for 6 minutes.

Put half the quantity of bacon, half the chicken pieces, half the quantity of onions and half the quantity of eggs in the baking dish. Lay on the remaining pieces of chicken, add the rest of the other ingredients and pour the sauce over all.

Cover with rich pie pastry, pressing down the edges with a fork. Brush with milk and make several slashes for the steam to escape. Bake in a hot oven (450°F) for 15 minutes, reduce heat to moderate (350°F) and bake 30 minutes longer. Serve at once with succotash.

Serves 6.

"I always heard it was a Methodist dish." — *Eudora Welty*

In *A Cook's Tour of Mississippi* by Susan Puckett and Angela Meyers. Jackson: *Clarion Ledger/Jackson Daily News*, 1980, page 97. Aunt Beck brings her Chicken Pie to the family reunion for Granny Vaughn's ninetieth birthday in Welty's 1970 novel *Losing Battles*.

Jackson: A Neighborhood

It seems, looking back, that everything that went on in Jackson was done in the unit of the family. When Livingston Lake opened, it was the family that responded. They went out in the family car every morning and took a dip before breakfast. In that first onrush of enthusiasm, you rode out from home in the rising sun, already in your bathing suit and rubber cap decorated with rubber butterflies, singing "Margie" all the way (that was the summer the lake opened) to learn to swim the breast stroke in a harness of water wings. As they went methodically splashing around you, their heads rising out of that warm brown water, it was neighborly; you saw all the same people every morning, much as you do at the supermarket now.

When you and I look back at Jackson, doesn't it seem that everyday life then very easily gravitated to the personal level? When the postman arrived with the mail (twice a day) at your door, he blew a whistle. It seems to me that the mail itself was all composed of **letters**. Could it even be true that junk mail had not then been invented? We children, of course, would have loved it, but I remember nothing coming that would qualify except what we sent off for ourselves—orders for signet rings in return for wads and wads of Octagon Soap coupons.

The scale of life was personal and manageable—manageable for children. There were a lot of three-digit telephone numbers. You gave your number to Central, and Central was a person—a lady, who said "Number, please," and "Sorry, the lion is busy." If you wondered what time it was, a normal thing was to use the phone and ask Central to give you the Fire Department. Nobody in the world had an answering service: you got **them**; not a recording: a fireman. Their line was doubtless often busy with people curious to know the time, but never mind: if you had a fire, there were fire alarm boxes fixed to the light poles on convenient street corners, little red iron boxes with glass doors. Any alarm would bring the whole fire department out on the street. This included, in my earliest memories, a wagon called "the steamer." There was a clanging bell mounted on the front and a kind of brass boiler filled the back, with white steam rolling out at the top. It was always a little late, behind the hook-and-ladder truck and the Chief; but the steamer alone was pulled by a pair of matching white horses, out from under whose galloping hooves live sparks flew. As it thundered up the street, it was something glorious, worth waiting for and running after.

When you think of your childhood, there are many people who seem to have gone by in a parade: the old familiars. Many Jackson familiars were seasonal; and they were punctual. The blackberry lady and the watermelon man, the scissors grinder, the monkey man whose organ you could hear coming from a block away, would all appear at their appointed time. The sassafras man at **his** appointed time (the first sign of spring) would take his place on the steps of the downtown Post Office, decorated like a general, belted and sashed and hung about with cartridges of orange sassafras root he'd cut in the woods and tied on. They were to make tea with to purify your blood, and quite cheap at the price, something like a nickel a bunch. And when winter blew in, out came the hot tamale man with his wheeled stand and its stove to keep his tamales steaming hot in their cornshucks while he did business at the intersection of Hamilton and North West.

On a day when my mother had taken me to the Emporium where Mr. Charlie Pierce was making some suggestions for a party dress for me, he suddenly said, "My dear Mrs. Welty—the gypsies," and without further warning, the flower spray and sash—he'd been showing us how they would go—were swept out of our sight and beneath the counter. And there the Gypsies ambled, down the aisle. You could count on Gypsies in Jackson, coming with the first hint of fall. Gypsies were seasonal too, like the locusts and katy-dids.

Entertainment was easy to come by. First of all there were the movies. Setting out in the early summer afternoon on foot, by way of Smith Park to Capitol Street and down it, passing the Pythian Castle with its hot stone breath, through the one spot of shade beneath Mrs. Black's awning, crossing Town Creek—then visible and uncontained—we went carrying parasols over our heads and little crocheted bags over our wrists containing the ten or fifteen cents for the ticket (with a nickel or dime further for McIntyre's Drug Store after the show), and we had our choice—the Majestic or the Istrione. At the Majestic we could sit in a box—always empty, because airless as a bureau drawer; at the Istrione, which was said to occupy the site of an old livery stable, we might see Alice Brady in "Drums of Jeopardy" and at the same time have a rat run over our feet. As far as I recall, there was no movie we were not allowed to see, until we got old enough not to see "The Shiek."

At a time when the Century was still a live theatre, a third movie house came along on Capitol Street. This was an open air theatre which opened after dark, on the Town Creek bottom. The creek itself was straddled by an enormous billboard, which in my mind's eye I will always see pasted with an ad for a coming attraction with Annette Kellerman. It portrayed Annette in a long white drapery, standing on the edge of a cliff, blindfolded. Her arms were straight out in front of her, and one toe already pointed over the abyss. At my urgent pleas, our family attended. And when we did, Annette never went anywhere near a cliff, and made not a single appearance blindfolded, or even in draperies. She just kept on her usual bathing suit, and if there ever was anything after her, she outswam it. I attributed the early folding of the Open Air Picture Show to this gyp, but it was laid officially to the heavy attendance of mosquitoes at all performances.

But once a year, and another part of summer, live entertainment came with the Redpath Chautauqua. The tent went up on a vacant lot somewhere near the West Capitol Street Methodist Church. My father always took tickets for the full week's performances. This meant we could ride on the streetcar at night, which only began the excitement: holding on to wicker seats by open windows and smelling the scorching rails as we made what seemed a sizzling speed through the calm of nighttime Jackson. "Where Will YOU Spend Eternity?" was even then a landmark sign looking down from under a light bulb onto the I.C. Station, from just beyond Mr. Tripp's Furniture Store.

Within the Chautauqua tent: the smells of newest sawdust and oldest canvas, plank benches down front for the children to sit together on, stage with green rep curtains fastened together in front, while you waited with your heart in your throat for them to be rattled back. Until then you could only keep reading over and over the hopeful sign that hung on a tent pole, "Kimball Piano Used."

The show might be an educational lecture on a distant part of the world, or a concert by a musical trio (generally all ladies), or the performance of a play such as "Turn to the Right" or, more blessedly, "The Bat."

On the final night, a play was performed one year with a cast of local children; we were encouraged to try out. I did, for a role that where all you did in try-outs was sit with your ankles crossed in a folding chair in the middle of the stage with all the others around you and singing to you. It didn't appear that there were even any lines to speak. Another girl, with naturally curly hair, beat me to the part. Imagine my surprise when, on the night, this character turned out to be Joan of Arc and what she was doing at center stage was being burned at the stake, while the rest sang to her (this was during World War I):

"Joan of Arc! Joan of Arc! May your spirit guide us through! **Allons, enfants de la patrie!** Joan of Arc! We're for you!" I'd had a close call.

I feel we were highly entertained as children, and quite well versed in ways of entertaining ourselves. Our play was unscheduled, unorganized and incessant—in our backyards, our friends' backyards, in the public parks and especially in summertime, we ran free. (Our mothers, however, knew right where we were.) At the same time, it seems to me, we read all day. We might read all day in a tree.

Summer nights, we "played out." We made "choo-choo boats"— steamboats—out of shoeboxes with windows in the shapes of the moon and stars cut out of the sides and tissue-paper pasted over, and a candle inside lighted to show through, and at first-dark, down the river of sidewalk, pulling our shining boats on a string, we met other boats, and passed each other.

"Choo-choo."

"Choo-choo."

Summer days we went to spend all day with each other. You might play paperdolls. You went carrying all you had in a bulging Bellas-Hess catalogue in which the dolls, families and families of them, and their outfits were filed flat between the pages. With paperdolls, the thing to be desired was **number**. The combined batteries of your paperdolls and your friend's paperdolls spent the day visiting and dressing for each other. They acted out exciting scenes we thought up. Though a certain number of the fathers of these families had nothing to wear but long underwear, or, if clothed at all, were obliged to carry a second pair of pants over their arms (they all came out of the mail order catalogues), this didn't cloud our day.

A child quite naturally thinks his own world—his house, his street, his town—is going to stay forever the way it is, in the same way that he thinks his own family will always be where he sees them now, and exactly the same. We of my day may have kept an unusually strong and reassuring conception of Jackson; for most of our childhood, the look of Jackson did indeed remain essentially the same. Buildings seldom came down, streets didn't get widened—or rezoned. Not only the streets and houses and "downtown" kept being just what they were supposed to be. Trees too seemed permanent. Trees you were growing up with remained where they were and you knew them in all their seasons. They just got bigger, still lining the same streets where you walked. In those days, the sidewalks yielded to the trees and went around them. The big tree in front of Carnegie Library at Mississippi and Congress took over the prime parking place in the street itself, and the curb ran out in a big half-moon to take care of the roots. Downtown traffic went around it. The tree at the Central Fire Station was given similar respect in Pearl Street until we, ourselves, at our age, let it be cut down.

I believe the Jackson of my day was really scaled for children. And then, in its very confinement to small and intimate size, it suggested the largeness of the surrounding world—you could see Jackson end and the country begin. The child's imagination could take this in with the use of his own eyes. The family car ride showed it to him—our relationship with the surrounding world. When it was night, there was another sense of greatness. This lay in our view of the night sky. Jackson's night sky, then, was not a blushing reflection of a neon city, but its own clear black—the perfect opposite, as it ought to be, from day. You could live anywhere in town and keep up with the stars. A child ordinarily could point out the constellations and name them, because they **shone**. And closer to hand, you could get the full effect of lightning-bugs, too—flashing from backyard to backyard, street to street, field to field along country roads, then so near home.

Jackson Landmarks, edited by Linda Thompson Greaves and others. Jackson: The Junior League of Jackson, Mississippi, 1982, pages 1–5.

A Note about New Stage

New Stage made its first appearance on January 25, 1966, in Jackson, Mississippi. In true theatre tradition, it was born backstage.

Its parent, the Little Theatre, had been a part of Jackson for a long time. Before they had a theatre of their own, members used a stage in the old Blind Institute, a tall Victorian building on North State Street. My introduction to what they were doing came when I followed my mother up the winding iron staircase of the Blind Institute's outside fire escape, helping her carry a tea table to the stage entrance at the top. She was a member of the props committee. Backstage and out front in the audience, I became attached for life to the pursuit of putting on theatre in Jackson.

Joining the Little Theatre in the '30s was to join a very social group. You came to a performance to see your friends, on the stage and off. Waiting at the playhouse door would be a receiving line, the ladies wearing corsages; refreshments were served at intermissions by coffee girls, and everybody took their time, because there were generally three acts and three realistic sets had to be changed.

If the sets for our plays were realistic then, casting was too. I suppose we reasoned that a doctor's part was safest in the hands of a practicing physician. Lawyers of whatever stripe, noble or villainous, were impartially cast from the Jackson bar. Maids were the exception: they were played by debutantes. They tripped out, smiled at the audience across the footlights, opened their mouths and said, "Tea is served, madame," and brought down the house. The Jackson identity of an actor on stage was never lost sight of, it mattering little how he might keep playing his heart out.

In the one-act play by J. M. Barrie, *The Old Lady Shows Her Medals*, a Scottish soldier, long thought to have died a hero's death in the war, returns to visit his old mother. He was played by the skillful Mr. Wylie Harris in a kilt. At first sight of him, the old mother refuses to believe this is her living son, until all of a sudden she cries, "Jamie! Jamie, it's you. I'd know ye anywhere by the hair on yer legs." But the next line we heard came from the front row of the audience: "Why, Wylie Harris doesn't have a bit of hair on his legs."

Our audiences were affectionate and indulgent. It would have been thought unfriendly to criticize any performance, though it was certainly very much the custom to wait until the last night to attend a play, so as to give the actors every chance to perfect their lines. Everybody was praised in the paper when the review came out, including the coffee girls. (Theatre criticism had to wait until the arrival of Frank Hains.) One old clipping reports on a play in full detail, including the dresses of the ladies receiving for the evening; all names in every capacity were listed—only the name of the play had been left out.

All this was of course perfectly consistent with the fashion, or the innocence, of Little Theatres across the country at that time. But Jackson was superior when it came to talent—our Little Theatre can hark back to the memorable Jimmy Hewes, Carolyn McLean, and Frank Slater, to name a few. And never did our Little Theatre lack devotion. When our theatre building burned, we all banded together and built a new one, much more ambitiously designed and with equipment brought up to date.

Performances, however, were not so quick to catch up with the times. We were trying very little that we hadn't tried before. It struck the younger members in particular that the predictable typecasting, the sets constructed so true to life that the very doors were outfitted with keys that would really lock, were not basically congenial with the idea of imaginative theatre. For the essence of theatre is the creation of illusion, illusion that successfully conveys itself to the audience and becomes a dramatic vehicle.

Jane Reid Petty was one of the members of the Little Theatre ready to speak up for a new approach—one that called upon imagination, and one that recognized the role a vital theatre can play in a growing community. A good local theatre ought to seek in every capacity, she believed, to bring its audience the best that the theatre at large has to offer.

Many of us were in accord with that idea, too. The logical next step forward was clear. Having sought and received the Little Theatre's parental blessing, New Stage Theatre came into being. Really, it *sprang*. Implicit in its first charge of vitality was the full intention of advancing—one day!— from amateur theatre to the professional.

Jane Petty herself, its founder and manager, an accomplished young woman of the theatre not only dedicated to her idea of New Stage but informed and full of resource, was blessed with the clear vision to make and keep to a straightforward longtime plan. At her right hand from the start was Frank Hains, theatre critic of the *Jackson Daily News*, a virtuoso designer, actor, builder, and director. Working together with them and forming the original board were Ford Petty as president, D. Carl Black, Patti Carr Black, James K. Child, Kay Fort Child, Howard Jones, Beth Griffin Jones.

Acquiring a home for itself was New Stage's first act of faith. Did ever an old and disused church building standing vacant (and leaking) in an old downtown neighborhood look as radiant with promise to a company in search of a theatre?

No proscenium arch? All to the good: see what we can do with a thrust stage. No wings, no flies, no backstage? Design our productions so that the limitations become advantages, by putting to use imagination and paint and cloth and hammer and nails and *lighting*. Church pews discouraging to an audience? Make cushions for all of them. No orchestra pit? There's a little box-like appurtenance sticking off to one side of the platform, as if made to measure to hold a piano and a pianist: what would stop us from putting on, say, a Cole Porter revue some day? Nothing ever stopped us. We were ingenuity in bloom, and our funding came along in healthy fashion too; Jackson proved to be behind us from the start.

New Stage proved to be a prodigal child. The opening performance, on January 25, 1966, was nothing less than *Who's Afraid of Virginia Woolf?* Albee's then new and controversial play was directed by Ivan Rider, and was performed by Jane Petty, Frank Hains, Sue Chancellor and John Wilkerson. New Stage had galvanized its audience from the first moment. It went on from there. The gifted Ivan Rider remained as resident director for thirteen seasons to come.

In its steady course over the eighteen years of its life, New Stage has brought its audiences plays of a wide range and variety—from *The Skin of Our Teeth* to *The Caretaker*, from *The Night of the Iguana* to *A Midsummer Night's Dream*, from *A Delicate Balance* to *The Miss Firecracker Contest* by Beth Henley, from *The Shadow Box* to *Dracula*. There's been musical theatre from *The Medium* to *The Robber Bridegroom* to *The Pirates of Penzance*—and that Cole Porter revue.

Visiting professionals—for example, Geraldine Fitzgerald and Inga Swenson—have been brought to work in productions with New Stage. Plays of local origin have been developed and produced. Social programs for the community, in which we have been helped by grants from the National Endowment for the Arts and the Mississippi Arts Commission, have meant free matinees for senior citizens, workshops for children and for young people, travelling productions into towns outside Jackson, the sponsorship of National Theatre for the Deaf.

Meanwhile, at the point when the old New Stage roof leaked be-yond repair and the walls could no longer be propped up, and moving out of the beloved church was imperative, we came into an agreement with the Little Theatre—which had incurred debts and was drifting toward an uncertain future—whereby the problems of both could be relieved. New Stage was able to take over the Little Theatre building along with its debts and move in. It became in a way our inheritance. When it had been extensively remodeled to our growing needs, it had, in addition to the Meyer Crystal Auditorium, a second, experimental stage downstairs: the Hewes Room, named for the Little Theatre's Jimmy Hewes.

In September of 1981, Bill Partlan arrived as our producing direc-tor. And we have most actively engaged upon our new phase of life. New Stage is the New Stage we have always made our aim. We are today a professional theatre.

New Stage Theatre Presents Standing Room Only! A Cookbook for Entertaining,
Jackson: New Stage Theatre, 1983, pages 9–11.

Jackson Communiqué

It's been unseasonably, and unreasonably, cold in the Deep South, and on hearing the other morning that Jackson, Mississippi, was all but paralyzed with chill we called up one of that community's most eminent residents, Eudora Welty, to inquire how she and her neighbors were faring. When she answered, her voice, to our relief, sounded quite cheerful, and she gave us the following report:

"My telephone's one of the few things that are working around here. I'm one of the real lucky ones. My electricity stayed on, so I'm all right, but, what with transformer fuses blowing out and trees falling down, many people have had no light or heat for three or four days, and they've been moving in with more fortunate friends or going to hotels. One of my neighbors has been making coffee over her hearth fire. We're pretty much iced in in Jackson. Nothing is moving. It's just impossible to get around. There's a heavy coating of ice on everything.

"You know, when I was growing up here we only had snow two or three times until I went to college, but now we seem to get some of it every winter. The difference this year is that the cold spell has been so prolonged. Usually, after a snowstorm it warms up again in a day or two, but I haven't been out of the house in five days. And we're due for more sleet this afternoon. Last time I checked the temperature, it was two above. Jackson is not inexperienced when it comes to bad weather. We've had our share of floods and tornadoes. We have a pretty good mayor—Dale Danks. Isn't that a nice name! He's taken us through other emergencies, like the flood of '79. First thing he did this time was to close up everything. No schools, only a few businesses open. I don't even know if he can get up in his plane to look at things, because the airport is shut down, and so are most of the roads. The Mayor has been warning people not to go out in their cars, because if the car stalls or they have an accident there's practically no way anybody can go and help them. Our interstate highways are closed stem to stern. The TV news this morning said there were many wrecks on the roads, but nobody knows about casualties, because the wrecks have only been spotted by planes. When the postman came by a couple of hours ago, he told me he's been skidding all over town, because he's supposed to deliver by vehicle, not on foot, and they don't usually issue tire chains for mail trucks south of the Mason-Dixon Line. The few people who have four-wheel drive have been volunteering to take other people to shelters.

"One friend of mine trying to come home by plane got as far as Atlanta, and then flew to New Orleans, and finally made it here by Amtrak. She said the train was full of people heading toward Jackson from all directions. Apparently, they had a big party en route. The children are having a grand time, too, with no school. They've been coasting on cardboard boxes and plastic bowls and cookie sheets. Everybody's got a snowbank near his front door for the children to slide on. The town's not very hilly, but the least slope is treacherous. If we have this sort of weather again next year, I suppose all the children will be getting real sleds. When I was a child and the snow fell, my mother always rushed to the kitchen and made snow ice cream and divinity fudge—egg whites, sugar, and pecans, mostly. It was all a lark then. I always associate divinity fudge with snowstorms.

"Some people have been going out—the joggers, of course, among them—but their dogs won't. My friend Charlotte's dog finally did go out, and brought her back a frozen mouse. I don't have any pets, because I travel so much—thank goodness, I have nowhere to go this week—but at a time like this I'd like to have a little creature in the house with me. There are birds in the yard, and they're having a pretty hard time, too. Well, I've enough food in the refrigerator, and I've been getting some writing done. But you feel somehow as if you were isolated on a ship. The funniest thing, in a way, is that a lot of Jackson people were planning to go to Colorado to ski, and now they can't get to the snow because of snow."

In the "Talk of the Town" feature in the *New Yorker*, 18 February 1985, page 33.

V. ON WRITERS

Place and Time: The Southern Writer's Inheritance

As this was being written, the new book by William Faulkner is about to come out in America—a long novel entitled *A Fable*. One never knows ahead what a new work by Mr. Faulkner will be like—that is one of the joys of living contemporaneously with a genius. Now in the prime of his life, in the mid-fifties, he may well be giving us his major work; the talk is that he himself has an inkling that this is so. We shall have it here before long, and meanwhile the American critics are all giving cry. They ought to know by now, though, that Faulkner's work is a whole, that cannot be satisfactorily analysed and accounted for, until it can be predicted—Lord save the day. That prose is indestructibly itself and alive, something passionate and uncompromising, that will never sit still and wait on what anybody thinks: it will never be a possum in the tree. It sheds its light from higher up than any of the boys can shoot it down.

In the present surge of writers coming out of the South, Faulkner is the Man—pride and joy and show piece. Still, Mr. Edmund Wilson has put himself on record as wondering why on earth Mr. Faulkner doesn't quit all this local stuff and come out of the South to write in civilization. He asks how writing like that can possibly come out of some little town in Mississippi. The marvellous thing is that such writing comes. Let Mr. Wilson try calling for some in another direction, and see how long it takes. Such writing does not happen often, anywhere.

In America, Southerners are always being asked to account for themselves in general; it's a national habit. If they hold themselves too proud, or let themselves go too quickly, to give a reasonable answer, it does not really matter—at least it does not matter to the Southerners. Now that the "Southern Renaissance" is a frequent term, and they are being asked to account for that, some try, and others just go on writing. In one little Mississippi town on the river, seventeen authors are in the national print and a Pulitzer Prize winner edits the paper. It is also true that nobody is *buying* books in that town, or generally in the South. It seems that when it comes to books they are reading the old ones and writing the new ones. Southerners are, indeed, apart from and in addition to the giant Faulkner, writing a substantial part of the seriously considered novels, stories and poems of the day in America, and the most interesting criticism. One might just think that they are good at writing, and let it go at that.

♦ ♦ ♦

There has always been a generous flow of writing to come out of the South. One can begin with Poe and come up through George Washington Cable, Joel Chandler Harris, James Branch Cabell, Julia Peterkin, Willa Cather, Ellen Glasgow, Stark Young, William Alexander Percy, and so on—there are many more. Before the famous *Southern Review* of the thirties there were two previous *Southern Reviews*, the first published more than a hundred years earlier in Charleston. There was the *Southern Literary Messenger*, to which Poe contributed, and there was, and still is, the *South Atlantic Quarterly*, which has been going on in Durham, N.C., for the last fifty years, with many creditable pieces in it, as Dr. W. B. Hamilton's recently published collection from it has made plain. There has been a high standard of journalism in the South, not everywhere, but continuously somewhere; one thinks of it as a tradition out of which came historians and critics like Herbert Agar, who edited the Louisville *Courier* before coming to England; of Virginius Dabney in Richmond, and of Hodding Carter in Greenville, Miss., the aforementioned Pulitzer Prize winner.

It is nothing new or startling that Southerners do write—probably they *must* write. It is the way they are: born readers and reciters, great document holders, diary keepers, letter exchangers and savers, history tracers—and, outstaying the rest, great talkers. Emphasis in talk is on the narrative form and the verbatim conversation, for which time is needed. Children who grow up listening through rewarding stretches of unhurried time, reading in big lonely rooms, dwelling in the confidence of slow-changing places, are naturally more prone than other children to be entertained from the first by life and to feel free, encouraged, and then in no time compelled, to pass their pleasure on. They cannot help being impressed by a world around them where history has happened in the yard or come into the house, where all round the countryside big things happened and monuments stand to the memory of fiery deeds still to be heard from the lips of grandparents, the columns in the field or the familiar cedar avenue leading uphill to nothing, where such-and-such a house once stood. At least one version of an inextinguishable history of everybody and his grandfather is a community possession, not for a moment to be forgotten—just added to, with due care, mostly. The individual is much too cherished as such for his importance ever to grow *diminished* in a story. The rarity in a man is what is appreciated and encouraged.

+ + +

All through their lives Southerners are thus brought up, without any occasion to give it wonder, to be intimate with, and observant of, the telling detail in a life that is changing ever so slowly—like a garden in a season—and is reluctant to be changing at all. Without the conscious surmise of how they may have come to find it out, they do habitually find out how to be curious and aware, and perhaps compassionate and certainly prejudiced, about the stories that can be watched in the happening, all the way—lifelong and generation-long stories. They are stories watched and participated in, if not by one member of the family, then without a break by another, allowing the continuous recital to be passed along in its full course—memory and event and the comprehension of it and being part of it scarcely marked off from one another in the present glow of hearing it again, telling it, feeling it, knowing it. Someday somebody is liable to write it, although nobody is quite so likely to read it. The main thing Southern writers learn is that the story, whatever it is, is not incredible. Of course, that is what they wind up being charged with—stark incredibility. Faulkner is all true—he is poetically the most accurate man alive, he has looked straight into the heart of the matter and got it down for good.

One thing Yoknapatawpha County has demonstrated is that deeper down than people, farther back than history, there is the Place. All Southerners must have felt that they were born somewhere in its story, and can see themselves in line. The South was beautiful as a place, things have happened to it, and it is beautiful still—sometimes to the eye, often to the memory; and beyond any doubt it has a tearing beauty for the vision of the Southern writer, in whose work Place is seen with Time walking on it—dramatically, portentously, mourningly, in ravishment, in remembrance, as the case may be—though without the humour this writing is full of, where would it be? It is a rural land, not industrialized yet—so that William Faulkner can still go out and get his deer—but threatened with industry now; and some towns are much bigger and are filling with strangers, though many, perhaps most, are still small, poor, self-contained, individual, only beginning to change round the edges. The South is in no way homogeneous and even in one state there will be five or six different regions, with different sets of notions, different turns of speech. And yet most of the South's body of memories and lore and states of mind are basically Anglo-Saxon or Celtic—with a small dash of Huguenot French here and there—all of it, most likely, having passed through Virginia at some time or other. In the eighteenth or nineteenth century everybody who was coming to the South came, and mostly they stayed. The Civil War and industry have brought its only visitors. And the writing, in a way, communicates out of this larger and older body of understanding, the inheritance that is more felt than seen, more evident and reliable in thought and dream than in present life, in all the racket of the highways with the trucks and the transports bearing down. Quiet places are still left, if you know where to find them; and inwardly, family life, customs, the way of looking at life, have hardly changed at all, and never will, it is safe to say, at the heart—pride and poverty and maybe a general pernicketiness prevailing. The essential landscape remains one to induce the kind of meditation from which real writing springs.

Place must have something to do with this fury of writing with which the South is charged. If one thing stands out in these writers, all quite different from another, it is that each feels passionately about Place. And not merely in the historical and prideful meaning of the word, but in the sensory meaning, the breathing world of sight and smell and sound, in its earth and water and sky, its time and its seasons. In being so moved, the Southerners—one could almost indisputably say—are unique in America to-day. One would have to look to those other writers of remote parts, to the Irish and the Welsh—to find the same thing.

Literature does belong in essential ways to place, and always invokes place to speak in its fullest voice. To Southerners that assumption is so accepted, lies so deep in the bones, as never to have needed stating among themselves. It belongs to the privacies of writing. The movement of the twenties that was called, to begin with, the Fugitive, might never have quickened and burned so bright except out of defiance—that defiance that habitually springs up in Southerners in the face of what the North wants out of them. The ravishment of their countryside, industrialization, standardization, exploitation, and the general vulgarization of life, have ever, reasonably or not, been seen as one Northern thing to the individualist mind of the South. This new defiance was the kind of emotion that called up a self-conscious power; and the group of poets and essayists clustered round Vanderbilt University in Nashville, Tenn., in those days put all that into an eloquent statement, into the symbol of poetry, into a systematized ethical idea eventually to be christened Agrarianism. What they did was simply to see the South as an entity—historical, geographic, economic, aesthetic—and to take their stand to treat it as such, do or die. Strangely enough, they *did*. Perhaps there was something romantic and heroic about agrarianism, which history has trampled on; but their cause was not lost, for their ideas about writing, perhaps the heart of it all, persevered and triumphed. Their little group flourished and reached out, for the reason that they were, first of all, a group of creative minds, charged to bursting point with the poetic impulse. This was too much to defeat.

✦ ✦ ✦

Their original organ was the little magazine called *The Fugitive*, green in the mind to-day for its poetry and criticism. The contributors have almost without exception been published ever since, all over the world; they were the original Southern galaxy of Robert Penn Warren, Allen Tate, John Crowe Ransom, Herbert Agar, Donald Davidson. The writers who came after them, whose early work was nearly all recognized by, and only by, the Agrarian group in its next established quarterly, *The Southern Review*, were not so consciously taking a stand; perhaps now it was not necessary. They wrote out of the same world, and the same instincts, inescapably so, but in their own way, echoing only by the coincidences of strong place feeling these earlier writers. It is likely that the new crop, paying all respect and honour to what had been done before them, would have written their stories and poems just the same, without the Agrarians: they simply would never have got published. *The Southern Review*, edited in Baton Rouge, La., by Robert Penn Warren and Cleanth Brooks and Albert Erskine—with Katherine Anne Porter, John Crowe Ransom, Allen Tate and others acting in close editorial connexion, while some of their finest work was appearing there—was of inestimable help to these new writers in giving them publication in austerely good company, under the blessing of discriminating editing, without ever seeking to alter or absorb them. This was to the good of everybody: the idea was, after all, to keep alight the individual vitality of the region. Eudora Welty is an example of the writers who owe publication of their earliest stories to acceptance by *The Southern Review*. Peter Taylor is another, published there and in a sister quarterly, the *Sewanee*. Of course there were up-and-coming Southern writers *not* appearing in *The Southern Review* or *Sewanee*—Carson McCullers, for instance, came out in Boston in a novel. But there were always enough writers to go round. For years *The Southern Review* did in fact bring out most of the best work of the time, by Warren, Tate, Ransom, Katherine Anne Porter, Caroline Gordon, &c., in an array seldom matched in the files of American magazines. Though *The Southern Review* is gone, *Kenyon* came, and it and the *Sewanee* have carried on the early ideas, though more critical than creative work is filling its pages these days.

Appearing this year in England are books by a number of these writers. *Brother to Dragons*, the brilliant long poem that is Robert Penn Warren's latest work, is an example of that act of Mr. Warren's imagination of drawing up together in one astonishing handful a hundred threads, of passions, deeds, convictions, curiosities and facts, symbols and searchings, holy and unholy, and shaking out before our eyes a resultant poem that is a wonder of dazzling pertinence and beauty. Always vigorous and magnetic, alive with thought and feeling, deeply probing, poetic, scholarly, proud and gay, bitter and affectionate, his work—poems, novels, stories, criticism—continues through the years to circle round the South, old and new, and illuminate it in new aspects and ways.

◆ ◆ ◆

The Days Before, Katherine Anne Porter's newest book, is a notable collection of essays. It is to be hoped though that her famous stories, too, will soon be available in new editions on this side. Born in Texas, a descendant, it is said, of Daniel Boone—who, as pictured in a current United States advertisement of something, did his writing with a knife on the bark of a tree ("D. Boon kilt a bar here")—Miss Porter has perhaps the greatest purity and elegance of style of all living American writers. In thirty years of writing her output has not been large, and at home she has been asked to account for that, but has serenely continued to put forth perfect things in judicious amounts, just as it suits her. Reproaching her for little output is as illogical as trying to take down the performance of the moon because it is not out every night. Miss Porter's prose has lucidity and radiance, but one would not say it was lunar, for it is neither unearthly nor dreamlike nor particularly feminine. It has the rather more masculine power of mental and moral strength. She deals with states of mind, moral journeyings, with good and evil. She is not especially identified with place, or rather with one place, with her South: Miss Porter is a cosmopolitan in the good and the literal sense both. Within a range of three books of stories she has written of Mexico, Colorado, Germany, Texas, New Orleans, and the remembered South as handed down (with great strength of mind and no vapours) from her grandmother. In retrospect her writing seems to have the most sparingly allotted sensory images of any Southern prose one can think of, but those it has (the "Flowering Judas," the "Pale Horse, Pale Rider") are all the more extraordinarily powerful and compelling; in their role of symbols they control whole stories with the force of magic. It is to be hoped that all three books of stories will shortly be put within the easy reach of English readers; that they are not now is surprising.

✦ ✦ ✦

Peter Taylor is another writer who one wishes were better known here. He is, in addition to being a good writer, and a young one, the authentic voice of a part of the South too seldom heard from out of the thick of the rumours and alarms of Caldwell and Cain—that of the "nice people." *A Woman of Means, The Long Fourth and Other Stories,* and the recent collection called *The Widows of Thornton* will all be known here, it is to be hoped, before long. Eudora Welty has a new book out this September in England, called *The Ponder Heart.* It is a long story, of comic design, set in a small town in Mississippi. One of Elizabeth Spencer's two novels, *This Crooked Way,* is published in England, but the unpublished one is just as good: *Fire in the Morning.* Young and richly talented, a teacher in the University of Mississippi, she is at present travelling in England and on the Continent on a Guggenheim Fellowship. Other strongly recommended new novels out of the South in recent months are *A Good Man,* by Jefferson Young, a sensitive study of race relations in a quiet, authentic, and tender voice; and *The Chain in the Heart,* by Hubert Creekmore, an historical novel of race, dealing with three generations of Negroes in the deep South and notable for its sincerity.

Published anonymously in *Times Literary Supplement,* 17 September 1954, xlviii, the issue entitled "American Writing Today: Its Independence and Vigor." Edmund Wilson replied, "I have never asked or wondered anything of the kind" and followed by quoting from his 1948 review of Faulkner's *Intruder in the Dust* (*TLS* 8 October 1954, page 641). Elsewhere in *Occasions,* see "Department of Amplification," Welty's letter to the editor of the *New Yorker* in response to Wilson's review.

Tribute to Isak Dinesen

Of the story she made an essence; of the essence she made an elixir; and of the elixir she began once more to compound the story. What is perpetual about the story form was one of the things that seemed to absorb her most; perpetuation became, in itself, a part of the story, and so did her delight renewed in its provocation. We can see a story of hers and its telling winding about each other like twin staircases up the tower.

Another thing one feels about her work, which is just as rare, is that she was proud in the practice of it. Because it was she who assumed it, we saw with its privileges and its demands. With whatever smile of irony, she made, and played, the role; in the end one feels she was humble before it.

Beyond the storyteller is the woman, and beyond Isak Dinesen's fiction stands Karen Blixen's book *Out of Africa*. This book came from within, out of living life—proud, but more than proud, vulnerable life. The book of her life is itself her best art. Isn't this, too, a rare thing?

Isak Dinesen: A Memorial, ed. Clara Svendsen. New York: Random House, 1965, page 94. First published in Danish in *Karen Blixen*, edited by Svendsen and Ole Wivel, Copenhagen: Gyldenal, 1962.

Tribute to Flannery O'Connor

In her cruelly short life, Flannery O'Connor wrote novels and stories whose distinguishing mark, to me, is their triumphant vitality. Her work speaks steadily of an exuberance of spirit, and straight out of this, it seemed, came the joyous command she always had of a talent of great lights and darks. She wrote with deep commitment about what put the greatest demands on her, and achieved a fiction of originality and power. Her concern was of course with the spirit, which in her stories made for richness with many faces. And I shall always treasure for my particular love and admiration her comic gifts. Work as good as hers makes all writers proud.

Esprit 8, Winter 1964, page 49.

Tribute to Allen Tate

Allen Tate was the first poet I ever laid eyes on. I met him in the early 1940s, in a publishing house on lower Fifth Avenue, where he was at the time an editor. I was in awe of him, but I had asked if I might call, because I had got the dream of starting up and editing a magazine to publish the work of young short story writers.

If I had never seen a poet, I knew very few writers at all, and knew nothing of editing or publishing, but being a young short story writer myself—I'd published my first book, at least—I was fired up to try. Allen Tate could tell me what I needed to know.

He told me "Don't do it." He surprised me with every word he said! He gave me succinct and caustic information, with stories attached, about the depths I'd be getting into, about how I'd flounder in my ignorance. His horror of my jumping into this venture he made a form of encouragement: he was ready right then to congratulate me if I would *refrain* from editing a magazine and concentrate from now on on the writing of my own stories. He told me that he had read stories of mine, that he thought well of them, and he shook my hand.

He was an interpreter. Characteristically, generously, he spoke to the question I didn't know I'd asked him. He gave me an answer that was not a denial but a deliverance. Thus our long friendship began.

Quarterly Journal of the Library of Congress 36, Fall 1979, page 354.

Foreword, *Self-Portrait:*
Ceaselessly into the Past
by Ross Macdonald

Kenneth Millar did not sit down and write an autobiography as such; it has arrived of itself, in its own time, and is an accretion— a circumstance that seems characteristic of this modest and meditative man. It is an autobiography, though—by virtue of occasional essays, introductions and prefaces to fiction, his own and others', and to a bibliography another prepared of his work. One foreword begins: "Most fiction is shaped by geography and permeated by autobiography, even when it is trying not to be." If the autobiographical content of what follows has been obliquely provided, it is not oblique itself. When this writer's concentrated gaze does take in himself, it is direct and central. What we have is the clear, the clarified, result of long thoughts. The ordinary autobiography is designed to give more information, but we are not begrudged here of something better; we are quietly offered not details but essences.

Major factors emerge: how the sea became, very early, the most deeply felt element in Ken Millar's life; how the sense of family became the generative force of his work and its true subject, not by way of a happy and secure childhood but through the uncertainties of being moved about constantly during his formative years, of knowing very young the unsettled lives of his parents, and the father's desertion of the home. We learn that his belonging by birth and by his raising in two different countries brought him, through his own deliberate struggling with it, to the profound and liberating recognition of what place meant. We find how the same migrations planted in that lively and curious mind a lifelong interest in the North American *colloquial* language, which became the closely studied instrument of his work.

Customarily, he brings up a fact of his life in order to clarify a point about the craft of writing. He thus remarks in the course of the excellent introduction he provided for Matthew J. Bruccoli's bibliography of his work: "The year I graduated (from high school), 1932, I counted the rooms I had lived in during my first sixteen years, and got a total of fifty"—to go on: "Novelists are made, if they are made at all, out of uncertain beginnings and long delayed completions, like their books." Of the writing of his "break-through" novel, *The Galton Case*, he says, "I approached my life from a distance, and crept up on it in disguise as one might track an alien enemy; the details of the book were all invented. But there was personal truth in its broad shape."

It occurs to me that this book with its personal truths might be more strictly thought of as a self-portrait. Reading the succeeding pieces, you are really allowed to see the author not in time stages but all at once. You see him writing what he has written over the years. Most self-portraits are painted by their artists with the aid of mirrors; a writer's work may reflect him only in part, but here, when he looks into it himself and knowingly, it shows him to his reader in a curious, and affecting, doubling of honesty.

The portrait is complex in a still further respect. There is the writer, and there is the private person; and there is also a third, Archer. The essay which tells of the relationship between them is an astonishing achievement in self-perception. The most significant fact in the close alliance between a writer's life and his fiction (however close, or however far apart, they might on surface appear) lies in his art, continuous and developing, of making one out of the other. Not surprisingly, the father figure appears in roles of significance in most Macdonald novels (as he appears in the Millar essays). A principle in the novels is that what was missing reappears—people, information, evidence, old crimes, buried victims, sometimes lost love. Solution is found when, and where, relationships reach full circle. It is human relationships that must be sought for, discovered, and at last understood.

Ken Millar had learned that for himself intensity of feeling, if it is to become accessible in fiction's terms, requires distancing, requires the perspective that comes of precise observation and of irony. This is one of the marks of his seriousness as a writer which makes so valuable what he can tell us about the crime novel. *As* this serious writer, he has respected the form, and has respected it best by making it his own. He is, as we know, its master: it responds to a very broad range of his powers.

We keep in mind his own work in the context of the essay written to introduce his *Great Stories of Suspense*, his brilliant analysis of the function and place of the crime novel, its form, its history, its relation to other branches of the novel, its significance in our national culture. In particular we can realize their force as a reflection of the life of our day. Just as Wilkie Collins's *The Woman in White* with "its dark and knowing look at Victorian society," remains a living portrait of Collins's England, *The Far Side of the Dollar*, *The Zebra-Striped Hearse*, *Black Money*, *The Underground Man* and other equally compelling Macdonald novels will continue to give back to their future readers the life, to its most sensitive fluctuations, of his changing California.

In the portrait yet another profile is to be traced in the eloquent introduction to Robert Easton's account of the tragedy of the Santa Barbara Oil Spill of 1969. Ken Millar's passionate and always active concern for the conservation of the natural world is vividly clear here. Of course, all his fiction too is shot through with his love for this beautiful world of mountain and sea where he lives. (I shall never forget his showing it to me.)

The spoilers of the natural world are also the spoilers of the in-nocent and vulnerable; his crime novels connect them in ways that reach far and far back. That same 1969 oil spill is the explosive force in his fine novel *Sleeping Beauty*, where it is given the full strength of his tragic insight into its human motivation, its pattern of family connection. One speaks to him of the other: the mistreatment of the natural world and the damage people do to their fellow human beings. Violence is all one language—or rather the same lack, deprivation, of any other language. One of the gentlest of men, Ken Millar has not found the basilisk face of evil to be inscrutable.

The superb dramatic structure he gives his novels carries full weight of their social implications; his suspenseful plots are vehicles of moral suspense. The intensity of his human concern has found its form, so suited to his demands and so perfectly controlled, because he is the gifted writer he is, and the kind of writer he is.

Introducing the 1979 trilogy *Archer in Jeopardy*, he writes: "The underlying theme of these three novels, as I read them now, is the migration of a mind from one place and culture to another. Its pur-pose, like the dominant purpose of my young life, was to repossess my American birthplace by imaginative means . . . In the end I possess my birthplace and am possessed by its language."

This is a poet's concept too. In a recent essay, Seamus Heaney, who is also of two cultures, writes: "Certainly the secret of being a poet, Irish or otherwise, lies in the summoning of the energies of words. But my quest for definition, while it may lead backward, is conducted in the living speech of the landscape I was born into. If you like, I began as a poet when my roots were crossed with my reading."

What this imaginative novelist has learned from his own migra-tions, what he retains indelibly in his memory, that long memory, what he continues through the changing times to learn and observe, exam-ine—all, in the sea-change of fiction writing, appear, are resurrected, in the invention of character, and in the development with all the bril-liant Macdonald complexities, convolutions, and stunning surprises, of plot. All this has come, and more will surely continue to come, out of what he calls in one essay "the inner shape of a man's life," which itself "remains as personal and hidden as his skeleton, just as intricate, almost as unchangeable."

One most important element in both the life of the writer and the writer's work, and one that closely connects them, binds them together indissolubly, has to do with his creation of the style by which we know him—I think it is the best way we do know him. But this is not one of the subjects that lends itself to words of discussion, much less revelation—it is not a subject for any autobiography. We can only observe that style lies very close to a writer's life, and in the completest way allows the writer's work to speak to us.

As it does here.

We are grateful for this book. One further thing about Ken Millar's kind of autobiography: it is open-ended. There will always be room for more, when the time is right and the inclination takes hold. As it now stands, it is a valuable and moving document of a most valuable man.

Santa Barbara: Capra Press, 1981, i–iv. The collection includes Macdonald's introduction of Eudora Welty at the 1977 Santa Barbara Writers Conference (pages 125–26). Ross Macdonald is a pseudonym for Kenneth Millar.

Foreword, *The Stories of Elizabeth Spencer*

Elizabeth Spencer is from North Mississippi and I am from Central Mississippi, so there needed to be a modest coincidence to bring us together. This occurred. Elizabeth came as a student to Belhaven College in Jackson and was unerringly made president of the Belhaven Literary Society; it was the year I published my first book, and I lived right across the street facing the College. Elizabeth made a telephone call to ask if I'd please step over to a session of the Literary Society so they could meet a real writer and seek my advice. It would have been unneighborly to stay home.

I met then a graceful young woman with a slender, vivid face, delicate and clearly defined features, dark blue eyes in which, then as now, you could read that Elizabeth Spencer was a jump ahead of you in what you were about to say. She did as nice Southern girls, literary or unliterary, were supposed to do in the Forties—looked pretty, had good manners (like mine, in coming when invited), and inevitably gig-

gled (when in doubt, giggle). But the main thing about her was blaz-
ingly clear—this girl was serious. She was indeed already a writer.

As a matter of fact, she was all but the first writer *I'd* ever met, and
the first who was younger than I was. (The other was Katherine Anne
Porter.) Elizabeth offered me my first chance to give literary advice.
But my instinct protected us both. This free spirit, anybody could tell,
would do what she intended to do about writing. What else, and what
better, could a writer know of another writer? It was all I was sure of
about myself. I imagine she was glad not to get advice.

Instead of advising each other, we became friends. To leap over
something like a decade's difference in age proved no more trouble to
either than crossing Pinehurst Street. It wasn't long before Elizabeth
herself, with degrees from Belhaven and Vanderbilt, published her
own first book, the novel *Fire in the Morning*: she'd gone right on her
way as she'd known she would, and as she always has.

In the Southern branching-out way, we met each other's families;
in particular, Elizabeth and I appreciated each other's mothers. In
Jackson in my family home, in Carrollton in her family home, and, over
the years, on the Mississippi Gulf Coast, in New York, in Florence, in
London, in Montreal where she lives now, sometimes by trustworthy
coincidence and sometimes by lucky planning, we'd meet, and though
we might not have written each other a line, we knew right where to
take up the conversation. It was as refreshing as a picnic—indeed it often *was* a picnic, and we talked over lunch on the banks of the Pearl.

Even though Elizabeth dedicated her book of stories *Ship Island*
to me, I see no reason why my pride in this honor should prevent me
from giving expression to my joy in the timely appearance of this full
collection. It is as her fellow writer that I see so well what is *unerring*
about her writing. The good South, bestowing blessings at the cradle
of storytellers, touched her most tenderly with the sense of place.
Elizabeth evokes place and evokes it acutely in that place's own choice
terms—take, for example, her story title "First Dark." She can fault-
lessly set the social scene; she takes delight in making her characters
reveal themselves through the most precise and telling particulars. I

think she would agree that Southern writers really don't have much excuse for writing vaguely or unobservantly or without enlightenment about human relationships, when they thrive in the thick of family life. They comprehend "identity" because it's unavoidable. One reason why Elizabeth has never hesitated in her writing is that she began by knowing who she is. In her scrutiny of recalcitrant human nature there's an element of participating joy in that nature's very stubbornness, or in the way it yields every time to the same old tunes. She cannot go wrong about the absurd. All these are Southern blessings— perhaps. But equally valuable to this writer is a gift *not* characteristic of the Southerner: this is her capacity for cool detachment.

It was never surprising that she has felt well able, early on, to strike out from her Mississippi base, to find herself new territories: her fiction has consistently reached toward its own range, found its own scope, its own depth. What she'll do next, after the broad variety of her accomplishments, is still unpredictable.

It would have been as reckless to predict for Elizabeth as it would have been to offer her advice, and for the same good reason. Indeed, how *could* I have guessed, for one thing, that a schoolgirl so fragile-looking (though she went with a determined walk that made her hair bounce) could have had so much *power* to pour into her stories? Without any sacrifice of the sensitivity and the finely shaded perceptions we expect of her, her cool deliberateness to pull no punches will time after time take the reader by surprise. Katherine Mansfield stunned readers by a like combination of means; and I should say Elizabeth Spencer has earned with these stories a place in her rare company.

Garden City: Doubleday, 1981, pages xvii–xix.

Foreword, *To the Lighthouse* by Virginia Woolf

As it happened, I came to discover *To the Lighthouse* for myself. If it seems unbelievable today, this was possible to do in 1930 in Mississippi, when I was young, reading at my own will and as pleasure led me. I might have missed it if it hadn't been for the strong signal in the title. Blessed with luck and innocence, I fell upon the novel that once and forever opened the door of imaginative fiction for me, and read it cold, in all its wonder and magnitude.

Personal discovery is the direct and, I suspect, the appropriate route to *To the Lighthouse*. Yet discovery, in the reading of a great original work, does not depend on its initial newness to us. No matter how often we begin it again, it seems to expand and expand again ahead of us. Reading *To the Lighthouse* now, I am still unwarned, still unprepared in the face of it, and my awe and my delight remain forever cloudless.

The setting of *To the Lighthouse* is generally supposed to be much like the place at St. Ives in Cornwall where the Stephen family spent the summers during Virginia Woolf's childhood; and the portraits of Mr. and Mrs. Ramsay are said to derive from Leslie and Julia Stephen, the author's parents. However great a part recollection played in informing the novel, what connects *To the Lighthouse* to autobiography seems meteorological in nature. Not slow recollection so much as a bolt of lightning runs between them; we enter a world that is lit by its flash and play and under its heavenly signs is transformed.

The physical surround, so continuously before us in its changes, its weathers, its procession of day and night, so seducing in its beauty, is not here as itself. What Virginia Woolf has us see is the world as apparent to *them*—to Mrs. Ramsay, to Lily Briscoe, to James, Andrew, and the rest of the characters.

From its beginning, the novel never departs from the subjective. The youngest child, James, is on page one cutting out a catalogue picture of a refrigerator which he sees "fringed with joy." The interior of its characters' lives is where we experience everything. And in the subjective—contrary to what so many authors find there—lies its clarity. There is nowhere in this radiant novel a shadow of detachment. Such is Virginia Woolf's genius. The business of living goes on—stockings are knit, the *Boeuf en Daube* is cooked and served—and she is a genius with the homely, piercingly precise detail too. But if there is a pull and lure and threat from the outside world, other threats, other lures, are greater: those that search the characters more fatally, from within.

Here, with this houseful of family and summer guests, on these few miles of shore and sea, with Lighthouse, life has been intensified, not constricted, not lessened in range but given its expansion. *Inside*, in this novel's multiple, time-affected view, is ever more boundless and more mysterious than Outside. And for the author, who is throughout this novel writing in her deepest element, there is more to risk, and farther to go.

"The hoary Lighthouse, distant, austere," in the perpetually changing sea beneath the unpredictable sky, standing at its tricky, illusory distance away, signals on eternally.

To some of the children it remains as a father's promise of destination, a promise that a tyrant of a father can break, or can withhold until it's too late to make amends. To Mrs. Ramsay it is indeed her husband's promise to her children and is as well, in plain fact, the home of the little boy with the tuberculous hip and the keeper, who regularly needs to be sent coffee, tobacco, warm stockings, and something to read.

We see that the novel, too, from the start is full of signals, many of them signals of danger; these take the form of questions in the characters' minds. Not only, Will the children ever get to the Lighthouse? but What has life in store? How far is Mr. Ramsay (his gift being to stand alone in his intensity of mind "facing the dark of human ignorance") able to think his way from abstract A to abstract B and then forward? Will Lily Briscoe succeed in putting her susceptibility, her apprehension, her adoration of the Ramsays, into color and shape on paper? What is reality?

Part One is thronging with possibilities. All is speculation directed toward the future. It is centered upon destinations, promises to the private self, to others; it smiles toward the beckoning of love. That what is in store might prove to be unbearable is news broken, in *To the Lighthouse*, by Time itself.

Persisting through the novel and playing a part in transforming it is a rhythm that moves as waves of the sea move, and the rise and fall of the heavenly bodies that pass over the sleeping house. Rhythm is visible in the silent strokes of light from the Lighthouse, and sounds in the pounding of the waves and the racing feet of children through the rooms. It is administered in the blows of chance or fate; and to an extraordinary degree the novel seems to partake of its own substance, to be itself a part of this world, for there is a felt rhythm, too, underlying the novel's structure and forming a pattern of waking and sleeping, presence and absence, living and living no longer, between clamorous memory and lapses of mind, between the rushing in of love and the loosening of the hand in sleep. In the "Time Passes" interlude, the novel works its way forward and backward and around, freely, within its own realm of time imagined, and can inundate the void, too, when people are no longer there.

Lily, who has been in love with the whole Ramsay family, thinks near the end, standing at her easel, "Love had a thousand shapes." Love indeed pervades the whole novel. If reality is what looms, love is what pervades—so much so that it is quite rarely present in the specific; it is both everywhere and nowhere at a given time. This is of course because of Mrs. Ramsay. The love between Mr. and Mrs. Ramsay is the centerpiece, yet we see them alone together only once. The beautiful Mrs. Ramsay, in contrast to the others, had "resolved everything into simplicity," "bringing them all together, saying, 'Life stand still here.'" The unforgettable dinner-party scene, as the day, and with it Part One, reaches its culmination, has the very texture of human happiness. With its lighted candles, the bowl of fruit, the wonderful *Boeuf en Daube*, the last-minute arrival of Minta and Paul, who come to the table, as hoped for, engaged—here is Mrs. Ramsay's triumph.

It could not last, she knew, "but at that moment her eyes were so clear that they seemed to go round the table unveiling each of the people, and their thoughts and their feelings, without effort like a light stealing under water so that its ripples and the reeds in it and the minnows balancing themselves, and the sudden silent trout are all lit up hanging, trembling."

The windows of the dining room give back to her "a reflection in which things wavered and vanished, waterily." And as the ladies rise and leave the table and go out through the door, in that moment the present—and with it the poetry of the scene—becomes the past; as the twilight goes and night falls beyond the bare panes of the dining-room windows, what is really out there is *time*. And in the brief thirty-page interlude that follows, time gets in.

The novel written altogether until now from inside a number of human minds is at this point divested of any of them, of the human point of view. Time is at work: the verbs of sentences—"nosing," "swaying," "fumbling," "stroking" (the Lighthouse beam), "blundering"—no longer stand for human action. We *watch*—outsiders now—as time moves, with slowness immeasurable or with the slide of elision, or with the speed of light, and the identities of the characters prevail only within parentheses. The tide swims over them, bearing here and there in its waves the power of sudden or random disintegration—the extinction of Andrew in a burst of wartime shellfire, the loss of Prue in childbirth, the death, on some night or other, of Mrs. Ramsay.

But Mr. Ramsay's expedition through abstract thought toward reality will never be given up, and never will it reach its destination. ("Try thinking of a kitchen table when you're not there," so Andrew once describes this to Lily.) Lily herself, painting on the lawn, finds her own way "from concept to work as dreadful as any down a dark passage. . . . *But this is what I see*" (italics mine).

Set down here in the surround of the sea, on the spinning earth, caught up in the mysteries and the threat of time, the characters in their separate ways are absorbed in the wresting of order and sequence out of chaos, of shape out of what shifts and changes or vanishes before their eyes. The act of thinking, the act of using a brush dipped in greens and blues to set down "what I see" on a square of paper, the giving of human love, of making the moment something permanent, are all responses made at great risk ("risk" is the novel's repeated word) to the same question, "What does it all mean?"

"Beautiful and bright . . . and feathery and evanescent on the surface . . . but beneath the fabric must be clamped together with bolts of iron . . . a thing you could ruffle with your breath; and a thing you could not dislodge with a team of horses." These are Lily Briscoe's private words to herself for her painting as she would have it be at last; by no coincidence they come as close as we could ask to a description of the novel. Radiant as it is in its beauty, there could never be a mistake about it: here is a novel to the last degree severe and uncompromising. I think that beyond being "about" the very nature of reality, it is itself a vision of reality.

To the Lighthouse is at once ethereal and firm, as perhaps only a vision can be. A presiding presence with streaming hair and muscles stretched, the novel's conception has the strength of a Blake angel. It

is an exertion, a vaunting, a triumph of wonder, of imaginative speculation and defiance; it is that bolt of lightning Virginia Woolf began
with, an instantaneous burst of coherence over chaos and the dark.
She has shown us the shape of the human spirit.

New York: Harcourt Brace Jovanovich, 1981, vii–xii.

Afterword, *Novel Writing in an Apocalyptic Time* by Walker Percy

My gratitude for the honor done me in giving my name to the Chair of Southern Studies at Millsaps College is deep. I am moved all the more through the awareness that long before the gift I'd come to know the givers. The LeRoy Percy family, whose benevolence has in such large part made the Chair a reality, were already dear to me in friendship. Walker Percy, whom I've valued from the beginning for the superb writer he is, is also a friend I cherish and count on. All these happy circumstances are bound up in what the Chair's inauguration means to me.

There was never any question as to who the inaugurator should be. Clearly, Walker Percy and no other. The searching essay he's brought us, about living and writing in our day, acutely sizes up the state our fiction is in—deep trouble. He is doubly qualified to draw his conclusions.

Walker Percy has spoken on another occasion of his strong fellow-feeling for another fiction writer who was trained as a physician—

Chekhov, "the literary clinician, the pathologist of the strange spiritual malady of the modern age." They both "brought a certain set of mind from medicine to literature." I add this, that the novelist equipped with a physician's cool control, precision, discipline and direction, *and* an artist's searchlight passion has a doubly-informed, doubly-driven tool of work.

Does this sound like a description of the NASA fountain pen, said to be able to write equally well under water and in the stratosphere? It performs, according to Hammacher-Schlemmer who has it in the catalogue, "flawlessly at any angle, under water, over slick photos, at minus 50 degrees and plus 400 degrees Fahrenheit, and writes on for three miles." Very well, that's not any too much equipment for the job of writing fiction about our fellow human beings on earth. Or any too specialized.

The physician's ear and the writer's ear are pressed alike to the human chest, listening for the same sign of life and with the same hope, and with a like involvement in the outcome. We both know our instruments are human and part of us. Each of us listens for the heartbeat with his own heart, scans the brain of his fellow man with his own brain, to find out whether mankind is living or dying at this moment. Diagnosis is a personal emergency. That is, the perception of what ails us, what is wrong with the world, is likely to arise in, and come back to, the self.

A novel completed, in being a reflection of human life at a certain time and place, is inescapably its author's unique vision of human life itself. The novel's structure is two strands in a spiral, a double helix. Walker Percy the physician recognizes that structure, but it takes the novelist in him to perceive the *drama* that also lies in it, equally implicit. It's the novelist that recognizes human experience for what it is to the man or woman living it. Experience is a colossal predicament.

And Walker declares in this essay: "There is something worse than being deprived of life; it is being deprived of life and not knowing it. The poet and the novelist cannot bestow life but they can point to instances of its loss, name and record them."

Thus, he tells us here, the real challenge to the novelist is *not to see things as they are not.* "What the novelist notices is not how awful the happenings are but how peculiar it is that people don't seem to notice how awful the happenings are."

So we're likely to find his own novels proceeding civilly, urbanely, until all at once a Percy thunderclap shakes us into apprehending the size and shape of the real but unbelievable things that are happening here in this world to us.

From time to time I get the notion that Walker Percy's work is brooded over—at a remove, but *there*—by the great genius of another century and another country, Dean Swift, who diagnosed and transformed into his masterpiece of fiction troubles in kind and character not too unlike our own right now. In our times we've reached extremes common to Swift's—scientifically, philosophically, linguistically, spiritually, psychically—to which the logical visitor to our society might be the same man. Not a menacing pointy-headed plotter from outer space but the good solid Gulliver might easily be cast up on shore at Ocean Springs, Mississippi, and start showing up in golf courses and K-Marts here and there. In such mundane settings—as Walker has prepared us—apocalyptic events may very easily get set off. Our Gulliver would remain unflappable; he'd exercise curiosity on seeing the sights, and might show an interest in our language, and surely he would make notes. The original Gulliver, be it remembered, was a physician before he turned into a traveller.

Walker's fiction on its own penetrates our scene, by way of its sanity and its wit, its resources of fantasy and satire, its uncompromising seriousness of concern. His observations tonight in their range and pertinence, in their pulling no punches, just have struck us all as *auspicious*—not only for the opening of the Chair but for its future role in Millsaps and the liberal arts it is here to support. The Chair has a life from now on.

New Orleans: Faust, 1986, pages 25–28. Percy's essay was first delivered at the 1982 inauguration of the Eudora Welty Chair of Southern Studies.

VI. ON FRIENDS

Nash K. Burger Jr. of Jackson, Mississippi

Nash and I grew up in the same town and in the same years; we were in the same grade and often the same room all the way through school. In those days the honor roll of the public schools in Jackson was considered news and was carried in full in both daily newspapers. Better than that, every boy and girl on the honor roll won a free summer pass to the ballgame. Nash and I would both end up in the grandstand, so we'd average just about the same—anywhere you like between 95 and 100. If he'd beat me on scholastic grades, I might beat him in deportment (prig that I was?), and of course we made the same 100 in attendance. Our set hadn't thought of dropping out. Of Davis School? You couldn't even have left the classroom without a written excuse from home, and then you'd still have to get past Miss Duling in the principal's office. You couldn't. Miss Lorena Duling would freeze you, maybe kill you, with the look of her eye. She'd have stared down a dropout the way Saint Peter would if he caught one trying to get out of the gates of Heaven.

Nash's own abiding wish, of course, was just the opposite. He was hellbent to keep on learning. I've had time to find out—I've known Nash all my life—that he may have been our class's earliest, perhaps only, real scholar. Being deft and witty, he managed to keep the rest of us, so busy laughing, from guessing his seriousness too early, say the 4th grade.

In our Davis School days, Jackson didn't spread out very far, and somehow that small size gave us more scope. Nash's house (it had once been in the family of L. Q. C. Lamar) was just a block from Capitol Street, mine only two blocks on the other side of the New Capitol, with Davis School right across the street from our front yard. We were both within a child's walking distance of everything—school, the library, the ice cream parlor, the grocery store, the two movie houses, Smith Park. On summer nights there were band concerts in Smith Park, and whole families—Nash's and mine included— would stroll there after supper and listen, and let the children dream in the swings, run up the seesaws, climb the statues, and drink lemonade while the band played selections from *William Tell*.

Without the exact approval of home, we children made free of the nearby State Capitol too—riding our bicycles down the steep terraces or the long flights of steps, flying our kites or playing ball on the lawns. We'd skate through the Capitol, skimming over the marble floors (very desirable echoes in the rotunda) and rounding a circle in the Hall of Fame, in the center of which, for an unknown reason, was exhibited an Indian mummy in a glass case. It's about the only inaccessible thing I can think of in Jackson, and it was a fake.

Nash was a movie-goer, State Fair goer, Chautauqua goer, Century Theatre goer, church goer, library goer, school goer. I never have yet received the impression that Nash would ever want to stop going to a one of these. In Jackson he grew up a part of every good crowd.

Everybody went downtown on the night of an election to watch the returns come in; these would be thrown on a screen outside the newspaper office above the street. The whole of Capitol Street below would be swarming. I remember one such night when my mother spotted Nash out in front of the crowd. There he stood, in the knee pants and long black stockings the boys wore then, and I think a baseball cap on backwards; at ease, his eye cocked on the screen, and all the while spinning a school tablet on the end of his finger—like a juggler with a platter. My mother said, "That's the boy with the brightest mind in your class." I think she must have spotted the tablet spinning for what it was—philosophical detachment.

High school gave us the chance to see what Nash could do with writing. In English class, he varied the monotony furnished by the rest of us by writing his book reports on imaginary books by imaginary authors. For the school paper, the *Jackson Hi-Life*, and the annual— he was of course on the staff of both every year—he would come out with some fine parody—of boy's books, westerns, sentimental novels of the day—the same thing Corey Ford did a little later on. He was a satirist at 16. No, 14? Both at work and play. I remember the Junior Jupiter Juvenile Detective Agency, which took up a page in our annual; Nash was its founder and the president. They even wore badges— ordered off for, Nash told me, in bulk, from the back pages of a church publication called "Kind Words."

Ours was a small class—we'd been picked to graduate a year early, for some special reason—and we all knew one another well, having been together after all since we were six years old. We all knew what each other was doing and what each other was reading. When I signed the card to take a book out of the Carnegie Library, I'd invariably see the signature of Nash K. Burger Jr. a line or two above—he'd beat me to it. And what else had he beat me to? I think now that he may have been the only one in our fairly smart class who had developed any real taste in books by the time we went off to college.

In wayward fashion, over the next four years, letters traveled back and forth between Nash and me—his from Sewanee, the University of Virginia, from Jackson or even from France, where he rode his bicycle over it one summer; mine from Mississippi State College for Women, the University of Wisconsin or Columbia. This didn't mean a letter from Nash wasn't likely to begin, "Your letter has finally reached me after being forwarded over all the islands in the South Pacific. We are on the return leg of a huge horseshoe which takes in the entire southeastern archipelago, on the good ship Uncle Ben." He could also give me gentle warnings about my false starts: "When I find a college student who does not agree with everything the *American Mercury* and James Branch Cabell have ever said, I intend to take up my bed and walk." He put me onto Sherwood Anderson, so I came to *Winesburg, Ohio*, but he also told me to read Joseph Hergesheimer, Joseph Hergesheimer, Joseph Hergesheimer, so repeatedly that I wouldn't then and haven't yet.

Nash edited something everywhere he went. It was *The Mountain Goat* at Sewanee, I recall, and back in Jackson he started, from Millsaps, a statewide college literary magazine, open to every college both white and black, called *Hoi Polloi*, which must have been a first. In the 1930s, same as now, Jackson had no good newspaper, and after graduation, which threw us all out into the Depression with no likely jobs in sight, Nash and another classmate, Ralph Hilton, saw no reason why that wasn't as good a time as any to start a paper of their own. Somehow they got hold of some space up over a store on a side street, a few rickety tables and a second-hand typewriter or two, and went at it. Nash and Ralph covered the news and wrote the editorials—sample subject: Prohibition; I was thrilled to be assigned the book reviews, and can recall turning one in written in heroic couplets. Up under that flat, hot tin roof, it was like working inside a popcorn popper. We survived briefly, even if we never put the notorious Fred Sullens and the *Daily News* out of business. (Ralph went on to the Associated Press and upwards.) Our Ole Miss-Yale graduate, Hubert Creekmore, started his own, earlier, *Southern Review* somewhere along then, too, to which Nash contributed a fine article and for which I aided Hubert in getting ads and reading proof. When we had to quit, we dumped all the copies we had left, with a short bridge-side ceremony, into the Pearl River. Hubert said they should at least be rare.

It was the unusual visitor that ever came through these parts in those days—we were a little off the beaten path. But Henry Miller was unusual. Fresh home from Paris, he was going to drive himself across the continent in an auto made entirely of glass, to see what his impressions of America might be. Along his way, Doubleday alerted their authors to take him in and help him in gathering information for the forthcoming book, which was to be called *The Air-Conditioned Nightmare*. I was now an author and Jackson was on his route, but my mother put her foot down. It wasn't that she gave a hoot what Henry Miller wrote in his books; where he'd made his mistake with her was in writing a letter to me. He offered, a little earlier, to put me in touch with an unfailing pornographic market that I could write for if I needed the money. It could have been a stranger's idea of a charitable suggestion to the author of a first book of short stories, but my mother didn't see the suggestion as charity. (I didn't either, I confess—I was ashamed of him.) "Well, he needn't expect to be invited into my house," said my mother, and of course neither would she have countenanced my begging off by saying I had to be out of town: that would be telling him a lie.

A good thing I knew whom to call on: Nash. Thereupon Nash, and Hubert Creekmore too, and I settled Henry Miller in the car and kept moving. (When he showed up, he wasn't in the glass car or any kind of car at all, so we used my family Chevrolet.) We showed him Vicksburg, Port Gibson, Natchez, the ruins of Windsor, the Mississippi River. Nash, who had in his command all the fact and history and lore Mr. Miller might have ever needed to gather, offered him tidbits now and then, while Hubert put knowledgeable questions to him about his work, and I drove. All of it, and our landscape, seemed to leave him imperturbable, though no less imperturbable than Henry Miller left Nash. I only remember that he stayed three days and never did take off his hat—even while we were having our picnic lunches. Was he really looking? We took him to the same place to eat every night—the best we could afford—and he thought it was three different steak houses.

When Robert van Gelder began editing the *Times Book Review*, he changed the old pattern of using the same reviewers over and over till they wore out, by inviting some brand new names. Nash's debut (from Jackson, where he was by then a schoolmaster, and the husband of one of his ex-pupils) was a review that delighted Mr. van Gelder so that he popped it right onto the front page. When it came under Mr. Markel's eye, it's told, he phoned Mr. van Gelder and demanded to know who in hell was Nash K. Burger Jr. "Nash K. Burger Jr.," Mr. van Gelder replied, "is the author of the book review we are using on page one."

In 1969, Nash came down to Jackson to make a speech at the Mississippi Arts Festival, which he delivered in the historic House of Representatives in the Old Capitol. It was a beauty, and here is a bit of it, which says something in the best way I know of, his own words, about Nash as the child and as the man:

> . . . It was early on a chilly morning in November, 1918, that I went out on the front porch of the house where we were living, just down the hill from the Old Capitol, to gather up the *Clarion-Ledger* and see how World War I was going; like most small boys I was excited by the war. I was elated to learn from the headlines on the paper that the war was over. Our side had won. Having taken this amazing news and the paper to my parents, I dressed quickly and scampered up the Amite Street hill to the corner of Capitol and State, where a few other early risers were also beginning to appear.
>
> On the grounds just in front of the Old Capitol . . . in a ramshackle scaffolding hung the historic antebellum Jackson fire bell that had escaped the Federal intervention of 1861–1865. Dancing about with excitement, I noticed the old bell and decided it should peal forth the good news. I dashed across to attend to this, but found the bell lacking a rope. Somewhere I found a piece of rope, clambered up the scaffold, tied the rope to the clapper and started yanking away, sending clanging sounds far and wide and alerting any citizens not already aware of it that the war was over. I continued banging for some time, receiving stares, smiles and jocular remarks from passers-by, until my arm got a little tired. I began to think of breakfast and that it was approaching time to be at Davis School. About this time an ancient colored woman known

as Aunt Nancy, who could tell fortunes and work other marvels, and was well known to almost all of Jackson's fifteen or twenty thousand inhabitants, appeared on the scene. She asked if she could ring the bell a while. I was ready to call it a day anyway, so turned over my job to her and hurried home.

Now we approach the point of this rather lengthy remembrance of things past. The next day in the *Clarion-Ledger* there was a long and glowing account of the zeal of Aunt Nancy, this fine, old-time colored woman who had patriotically appeared at the Old Capitol early on the morning of Armistice Day and despite her age and obvious infirmity had continued for several hours to sound the old fire bell in celebration of the historic event. Moreover, the article informed us, appreciative Jackson citizens had stopped to press nickels, dimes, quarters, halves, even a few dollar bills on Aunt Nancy as a reward for her enterprise. No mention of me, of my scrounging rope for the clapper, of my long hour or so of banging (my arm was still sore from the effort) and, of course, no financial reward.

So it was that I first learned—and this is the point, so long delayed, of my story—of the gap between the printed word and the facts of life, between what we call truth and the way a writer, either deliberately for a planned effect, or innocently out of ignorance, distorts reality. Having been raised to believe in the inerrancy of the King James Bible and the Book of Common Prayer, I was startled to discover at the age of 10 that this inerrancy did not extend to all that was printed. In subsequent years I have come to realize even more just how wide this gap between the facts of life and the printed word can be, whether in newspapers or books—to say nothing of reviews of books.

And so on. It's a mind both clear and wise, responsive and reflective, that has yet to be amazed for the first time at the human comedy around him. Just as always, and of course from now on too.

What will he do at this point? Teach at the University of Virginia, or just enroll—or should I have put it the other way. Grow figs? Re-read *Quiet Cities* by Joseph Hergesheimer? He won't stop living with books, whatever he does—he'll write or edit or publish. Nash used to say off and on that one day he'd have a press of his own. He even said once he might let me design the type. Well, for my part, I'd be willing to learn, if we could some day still carry that out.

Comments written for Burger's retirement in 1974 from the *New York Times Book Review*. Published in *The Road to West 43rd Street* by Nash K. Burger, Jr. Jackson: University Press of Mississippi, 1995, pages 178–84.

Foreword, *The Capers Papers* by Charlotte Capers

Charlotte Capers never thought to collect her papers. Her colleagues in the Archives have now done it for her, making their choices from a large number that go back for several decades. Here they are for our delight.

We will all have to agree at once to this: they represent Charlotte but they cannot convey her. They weren't written with that in mind, for they came about by circumstance. Many of them—some of the best, in fact—are samples of her warmly remembered Sunday newspaper column, "Miss Quote," set down spontaneously in response to an occasion. The occasion would have been local; it might have been of public or personal import, might have been anything that flagged the author down as she came its way or it came hers. They were crowded by space limitations and pressed by the deadline, but they were tossed off with ease and speed. And they acutely reflected their day. They can still call it up, and remind us well that Charlotte Capers never missed a thing in the passing scene.

She's such a part of it herself. Charlotte does a variety of things well and enthusiastically besides write. She'd rather rise up and dance than sit down and type. She favors the spontaneous, she enjoys the immediate response, the give-and-take of conversation, in which she is a virtuoso. Writing is something you do by yourself. This is the most serious strike against it, or Charlotte may jokingly let you think that; but in the judgment of another writer who has kept urging her on, she writes entirely too well not to take an honest satisfaction from doing it. When we read the collection here we want still more.

Most of these pieces were written to amuse, and they abundantly do so. If some of them are fleeting, so was, and so is, the passing scene. The point is that Charlotte *caught* something. Her perceptions are not only quick and bright but accurate and wise. She knows her world. She sees the social world we all move in with its history behind it, too, that built and shaped, and sometimes shadowed, our times. She is a viewer with perspective.

It is above all, though, the sense of people, of human nature and intractable human behavior that intrigues and stirs and delights her mind, and fairly often confirms her expectations. It's the rest of us that set her off. Herself too she can take on as an equally qualified subject; her own adventures make her best pieces. Her writing might spring out of that sensitivity to human idiosyncrasy which very often brings about such a satisfactory evening of conversation between friends. (*Southern* conversation, as we know and practice it.)

They are wonderfully conversational, these flowing pieces. However she makes it appear, the conversational style is not at all easy to get down on paper. Charlotte has mastered her style without seeming to try; this is characteristic of her. The Capers style, in her papers as in her character, is intuitive, receptive, hospitable, unpredictable but *succinct*.

To relish human nature (which is a talent all its own—you probably have to be born with it) is to pretty well know it, to be well-prepared and seasoned to its surprises and revelations. She applies the extravagant idiom, the outrageous now and then: it offers her a reasonable amount of scope in a small column of type, and comes in generally handy for reporting what goes on here. Exaggeration is one of her splendid accomplishments. Just as a towering skyscraper can only be built on bed rock that goes deep and stands unquivering, to exaggerate as tellingly as Charlotte can, you need to be pretty firmly based in human truths.

These pieces vary in subject and mood and kind. But they convey in common a warmth of feeling you won't fail to recognize as Charlotte's own. In reading the Capers papers we hear the Capers voice.

The beautifully written "God and My Grandmother," an essay given the full development it deserves, has the power to deeply stir us. "Pawley's Island" is a sensitive and very special evocation of a place. The exemplary portrait of the "Tiny Tenant" is made up of one part clear eyed observation, one part headlong devotion, and no part whatever of sentimentality. You will decide which are your own favorites. In any case, the last piece, "Autumn Light," an elegy of our state in 1954, is likely to remain a picture in all our minds, not fleeting but indelible.

Jackson: University Press of Mississippi, 1982, pages 9–11.

Celebrating Reynolds Price

Though I am fond of birthday celebrations, I've always tended to forget the exact age they make us—my friends and myself—in the process. Reynolds, though, who laughs at me for this, knows and remembers what that age is: he knows the verity of it. But the fiftieth birthday is one that announces itself; all can look ahead and see it coming, and those who pass it can look back and see it behind. Reynolds Price reaches this milestone on February the first. With all my heart I can celebrate it for him.

His vitality, heroic in youth, has flourished right on, steady as a flame. And like a number of his other endowments—his imagination, his generosity of spirit, his communicative delight—it has not only strengthened but informed him, increased him, in his work. We can with his newest, as we could with his earliest book, take deep breaths of the *freshness* of his writing. We can at any point return like a home-sick visitor to the gentle hills of his Piedmont, to share keenly as ever his awareness of its sentinel mountains never far away, to enter, by yet another turning, into his reverence for the mysteries and comedies of people and place. If he knows his own terrain like the back of his hand, he remains perpetually able to *see* it afresh, learning it for himself anew. Nurtured in the traditions of the world he knows so well, brought up in its story, in its own family, he searches its secrets like some original explorer, moving always, we read to find, according to the direction of love. His vision of work is the deeper, the more compelling, for his fifty years.

While I may forget about birthdays in the general, what I remember very much in the particular is meetings. First meetings are indelible.

My initial meeting with Reynolds took place on the railroad station platform of Durham, North Carolina, in the early spring of 1955, at somewhere around two o'clock in the morning. I was arriving on a train from South Carolina to speak and meet with the students of Duke later that same day. Since I couldn't bear the thought of anyone's meeting me, or of meeting anybody myself, at that hour of arrival, I'd firmly requested of the University that I be allowed to manage for myself. The train came to a stop, and I, the only passenger to descend, stepped down into the black of 2 A.M. The station, like the town around it, was without any light that I could see. No porter, no taxi was visible. Then I saw emerge a solitary figure—he was surely wearing a white suit in that darkness—of a slim young man. He introduced himself—Reynolds Price, a student at Duke; he'd been waiting for me. He said in the kindest way that I was not to trouble to speak a word, but just allow him to carry my bags and take me safely through the deserted streets to my hotel. He had imagined so well the plight I had arbitrarily set to find myself in, and had taken it upon himself to rescue me anyway. And I spoke a word anyway—"Thank you." Our long friendship began right then and there.

Since that time, we've met in all kinds of places and at all sorts of hours, and have never *stopped* talking. That first meeting may actually have been the only one in twenty-eight years when we didn't end up laughing.

Dear Reynolds, I celebrate your fiftieth birthday with joy, and with love.

For Reynolds Price 1 February 1983. Privately printed.

"That Bright Face Is Laughing"
for Robert W. Daniel

I prize a snapshot of Robert that I took the summer we met. He is a teenager. In shorts, sneakers, and a baseball cap, he's sitting on the porch steps, just looking up to say something—of course that bright face is laughing. He'd come down to Jackson, where I live, to visit a friend of us both, Frank Lyell, whom he'd met in Sewanee. Robert and I became fast friends then and there. Through all these decades, I've never felt we were out of touch with each other's life and welfare, or that we'd ever meet and be found wanting of a fresh story for the other's laugh.

A sense of the absurd is the most congenial tie in the world—more congenial than the love of literature is in general, though we have a good one there too, as it happens. Robert's sense of the absurd is acute, elegant, not to be deflected, and impossible to match. I knew it then, and I can add now that it's also as sound as an apple and has never gone sour with the increasingly absurd years.

One of those early summers, Robert, along with myself and the same Frank Lyell and one or two other friends, got up a burlesque poetry anthology; we made up the poets, their wonderful names, their biographical sketches, and their poems; and Robert bestowed the title on it, "Lilies that Fester." We did it entirely by mail; the edition consisted of one copy. Not long ago Robert ran across this, and when next we met he brought it out. We both still thought it was absolutely wonderful. The more so, maybe, when you see it now as the kind of pastime we all used to carry on, as a timeless *joie de vivre* that was a resource during the Depression.

Before scholarly criticism put its claim on Robert, poetry (the real thing) already had a hold on him—his *Tennessee Eclogues, A Garland of Seven Poems*, won the Yale University Prize for 1939—and his critical imagination has this double power, double blessing, that runs through all he's written. It fills me with gratitude to Robert to think of what he has written and said of my own work: as long as thirty years ago, he gave his perception and his sympathy to what I was trying to do, which confirmed and steadied me in my purpose and hope in a way that I have never forgotten. Indeed I felt that confirmation was still going on when Kenyon College, with Robert's citation, gave me its honorary degree just recently.

There's still another thing that Robert and I have in common— our birthdays. I'm an earlier year, but we share the month and day, the same fateful thirteenth of April. Neither of us ever forgets to find some awful card in our local drugstores to press this home. So how much finer is my unique opportunity to say happy birthday to Robert on this occasion in the auspicious pages of his own *Kenyon Review*. Happy birthday and love, dear Robert. Many happy returns!

Kenyon Review, 5 new series, Spring 1983, pages 120–21.

Tribute to Walker Percy

Let us for a moment imagine a scene wherein the two Walker Percys confront each other for the first time: the doctor who now intends to desist from practice and the writer who now intends to begin. When the writer presents himself in the doctor's office, the doctor says, "You propose to write, as Walker Percy? Let me advise you, you've had no experience. As a writer you're in your infancy. You think you are ready to take over what I have to say? Let's see you prove it." So the infant climbs up into the doctor's chair, gives it a spin, and writes *The Moviegoer.*

Of course, the significant fact about Walker's self-initiation to the writer's life is that he *didn't* begin as a wide-eyed young dreamer setting out to find his way in the literary world. He already *knew* the world, he already knew its literature, and he must have early begun to heed and to explore what was already a trustworthy insight into himself the man. It would be unlikely that he was not entertaining some compelling thoughts and observations about the rest of us. I suspect that he had prepared for becoming a novelist for as long as he had lived.

Art and science both are ways of exploration; either way, evidently, Walker Percy was a man after the truth. It seems possible that personal truth yields itself more obligingly to art—the indirect way, the allusive, suggestive, and ever-changing route, guided by the imagination.

On first reading a novel by Walker Percy, we might rather soon ask ourselves, "Where are we? Where in the world is he taking us?" We'd set off in a comfortably familiar world, the novel had proceeded civilly, urbanely, on its way, until all at once a Percy thunderclap had shaken us into apprehension. There was some real, everyday, but mysterious happening going on in the country around us—right up our road, in fact. What was until a moment ago a familiar time and place (even, perhaps, "Southern") is signaling "Danger!" In Percy novels, ordinary lives do get subjected to these occasional quick, glancing, comical, or metaphysical jolts. Thereby much goes on to be revealed.

Where is Walker Percy taking us?

But we are still at home. Home lies before us in a different light, and its face is turned toward a new perspective, but it's still where we live. Only *we* may have altered. We, who had once seen ourselves as comfortable homebodies with our names on the mailbox out front, with a zip code, a social security number, a MasterCard, were signed up with Blue Cross and Medicare and insured against fire, flood, and maybe earthquake—but not, it seems, against the intrusions of fantasy, poetry, or prophecy, which Walker Percy so calmly levels against *our* calm.

He had elected not to practice medicine, but Walker the novelist was a brilliant, perhaps a born, diagnostician. He knew, for he was always a student of life, the prognosis of a serious spiritual malady; he could read the signs and portents of despair. He could detect how easily a spiritual disorder can overtake a fellow human being, a familiar society, or the nation that we live in and normally take for granted.

The physician's ear and the writer's ear are pressed alike to the human chest, listening for the same signs of life, and with the same hope and with a like involvement in the outcome. Each listens for the heartbeat with his own heart, scans the brain of his fellow man with his own brain, to find out whether mankind is living or dying at the moment.

Walker declares in an essay, "There's something worse than being deprived of life. It's being deprived of life and not knowing it. The poet and the novelist cannot bestow life, but they can point to instances of this loss, name and record them." Thus, he tells us, "the real challenge to the novelist is not to see things as they are not. What the novelist notices is not how awful the happenings are, but how peculiar it is that people don't seem to notice how awful the happenings are."

His reader is free to conclude—and I do—that Walker's work—novels, essays, all the forms he reached for as needed—is in its strongest intention concerned with truth. I think that only a judicious portion of this truth is the factual kind; much of it is the truth of human nature, and more of it is spiritual. Walker Percy was empowered to deal with this through being—only through being—a writer of fiction. His reader catches sight of a novel's truth through the movements of his characters (sometimes in opposition to their protestations), overhears it in what they say or do to one another or in what they fail to say and omit to do. In a work of fiction, truth has to be not told, or explained, but shown. Walker Percy, showing it, could be as indirect as a magician. Truth appears to act itself out; it is transformed into the believable.

Walker Percy shared with Swift a hatred of human folly and a concern for human souls. In Walker's hands, satire made its passion known, but it never lacked for comedy or for grace.

Good, severe thinker that he was, he allowed nothing hazy into his prose. Yet we see the completed novels, crystal-clear, stand before us filled to the full with mystery. The fact is that *they*, the novels, are clear, *they* are consistently lucid—and the *subject* is mysterious—eternally so: *we*, human beings, are the subject, and able to read his novels with an enchantment of discovery and recognition.

Memorial Tributes to Walker Percy, 1916–1990. New York: Farrar, Straus, Giroux, 1991, pages 13–17.

Introduction to *The Norton Book of Friendship*

From the beginning of our plans as editors for the *Norton Book of Friendship*, we found ourselves the richer for the differences between us. One is an academic, the other a writer of fiction. One is a man, one a woman. We are of different ages and backgrounds and come from different parts of the country, though we both were graduated from colleges in the Middle West. The scholar-professor was born to be at home with statements on the nature of Friendship and what defined it—or indeed was proof of it; the fiction writer bound to seek among works of the imagination, showing forth Friendship, obliquely and dramatically, through its various aspects. We found our separate approaches congenial and promising. When we set our various choices side by side (each of us chose in either category) we found that rather than denying, or diminishing, each other, they opened ways for each other. Sometimes they suggested an unexpected tie.

In any case, we join in the two best ways for the purpose of editing a reader on Friendship: we both are readers, and we both are friends.

Ronald Sharp and I are even friends of the same old friend; some years ago when I was visiting him in Ohio, he introduced us to each other.

That is to say, friendship was blessing our partnership. It *is* a blessing. As is true of all friendships: it might not have happened—and it did.

Not surprisingly, our search for entries took on the character it did because of the essential nature of the subject. "Friendship" is inherently a magnet. As with its own drawing power, it locates and draws to the surface, spreads before our eyes poems, stories, essays, letters, in the widest variety. The qualities of playfulness and frivolity adhere to friendship as rightfully as those of devotion, heroism, sacrifice, of meditation and retrospect. The Irish drinking song "The Rakes of Mallow" has a place here as well as Yeats's poem "The Municipal Gallery Re-visited."

Certainly friendship has proved a magnet to literature, an everlasting magnet. History, poetry, drama, letters have been drawn to the subject of friendship, not simply to celebrate it but to discover, perceive, learn from it the nature of ourselves, of humankind, the relationships we share in our world.

Friendship has inherited its literary treasury; it lies in the language. In the pages ahead are the classic statements; the indispensable questionings and answerings; the reasonings, the definitions. And in that treasury's further stores of pure gold are the works of the imagination, some old as time, some coined only yesterday.

A resident sense of discovery led the editors on; so did memory. (The pleasure of running to find a passage in a beloved book and finding what was supposed to be there *still there!*) Sometimes we could claim equal reward: we had made the identical discovery—at the same time, but while Ron was in Ohio and I was in Mississippi. How reassuringly filled with coincidence is friendship itself!

We counted on our meetings: showing our finds, making proposals for where each should go, offering our trades, then finding room for everything—for the time being. Ron generously undertook all the traveling; the book was made, unmade, and remade in Jackson. And yet, all the way, it seemed that a very solid undertaking was on serene and unendangered course. Its movement was steady, even on balance, I thought. And certainly, the reason for its progressing in safety was, once again, its subject.

Through our method of setting out our combined choices into the single sweeping view on the table or the floor, unexpected affinities offered themselves sometimes before our eyes. That was one way by which our work advanced. In the sheer pleasure of being led on by our own book, we often broke out laughing.

We spotted irresistible pairs of poems, entries whose origins were more likely to have made them incompatible. Seen together, their differences were not as interesting as their kinships. We saw again that friendship acts as a magnet, draws to it something of a circle of its own, poems, stories, or letters. We were looking at a form for putting together our book: the constellation. The one that was apparent from the first is the one that leads off our book: we gave it the name "Invitations."

Should we try to include the novel? Which novel? Any specific question comes down, of course, to the basic question: which would be preferable, too little of Jane Austen, or none at all? If you cut *Emma*, such a wonderful novel of friendship, you would have to curtail Miss Bates, and this would be intolerable all around. We must leave out *Emma*. Miss Bates, who always found it hard not to go on talking about the blessings of friendship ("How shall I ever enumerate the dishes?") will go slighted one more time.

Of course we couldn't have A *Passage to India*, or any partition of *Swann's Way*. But neither could we include "Death in Venice," or *Fallen Idol* by Graham Greene, or *The Turn of the Screw*, where James slowly turns a household friendship for us until it shows a side of spiritual possession. All are novels on the subject of friendship and none will permit us to cut them. Nor the still shorter novel, like *Billy Budd*, which through its very tightness and tautness is the more vulnerable to loss. Just as one word could not be added to this penetrating novel of a friendship, not one word must be allowed subtracted from it.

Excerpting *must* diminish a novel, in respects still other than its length. Its charge of intent, its buildup of moral force, the full chord of its implications of meaning, its full stretch of time and reach of place, its power of drama—of course, most of all, its drama—are affected by meddling with its form. Interfering with its place, its timing, its focus, its symmetry and harmony of structure, would rob it of its identity, something which without any question goes in one piece.

A work of fiction is a world, single and complete and self-contained—altogether unlike life, though *like* life is what it must seem. It exists, as it was made, by one imagination. Any part of it partakes of its whole, and the pleasure of reading the novel comes partly from experiencing the delicate intimacy of its construction.

Lack of space is not the only reason for our omitting novels. The flawless comedies of P. G. Wodehouse, in which friendship takes most often a leading role (the Code of the Woosters calls for deeds of rescue, following which—the way it turns out—the rescuer must in his turn be rescued), will not transplant into the wide, general garden of the Friendship Book. As V. S. Pritchett has pointed out, Wodehouse's gift lay in writing fantasy; he was constructing a sealed-off and perfectly consistent world to itself which, to the very extent of its perfection and consistency and delight, does not exist at all except on its own terms.

The letters the *Book of Friendship* brings together have been written, at some point, from a battlefield in France, from a stretch on the Concord or the Merrimack River, from a deathbed in Rome, from a medieval tower in Ireland, from a cell in Reading Gaol, from a stagecoach bounding over a road in Austria with the youthful Mozart inside it jotting down a note to offer Joseph Haydn the dedication of his Six String Quartets.

All letters, old and new, are the still-existing parts of a life. To read them now is to be present when some discovery of truth—or perhaps untruth, some flash of light—is just occurring. It is clamorous with the moment's happiness or pain. To come upon a personal truth of a human being however little known, and now gone forever, is in some way to admit him to our friendship. What we've been told need not be momentous, but it can be as good as receiving the darting glance from some very bright eye, still mischievous and mischief-making, arriving from fifty or a hundred years ago.

The letters here are many and different, but they make us positive that the story of a life is ever present in each one, running just beneath the skin of its words. To some extent this is true of all letters for the reason that their writers' lives *are* still attached to them. Their lives have been attached to their letters since the day they were written.

Of all our entries, the letters offer the fewest generalizations on the subject of friendship. They lead us into a gallery of portraits. Some, with or without design, are self-portraits.

Edward Lear, who is everywhere known now for his inspired nonsense writings and drawings, in his own time made his living as a painter of landscapes. While living in Hastings, he was a neighbor of Tennyson. They became friends; the two regularly took their walks together, Tennyson reciting to Lear his day's achievement. And how congenial the cadences must have been to the author of "Far and few, far and few / Are the lands where the Jumblies live. / Their heads are green and their hands are blue, / And they went to sea in a sieve."

Lear worshiped Tennyson for his love of beauty. Under the inspiration of friendship and admiration, he was struck with the idea of illustrating Tennyson's poems: he wrote to ask Mrs. Tennyson.

It was the poet's "genius for the perception of the beautiful in landscape," he wrote, "which I am possibly more than most in my profession able to illustrate, not—pray understand me—from any other reason than that I possess a very remarkable collection of sketches from nature in such widely separated districts of Europe, not to say Asia and Africa." Tennyson, Emily let him know, did not object.

Edward Lear made his uncertain living by painting landscapes on commission. The hoped-for opportunity would come through various titled friends and acquaintances who had a desire for large paintings of remote sites in the reaches of the Empire or beyond. Lear would spend months in carrying a commission out.

He was a lonely man who loved children. He would go alone, traveling by necessity on foot into Syria, for example, then setting up his easel to make his delicate pencil and watercolor sketches (that are today so highly prized) which were intended to serve him as a notebook of information and color cues. He was unable to resist penciling in the margins nonsense notes to himself, still visible today. On return to his studio back home, he would spend the winter working the sketches up into oil paintings. He would carry them out according to Victorian standards: of giant size, densely and meticulously filled in, suitable for hanging in castle halls.

Lear worked when he could, for thirty-five years, proceeding from paintings to engravings, "vainly seeking," he wrote Mrs. Tennyson, "a method of doing them whereby I can eventually multiply my 200 designs by photograph or autograph or sneezigraph or any other graph." Toward the end of his life, tired and ill and unable to work, he lost heart and admitted that his plan had come to grief. The sheer size of his attempted gift had defeated him.

His genius lay in the effortless and spontaneous creation of nonsense. Any sample of it lives for us now, as fresh as the day it was first set down on some scrap of paper, perhaps to please a child the artist might have noticed running about in a lonely hotel dining room. What Lear would have wished to live forever was the set of illustrations to Tennyson's poems: the two hundred of them completed and dedicated, a monument to his friendship with the Laureate.

We include here some of his letters of progress; he only dared write them to *Mrs.* Tennyson.

Friendship pervades English literature, but not absolutely. It had better not be looked for in Mother Goose. Our nursery rhymes are in every respect callous, impervious to feelings. This callousness may have been deliberately cultivated in the earliest moral tales for children, to make childhood stronger, the better able to hear without tears anything that life ahead had in store.

We take note in this book that friendship sometimes simply does not "take." "I do not love thee, Dr. Fell" is the riddlelike expression of this.

We acknowledge friendship that has gone down to failure in its inception. Francis Parkman's great historical account of early European arrivers in North America tells how the native inhabitants, who watched their sails approach, greeted the strangers as they stepped ashore by offering them gifts and hospitality and shelter; with guidance into the wilderness that lay ahead. Thus began one long career of giant failure in friendship, never to be eradicated.

It will have been noticed that we have not omitted love from the *Book of Friendship*. Friendship and love are not arbitrarily divided here, any more than they are in life. They know each other and avail themselves of each other. The solidest friendship is that of friends who love one another.

Neither have we omitted death. A lasting literature of friendship has risen out of grief. Lines written in mourning fill some necessity for a completion to the celebration of a friendship: the Chinese poems of farewell upon a journey; Achilles' storm of pure rage at the messenger's news of the death of Patroclus in the *Iliad*; Lorca's lament for the death of a great bullfighter: his compulsive reiteration that it had happened at five o'clock in the afternoon. There is the unbearable: Keats's message of the close approach of his own death, written in the last of his letters to his friend Brown: "I can scarcely bid you good bye even in a letter. I always made an awkward bow."

And the indomitable: Swift's "Verses on the Death of Dr. Swift," the poem that erects the poet's own life to memory, the ferocity of a passion that stands alone, as a giant rock stands, assaulted by the thundering sea around it.

Lately, in my old age, it has seemed to me, when friends meet to hold a public service to pay tribute to one of their number who has died, that without words to that effect ever being said, they are drawing a circle around that friend. Speaking in turn one after the other, joining themselves together anew, they keep what they know of him intact. As if by words expressed they might turn friendship into magic, the magic that now, so clearly, it had been.

Did friendship between human beings come about in the first place along with—or through—the inspiration of language? It can be safe to say that when we learned to speak to, and listen to, rather than to strike or be struck by, our fellow human beings, we found something worth keeping alive, worth the possessing, for the rest of time. Might it possibly have been the other way round—that the promptings of friendship guided us into learning to express ourselves, teaching ourselves, between us, a language to keep it by? Friendship might have been the first, as well as the best, teacher of communication. Which came first, friendship or the spoken word? They could rise from the same prompting: to draw together, not to pull away, not to threaten any longer.

Friendship lives, as do we ourselves, in an ephemeral world. How much its life depends on the written word. The English language itself is friendship's greatest treasure. The title of a dedicatory poem by Ben Jonson is "To the Memory of My Beloved, the Author, Mr. William Shakespeare, and What He Hath Left Us." Do we not *owe* friendship, as we owe Shakespeare, to language?

Ronald Sharp and I thought, on completing our choices for *The Norton Book of Friendship*, that friendship could be said to begin at the point where it offers itself: with invitation. Now we bring the book to a close in the same way, with an ancient song called "The Irish Dancer":

I am of Ireland
And of the holy land
    Of Ireland.
Good sir, pray I thee,
Of sainte charity
Come and dance with me
    In Ireland.

Eudora Welty and Ronald A. Sharp, eds. New York: W. W. Norton, 1991, pages 35–41. Sharp contributed a separate introduction.

VII. PUBLIC ENGAGEMENTS

Voice of the People, Letter against Gerald L. K. Smith

Jackson, Mississippi
Dec. 20, 1945
The Editor
Clarion Ledger
Jackson, Mississippi

Dear Sir:

Has any Mississippian bothered to inquire exactly what the fascistic Gerald L. K. Smith came to do in our state, and asked him to get out? Both Jackson papers today print unconcerned news accounts of this visit—a visit for which the word sinister could not be at all too strong—and let it go. No editorial comment, no questions asked in any quarter, it seems.

Nothing Gerald L. K. Smith could do is likely to be innocent, when he comes around poking his nose in, but this visit is not even pretending to be innocent. The news story you print says he "was in

Jackson yesterday for the purpose of contacting committeemen and laying down the foundation for the development of Nationalist organizations in the South." Isn't there anybody ready with words for telling Smith that smells to heaven to us, that we don't want him, won't let him try organizing any of his fascistic doings in our borders, and to get out and stay out of Mississippi? Or is it true that he is actually organizing? Then we need to know facts indeed.

It seems Smith after laying a wreath on the grave of Huey Long came up here with two more wreaths for the heads of Bilbo and Rankin—both of which they would fit too well, no doubt. But this is more scathing comment on our state; and deserving it or not for having elected men like Bilbo and Rankin to stand for Mississippi, is there still nothing we can do to atone for our apathy and our blindness or closed minds by maintaining some kind of vigilance in keeping Gerald Smith away?

It would be sad to cringe under shame of our Bilbos and Rankins forever and to the extent that we can't do anything about Gerald L. K. Smith. Far worse than sad. Most of our readers surely feel as does the undersigned—that we will get Bilbo and Rankin out when their time, election time, comes, God willing, but it's high time now to put the exodus on this public enemy we aren't even responsible for. Can't our papers speak up? And hadn't they better?

Sincerely yours,
Eudora Welty

Jackson *Clarion-Ledger*, 23 December 1945. The paper had no "Letters to the Editors" section at that time. Welty references also the Jackson *Daily News*.

Department of Amplification,
Letter in Defense of
William Faulkner

Jackson, Mississippi
December 15, 1948

To the Editors, *The New Yorker*,
Gentlemen:

How well Illinois or South Dakota or Vermont has fared in *The New Yorker* book-review column lately, I haven't noticed, but Mississippi was pushed under three times in two weeks, and I am scared we are going to drown, if we know enough to.

It's that combination "intelligent . . . despite" that we're given as a verdict each time. The "intelligent" refers to the books or their characters and the "despite" refers to the authors' living in Mississippi. Now there's one who is not only intelligent despite, but, it appears, not quite intelligent enough because of. In fact, one of this country's most highly respected critics writes three or four pages in a recent *New Yorker* on one of the great writers and begrudges him his greatness, and I do feel like "noticing."

Edmund Wilson, reviewing *Intruder in the Dust*, by William Faulkner, reaches one of his chief points in the paragraph:

> To be thus out of date, as a Southerner, in feeling and in language and in human relations, is, for a novelist, a source of strength. But Faulkner's weakness has also its origin in the antiquated community he inhabits, for it consists in his not having mastered—I speak of the design of his books as wholes as well as of that of his sentences and paragraphs—the discipline of the Joyces, Prousts, and Conrads (though Proust had his solecisms and what the ancients called anacolutha). If you are going to do embroidery, you have to watch every stitch; if you are going to construct a complex machine, you have to have every part tested. The technique of the modern novel, with its ideal of technical efficiency, its specialization of means for ends, has grown up in the industrial age, and it has a good deal in common with the other manifestations of that age. In practicing it so far from such cities as produced the Flauberts, Joyces, and Jameses, Faulkner's provinciality, stubbornly cherished and turned into an asset, inevitably tempts him to be slipshod and has apparently made it impossible for him to acquire complete expertness in an art that demands of the artist the closest attention and care.

That last sentence, born in New York, has the flaw of a grammatical mistake; I don't know what being out of date in feeling means; and I didn't mind looking up "anacolutha"—but to get through to the point, *Intruder in the Dust* itself having been forgotten earlier in the piece, I shy at this idea of novel writing as a competitive, up-to-the-minute technical industry, if only for the picture it gives me of Mr. Faulkner in a striped cloth cap, with badge and lunch box, marching in to match efficiency with the rest only to have Boss Man Wilson dock him—as an example, too—for slipshod bolt-and-nut performance caused by unsatisfactory home address. Somehow, I feel nobody could go on from there, except S. J. Perelman, and he works in another department.

It's as though we were told to modify our opinion of Cézanne's painting because Cézanne lived not in Paris but by preference in Aix and painted Aix apples—"stubbornly" (what word could ever apply less to the quality of the imagination's working?).

Such critical irrelevance, favorable or unfavorable, the South has long been used to, but now Mr. Wilson fancies it up and it will resound a little louder. Mr. Faulkner all the while continues to be capable of passion, of love, of wisdom, perhaps of prophecy, toward his material. Isn't that enough? Such qualities can identify themselves anywhere in the world and in any century without furnishing an address or references. Should this disconcert the critic who cannot or does not write without furnishing his? Well, maybe it should.

Mr. Wilson has to account for the superior work of Mr. Faulkner, of course he has to, and to show why the novelist writes his transcendent descriptions, he offers the explanation that the Southern man-made world is different looking, hence its impact is different, and those adjectives come out. (Different looking—to whom?) Could the simple, though superfluous, explanation not be that the recipient of the impact, Mr. Faulkner, is the different component here, possessing the brain as he does, and that the superiority of the work done lies in that brain?

Mr. Faulkner (if report of his custom is true) has probably not bothered to look at the reviews of his book; he certainly doesn't need a defender of any sort; but it's hard to listen to anyone being condescended to, and to a great man being condescended to pretentiously. Nearly all writers in the world live, or in their day lived, out of the U.S. North and the U.S. South alike, taking them by and large and over random centuries. (Only Mr. Wilson is counting for the city vs. the country, to my sketchy knowledge.) And it does seem that in criticizing a novel there could be more logic and purity of judgment than Mr. Wilson shows in pulling out a map. In final estimate he places Faulkner up with the great, as well he might, but with a corrective tap asks him—maybe twice—to stand on just a little lower step for the group picture, to bring out a point in the composition. I still don't think the picture turned out too clear, somebody was bound to move.

For of course there's such a thing as a literary frame of reference that isn't industrial New York City in 1948, just as there's a literary frame through which one can look and not find "pages" of Mr. Faulkner's "The Bear" "almost opaque." "Opaque"— to whom? To Mr. Wilson I would say that I believe they are clear to me (for one example—((queer eyesight and all))), remembering too that each of us is just one looker. The important thing is that Mr. Faulkner's pages are here to look *at*.

Yours sincerely,
—Eudora Welty

New Yorker, 1 January 1949, pages 50–51. The Department of Amplification, beginning in 1937, prints Letters to the Editors of the *New Yorker*. Wilson reviewed *Intruder in the Dust* under the title "William Faulkner's Reply to the Civil-Rights Program" in the *New Yorker*, 23 October 1948, pages 120–22, 125–28. Welty's review of *Intruder* was published in *Hudson Review*, Winter 1949, pages 596–98.

What Stevenson Started

An invitation to send a New Year's message to you is a high honor and I feel it. Maybe this greeting can find its place as word from a little group normally quiet. This writer knows of people here and there like herself, previously political ignoramuses (we now feel a fellowship)—well-intentioned ever, but not ever, in the sense of being personally involved, concerned deeply by a political campaign until this year. Then, with your appearance on the national scene, we found out how deeply concerned we could be. The climax of the election changed nothing of that (but for the heartbreak) and we are finding that the conception you gave us of politics prevails steadily over the news of the day, and stirs us still—that we think more about what your campaign revealed, through its challenge and its defeat, than about anything that could happen to obscure it.

The moving fact emerged for us that the voice of the passionate intelligence speaks to the whole range of the mind—in politics as well as in poetry. This intelligence so charged to communicate, so shaped in responsibility and impelled with learning and curiosity, so alight with imagination, from the start couldn't be denied for what it is; it could be resisted only—another kind of recognition. It challenges still, and what was said in the campaign remains said, clear to and beyond the finish of any race. If defeat has obstructed our hearing it just now, the wait is not silence but suspense. One of our problems as voters (for all I know, the oldest and hardest problem) is how soon and how fully we can accommodate greatness—honor it, not punish it, because it *is* greatness, and different all in courage from the run of things. If you yourself were remote from us now, and off in history, we'd take you for granted like a shot.

It was an odd sidelight, and not in the human way belittling of the events, that while this campaign was going on, it was to a good many people like something symbolic of what happened inside themselves at a crisis. Besides everything else, it was also that modest struggle, at home in any breast, between cherished hope and ardent belief and what always assails it—being played out clear across the American continent on crowded platforms and from the back ends of trains. (This illusion may of course have been the case with the other side, too, though Stevenson people were the only ones I heard mention it.)

If it *was* their chiefest inner convictions translated for the time being to the huge fateful stage of the outside world—to politics—there to get whacked, too—it was because at last somebody had got up and represented those convictions and brought them to bear on the scene, life-size and first-hand.

The support—the non-support, too—of any candidate must needs be a personal matter—one that will explore the voter's will, and willingness, his capacity, his vision, as well as the candidate's out front. But when was that ever as clear as this time, or as challenging?

Governor Stevenson, we brag on having you, and send wishes to you on New Year's to keep your health, but that's just our pleasure. Practicality at the earliest opportunity would become well-wishers more. We don't want to lose to even a short oblivion the candidate whose declared guiding concern it is to see man stand up in the dignity of reason, to take his place as a being of sentience and nobility in the sight of God. With that we were shown the compassionate side of a coin that rings forever with the purity and fierceness of that desire whose other side was the anger of Swift.

As our candidate you put that wish into the act, and took part in a campaign that would have cost any man a great deal, the man with selfless vision the most; for which we owe the debt. We are grateful for what you did, and our confidence reposes in you.

Some plan is doubtless in the making somewhere to ask more of you. Whatever your own design for the future may be, our belief in you has implicated us already. And whoever feels this must want to say on New Year's, as I have the chance to, that all we've learned from the year past is now a start on the future, so that we can give more practical evidence of our belief in working along with you when the time comes.

New Republic, 5 January 1953, pages 8–9. Following Adlai Stevenson's loss to Dwight D. Eisenhower in the 1952 presidential election, the *New Republic* invited "leading writers, artists and scholars to evaluate" the "Stevenson Spirit" and "to indicate what present and future contributions might be made to continue it." Other contributors were Marshall Field, Howard Lindsay, Lewis Mumford, Duncan Phillips, Elmer Rice, John Steinbeck, and Mark Van Doren.

Is There a Reader in the House?

I'm not trying to tell teachers news about their children—how could there be any news they don't know?—but, being asked, I could report something about children that was news to me. They don't read. The way I found out was their invariable response to my invariable response to a question asked me as a writer about the best way to learn to write. "Read," I replied. To which they replied, "*Read?*" They were incredulous that reading had anything to do with it. And the implication was that if it had, then that was just too high a price to pay.

So it shouldn't shock me the way it's been doing when a batch of children's stories comes in to me to be judged for some contest here or there, and I see before my eyes stories that are not like anything ever conceived of for the printed page. This stuff (and presumably each story represents some teacher's desperate choice for the best in the class) would merge with no sea-change at all into radio soap-operas, into TV dramas, or into the funny-papers, but none of it belongs to the world of books—and the world of books wouldn't want it.

Real life, honest experience (everybody alive has experience), sensible observation, any sort of real perception, feeling, thought—these sources (to and from which all good books lead) are the last sources on earth the writers of these stories would ever dream of consulting. The subject matter—brain tumors, and the surgery to go with them (there are constant calls for the doctor in these quivering but lifeless stories), matricide, fratricide, patricide, suicide, end of the world, hopeless insanity, worse—is all sensational. The treatment—present tense, staccato first-person narrative, asides and interludes that baffled me until I imagined the voice of some sponsor without portfolio—is equally shallow, equally tasteless, equally remote from anything that has to do with life, and hence with literature.

So far as the young authors of these stories are concerned, stories are something to be *listened* to (they are full of sound-effects, but almost no visual imagery), shuddered at, and mercifully, one hopes, forgotten. The meaning of words, their poetry, sense, significance, beauty, coherence in the way they're used—none of this is ever experienced, to judge by that anguished cry, "*Read?*"—and to judge by what these children suppose, from hearsay, must be a story.

Certainly there are exceptions. Let me say that a notable exception is the annual scholastic Magazine Contest. These stories from all over the country, which it's been my pleasure to judge a time or two, are of a consistently high order and show evidence that a teacher's influence can surmount anything! I have read stories by young people that surpass, in technique at least, anything that I or most of my contemporaries were able to write at that age. And these stories reflect good reading, not sometimes, but every time. They don't imitate, often; they rather show something learned and applied; but even imitation conceives of a goal and is better than uttering in a vacuum.

We must suppose and hope there will always be children who discover books (in their own homes, of course, would be the best place), value and cherish literature as literature, feel aware of the history and beauty and profundity of what exists there for them.

But the fact remains that the majority of these young story writers who enter the contests carry on blithely without the slightest suspicion that there's anything to be learned about writing from reading, that there's anything to a story that couldn't just as well be conveyed in a comic strip, in the language of zoom, biff, bang—or most frequently, ow. Recently the British magazine *Punch* carried a burlesque comic of *Ulysses*, telling the whole story in picture and caption on two pages, "Capsulysses." One of the capsule characterizations was Polyphemus's: "His eye is too close together!"

Think what they miss! That is the saddest thing. It isn't the point of my lament that most of these children will never understand how to write a story, or care why—there will be enough of them that do. I only wish these children—all of them—partook of what reading can give. You hate to see a whole world of pleasure and excitement and wisdom and glory go lost, its very existence unsuspected.

I certainly don't blame teachers, for teachers, by and large, are almost the only ones left to point the way. But I keep wondering what combination of teacher, parents, pupil, *books*—physical, openable, uncondensed, real books, in a house, beside a lamp and a chair—will somehow, with all its syllables, spell "Sesame." Something does tell us the letters TV don't belong in it, but I still think we can spell it with the thing in the room. Let the real *Ulysses* once begin—*The Odyssey* of Homer in E. V. Rieu's translation, say—and the world will be lost to him. As always and forever.

Mississippi Educational Advance 47, November 1955, pages 12–13, journal of the Mississippi Education Association. Reprinted as "Eudora Welty Blames Lack of Reading for Lack of Creative Ability in Child" in the Jackson *Daily News*, 17 November 1955, section 2, page 4.

English from the Inside

The U.S. Senate Committee on Labor and Public Welfare made a report in July of 1964 on the state of teaching of English in secondary schools over the country. Maybe the report surprised the country, but it couldn't have surprised the teachers. The Committee found the state of English teaching "so serious that it threatens the foundations of our educational enterprise and of our progress as a people." No wonder! The average teaching experience of nearly 7,500 secondary teachers sampled was nine years. Two-thirds of them did not consider themselves well prepared to teach composition; almost half of them did not consider themselves well prepared to teach literature and language.

And though they might teach their hearts out—and that's what most of them were doing—how were they to have felt other than they did? A sampling of elementary English teachers in every region showed that close to half of them began teaching without a bachelor's degree, that fewer than 10 percent had a major in English, and (is this perhaps most depressing of all?) that 54 percent had majored in education rather than in any academic subject.

And there hasn't been much that the teachers themselves have been able to do about improving their qualifications. This costs money, which not very many teachers can spare. And in the whole country, the report went on to say, the number of secondary school teachers of English receiving any form of financial help from the Federal Government for graduate study had, so far, totaled—out of some 90,000—no more than 800. (The teachers of other subjects the Government had so helped numbered more than 51,000.)

In the summer of 1965 something was done about the English teachers. A nationwide program of English institutes was set up under an amendment to the National Defense Education Act. One of these institutes, held at Tulane University in New Orleans, was directed by Dr. Marvin Morillo, associate professor of English at Newcomb College, the women's liberal arts division of Tulane. I was invited to go down for a day and watch the institute in action.

Thirty qualified teachers of English in public, private, and parochial secondary schools, grades 7–12, were taking six weeks of intensive, full-time work in graduate-level courses in literature, language, and composition. These courses gave them, upon completion, six hours of graduate credit toward advanced degrees. The thirty were exempt from tuition fees; they received $75 a week plus an allowance of $15 a week for each dependent.

While the U.S. Office of Education determines the basic eligibility for admission, the choice of applicants in each institute is left to those who administer the institute. At Tulane—even though the announcement had come late in the year—there had been, for the 30 places open, 350 applicants. The Tulane committee had, in consequence, the difficult and unhappy task of eliminating many qualified and deserving teachers. Its work of selection was hampered further because many students had, understandably, sent in applications to more than one institute; the result was duplication of acceptance and a great long waiting list of applicants who might meanwhile have been accepted somewhere else. Next year, it was hoped, some of these difficulties will have been ironed out. But next year the institutes will be announced earlier, and a still greater number of teachers is expected to apply.

"The facts are sobering," said Dr. Morillo. "Not only do the teachers themselves feel unprepared and inadequate, but their students are reflecting inadequate preparation, not only in their English courses but in other fields which require verbal and written skills."

The Tulane institute ran from June 14 to July 23 in utter comfort. Tulane is an air-conditioned university—the summer student works, studies, eats, sleeps, and plays in the cool. The new residence hall on campus had been set aside for the summer for graduate and professional students. The classes for the institute were held a few minutes' walk away in the University Center—a big, light-filled, well-designed, busy building, with cafeteria, snack bar, bookstore, bowling alleys, ping pong tables, music room, and swimming pool in addition to a variety of assembly rooms large and small. Classes for the institute were all held in one of the smaller rooms on the second floor.

"There's a wide variation in ability. What else would you expect?" one of the staff remarked to me as we walked up to begin the day with the literature class. Some of these teachers graduated as many as 20 years ago, and for the whole time ever since have been teaching their hearts out in some small-town school."

The teachers, most of them appearing to be somewhere in their thirties, a few in their forties, sat up and down two long tables, which the teacher's desk formed into a U, in the well-lit, soft-panelled room. Most of them were smoking. They were a pleasant-looking group, comfortably dressed, the women in summer dresses, the men in short sleeves and slacks; there was one nun in her habit and, I later learned, one young priest out of his clerical dress, wearing a bright sport shirt. They were exactly 50-50 white and Negro; in selecting the class, numerical fairness in regard to race had been a deciding factor. For the most part, white students sat along one table, Negro students along the other. This had been their own choice at the first meeting of the class, I was told later, and they had kept to it with the exception of one or two Negro students who had moved to the white side and one white student who'd moved to the Negro side. It spoke of self-consciousness, and I mention it in order to say that nothing else, to my eyes, did. There was certainly no self-consciousness when we all went later to the cafeteria; eating, laughing, talking together, the teachers sat down anywhere. Perhaps it was in some part the simple difference between the straight tables in the classroom and the round tables in the cafeteria.

Today Dr. Morillo was winding up *The Sound and the Fury*. Sitting there as a writer, I thanked heaven that this good teacher spoke of the novel throughout in terms of a work of art. He was informative, he was lucid, he was generous with suggestions as he went along. He discussed thoroughly, for example, such technical things as point-of-view—what Faulkner is doing in the three "I" sections of *The Sound and the Fury* and in the third-person Dilsey part, respectively.

With the selection of any Faulkner novel, in particular *The Sound and the Fury*, not only one of the most difficult novels written in our time but the novel containing, and in one sense dominated by, the Negro character Dilsey, there *could* in this class and in these circumstances have arisen some misunderstanding.

Subject matter, long before now, has been confused with its fictional treatment, objective reality with its imaginative interpretation. There could eaily, here, have been confusion in the students' minds between the behavior and speech of the Mississippi characters and the purpose and commitment of the author who put them into the novel. It would have been almost routine confusion, a commonplace in any classroom at work on any novel; indeed it prevails in discussion of fiction anywhere, as any novelist has found out for himself. But such was the quality of this lecture, and such was the attentiveness of this class as listeners and as participants, that I felt the effort came off. The articulate Dr. Morillo and the animated class made connection: what more can happen? What emerged, as they sat talking, smoking, pursuing the thing, was a sense of the *greatness of the novel*. How long they keep this sense of greatness must depend on them; but no other objective would have been worth a teacher's trying for.

In order to give myself a chance to learn more and to round out my picture of the Tulane institute, I visited the two other classes being offered.

I was unlucky enough to drop in on the composition class on a day when no student compositions were being read. I was able, though, to get some idea about the class from the teacher, Professor Harvey M. Craft, assistant professor of English, College of Arts and Sciences, Tulane. His method of work seemed both sympathetic and very well tailored to the needs of this class—it had had good results. He assigns a variety of compositions during the course: expository, narrative, and so on. For example, he gives them four or five plot situations and asks them to write, on the spot, dramatic monologues based on one of them, then read them aloud for the class. Or he asks them to write Haiku—a Japanese form of poetry—also on the spot, and then read them aloud. He has found that an immediate response to an assignment frees the student, is far less likely to produce self-consciousness, over-elaborate expression, and similar failures in using the language effectively. In the main he wants his student-teachers to realize, he told me, that there is no such thing as separating language from literature.

I asked if I might see some of the Haiku poems. Here are a few of the spontaneous efforts to use this ancient Japanese verse form to express some present observation of the life around them. They are nearly all neat and, I think, delightful abstractions of the heat.

A mosquito drones
The moss makes web-like tracings
Over the bayou
   —Anita V. Guillot

The heat waves shimmering
Playful noises of happy children
Evaporate too
   —Rev. William Alerding

The dancing demons . . .
Sun-blasted vegetation
Droops with thirst unquenched
    —Floyd Beeson

Mrs. Gail B. Little, Chairman of English, Louise S. McGehee School, New Orleans, held a workshop in the practical problems of secondary school textbooks, curriculum, grading, and the like. On the day of my visit, the subject under discussion was "which system of grammar to teach?"

"People feel, if you attack a child's dialect you are attacking his character, self-respect, home, and the rest. But we have to struggle. The question at hand is whether you are happy with the traditional approach to grammar," said Mrs. Little, a pleasant woman with an air of no-nonsense about her.

One of the class said, "Our job is not just to teach the children command of the language, but to give them some feeling of language as language."

"The child has internalized the basic structure of the language before he ever gets to school," said someone else. (I felt rather lost, myself, in the thickets of remarks like this, and wondered what I was letting myself in for when I came to hear about the "new grammar." I can't remember that I ever learned very much of the "old" when I was in school.)

There was an attempt at open discussion about the relative worth of linguistics and the traditional approach to grammar; but beyond linguistics being declared the winner I didn't receive the impression it got very far. My own ignorance could well have barred me from following it properly.

Mrs. Little's own vote was firmly for linguistics. "Linguistics seems to me a more accurate and realistic view of what goes on in the language." she said. "The linguistic approach sees language as dynamic." I felt that the class was sold on it.

Mrs. Little remarked to me, "Most of these people have been poorly educated in grammar. But this new grammar is *in* just now—so if they think that, they don't want to show they're scared of it; they wouldn't want to show shock." She added, "What I really hope to do is give them enough vocabulary, enough of an approach to it, to allow them to sit down and *read the textbooks* on structural approach."

I was impressed and interested all the way through my visit at the Tulane institute. I felt there was a great honesty about it in several manifestations. For instance, in the matter of race. Race was an element and faced up to. In the grammar class, the special difficulties of teachers confronted with all Southern speechways were faced up to realistically by Mrs. Little and by the class; there was no useless pretending that some of the problems close to race problems weren't there, and no disrespectful waste of time skirting around them. There was no inhibition because of race apparent anywhere to me. To the contrary, I had the feeling that members of the class in general enjoyed one another, and that this enjoyment did not end with the end of classes.

On the other hand, I felt another sort of inhibition present. I saw little evidence, on the day I happened to be there, of any spontaneous free play of the *imagination.* Any exercise of the imagination had to be dug for by the teacher. This is not to say that the class was altogether short on *having* imagination—that great resource on which all education has to draw. Indeed, their responsiveness to Dr. Morillo's lecture, the dashing off of their own Haiku, their general alertness and liveliness, all testify to its presence. Yet it never appeared articulate that day to me. The young teachers never, while I heard them, put an abstract idea about literature into words or ever quite clearly placed the achievement of a work of imagination above what they supposed to be the author's *opinions.* I felt that all Dr. Morillo's not inconsiderable efforts had been needed and called on, and that they'd been given, too.

I had a chance to talk with some members of the class and I asked several what they thought of the institute. Problems among teachers differ, some of them told me, but in general the institute had recognized and was grappling with the big ones, the basic ones. Most of the teachers said they felt rewarded by the course, and nearly all of them added that personal relationships they formed during the Tulane session had meant at least as much to them as had the work of the classroom.

American Education, 2 February 1966, pages 18–19.

From Where I Live

Southerners on their travels are always being asked to account for living in the South. I think every answer is personal (mine is that I like living in the South), and I think all personal reasons are valid ones. Southern writers, too, are perennially asked to give their excuse for not moving North or East. When, in one little Mississippi town on the river, one year, 17 authors were all in the national print and a Pulitzer Prize winner was editing the paper, Greenville in general was asked to account for that. Some citizens tried, others went right on writing. Mr. Edmund Wilson, a very considerable critic, once put himself on record as wondering why on earth a writer like William Faulkner didn't quit all his local stuff and remove himself to civilization to put his genius to work. He asked how writing as good as Faulkner's could ever have come out of Mississippi. Of course, the marvelous thing is that it came. Had Mr. Wilson tried calling for *The Sound and the Fury* in another direction, he would have been wise not to wait.

Reasons for wanting to live where you live and write where you live are personal, but taken all together they may also be general, far-reaching, and profound. The group of poets and essayists clustered around Vanderbilt in the 1920s went to the root of the matter. By the use of eloquent statement, the symbol of poetry, a systematized ethical idea which was christened Agrarianism, they sought to make their combined view of the South an entity—historical, geographic, economic, aesthetic. Perhaps there was something romantic and heroic about *I'll Take My Stand*, which history has not left untramped on, but their cause is not lost even yet, for their ideas about writing—perhaps the heart of it all—have persevered.

Better than all the rest of Southern writing, Faulkner's creation of Yoknapatawpha County stands for what I take to be a truth, that deeper down than people, farther back than known history, there is the Place. All Southerners must have felt, must feel now, that they were born into its larger story, and can see themselves, here where they came from, in chronological line—long, straggling, many-colored, not always pulling in the same way, but all touching, joined together, and still reaching. Part of the story.

And Southerners write it. Probably they must write it. It is the way they are born, to love a good tale. They are born reciters, great memory retainers, diary keepers, letter exchangers and letter savers, history tracers and debaters, and—outstaying all the rest—great talkers. Southern talk is on the narrative side, employing the verbatim conversation. For this, plenty of time is needed and it is granted. It was still true not so very far back that children *grew up listening*—listening through unhurried stretches of uninhibited reminiscence, and listening galvanized. They were naturally prone to be entertained from the first by life as they heard tell of it, and to feel free, encouraged, and then in no time compelled, to pass their pleasure on. *They* were telling it.

It was all part of Place. It wasn't only that history had happened in the front yard or come up into the house, once upon a time. But stories could be watched in the happening—lifelong and generation-long stories watched and participated in, first by one member of the family and then without a break by another, allowing the continuous and never-ending recital to be passed along in full course and to grow.

The event and the memory and the comprehension of it and taking a role in it were scarcely marked off from the other in the glow of hearing it again, telling it anew, anticipating, knowing the whole thing by heart—and all right here where it happened. A family story is a family possession, not for a moment to be forgotten, not a bit to be dropped or left out—just added to. No good story ever became *diminished*.

And, if one thing is consistent among the many Southern writers, different as they are from one another, it is that each feels passionately about Place. Not simply in the historical or philosophical connotation of the word, but in the sensory thing, the experienced world of sight and sound and smell, in its earth and water and sky and in its seasons. Place, so does it fire the imagination, must have a great deal indeed to do with the fury of writing with which the South is so continuously engaged.

Today the South is not the same to the eye as it was, and no longer can it be quite the same to the storyteller's memory; there are other reaches to the old perspectives that have opened to our searching minds. Place must be seen with Time walking on it.

Yet Place, ancient Place, remains in essence the same; it is the fleeting scene that changes. And while it used to be that the story was written about what had already happened, even if it was no later than yesterday, now the story is in the present with the writer—all of it is happening now, and fast, racing against the words.

Yet, for all its turmoil, for all its surging in the mass, the action of today's scene has moved only a fraction this way or that from the same track it has followed since the beginning. As earth and sky are the same, man's nature and his aspirations are the same. His motives for good and ill do not change. They never age, they will not vanish till we ourselves vanish and this place with us.

And just as ever, or so I believe from here, the story we tell or write is good only according to its faithfulness to the truths of the human heart.

Delta Review 6, November–December 1969, page 69.

Opening Remarks, Governor's Conference on the Arts: New Audiences/ New Creators

Governor Waller, Mayor Davis, Dr. McCain, Miss Hanks and other distinguished guests, members of the Governor's Conference on the Arts; ladies and gentlemen:

Just last Sunday, nearly coinciding with the date of this meeting, an exhibition of abstract art by some underground painters opened on the outskirts of Moscow. Was this the result of encouragement by the local Arts Commission? Had the National Endowment for the Russian Arts sent the artists—even though they were abstract artists—some form of support? What the government sent, and straight to the scene of the exhibition, was a bulldozer. The paintings on show were torn down and thrown under its treads, and the artists themselves were all arrested and thrown in jail for fifteen days, on a charge of "hooliganism." Government supported? Not even government-tolerated.

While here, in another part of the forest, another outskirt, what do we see going on? Here to be with Lida Rogers and her workers in the Mississippi Arts Commission have arrived in Jackson, Michael

Newton of the Associated Councils of the Arts, a number of our distinguished leaders in the National Council on the Arts, and Nancy Hanks, Chairman of the National Endowment for the Arts. Nancy Hanks, it appears to me after several years of seeing her at work, reveals herself through her accomplishments as a human dynamo and an all-purpose miracle worker. I don't know which came first. She instills life, at any rate, into the works, and it is a mark of her usual generosity of spirit, of giving forth, that she is here in person from her demanding job in Washington to be with us and galvanize our meeting. Here with these visitors, and all about to go to work this morning, are able leaders of our community in their own various fields of arts, education and civic life, to meet in direct conversation and exchange of ideas.

I am not a speaker and this is not a speech, but I feel honored to be here because I am keenly aware of the importance of this occasion. It is important to art, and it is important to people—to the people in Mississippi.

There has to be set in motion a machinery to disseminate art—and this is the most carefully made to be a good one. And this in itself is remarkable, for of course art itself has nothing to do with machinery. It is a human endeavor, springing from human passion. There is something unique in every true work of art that exists there only because of some one person's vision of mind and the work of his hands or his body, or his voice, or his imagination put on paper. Art is of human origin. And only human understanding, human experience and feeling can respond to it and appraise its meaning. We remember that the renowned art critic and historian Bernard Berenson characterized the central quality of a great work of art as "life-enhancing." I believe that the importance of all we are doing here lies in this quality of the "life-enhancing" in art. And the machinery of disseminating art to the public as we work with it here is subservient to the nature of art. It strives not to encourage art in the mass, but art in its excellence. It is really, I should say, directed toward an understanding of art on the part of the public.

We all know that there is no way in the world that understanding of the arts can be instant. Understanding comes as a result of exposure to something we find valuable in life. Understanding, like the art it would confront, is the product of a growing process. Again, just as it comes to the aid of the working artist, these Councils and Commissions of the Endowment, these meetings, among leaders, bring ways to help to set this art before the public in a context of meaning, significance.

In our working terms, as I see it, art implies two parts: there is the giving end—an artist who produces—and there is the receiving end—the viewers, the audiences, who stand ready to know what's there to be seen, heard, delighted in, ready to respond with a quickened imagination.

Indeed, the two overlap. Often the artists are themselves viewers of their own and other arts, members of different audiences. Many a viewer is an artist too—even if no further advanced than the amateur, the Sunday painter. Art can, in fact, involve just as many of us as want to be involved.

A member of the State Commission said the other day, "We want to show that art is for everyone."

When we are asked, what kind of art would be "for everybody," there can only be one answer: the best. Not a Gerber's puree to spoon-feed beginners with what might be thought simple enough for them to digest. Not a placebo to humor the long-hungry and the long-deprived in art, on the wretched assumption that they will think something is good only because they've never seen or heard anything better. But the real, honest-to-God thing—the best we are capable of making and giving. The feast itself. They must be brought up to the table.

And certainly if we give the best we are capable of, and if we receive the best we are capable of, our capacities will grow. Our art will grow.

In Mississippi we are proud of what we have been able to achieve in the arts. But we have no time or inclination to pause in order to brag on ourselves. Here we are to work, to learn all we can in two days, then to return to our vocations. We only work in order that the artists may make new things of truth, that their audiences and viewers may learn more of what it is about by opening minds and feelings to it, being willing to accept its beauty in all the manifestations in which it may appear. So we shall all experience in a way of our own some of the joy of art's making.

So the privilege of understanding art is what is being offered "everybody." The knowledge, the enjoyment, the experience of art can be shared by all the comers to the feast. Thank you very much.

Typescript, two pages. Subject File, Mississippi Department of Archives and History, Jackson, Mississippi, 19 September 1974. The 15 September 1974, "exhibition of abstract art" that Welty refers to became known as the Bulldozer Show. The Second Fall Open-Air Show of Paintings took place two weeks later on September 29.

Letter to the Editor of the *New York Times Book Review* in Defense of *The Surface of Earth* by Reynolds Price

To the Editor:

Your reviewer Richard Gilman protests (June 29) any sort of attention still being paid to the South, "as though it were an ongoing cultural reality," arguing that it has "only the most marginal place in general consciousness now." And Southern literature—all of which he is able to write off in a block ("downhome storytelling")—was finished, such as it was, in the year 1964: that was when Flannery O'Connor died. He had felt confident of hearing no more out of the place.

A column-load of such remarks were due his readers, Mr. Gilman explains, in order to provide a "perspective" down which he can look at *The Surface of Earth*, by Reynolds Price of North Carolina, just out. Mr. Gilman, let him tell you, has never caught sight of such an antediluvian monster—"a mastodon, sprung to life from beneath an ice field"—as this: a Southern novel, a regional novel, a novel that is written about a family—two families! Don't ask him how many generations.

"Who could have imagined that any novelist presumably sensi-tive to the prevailing winds of consciousness . . . could have written a relentless family saga at a time when most of us feel self-generated inheritors of obliterated pasts?" he asks.

This affording us a return-perspective on Mr. Gilman, we are not much surprised when he reacts blankly to the vocabulary of Reynolds Price. He is rather shocked by the terms Mr. Price uses to describe and express love. (Love is, to use Mr. Gilman's own term, Reynolds Price's "obsession.") "For against the hugely dominant literary tradi-tion of love as mystery, revelation, disaster or derangement . . . Price sets a vision of it as 'simple peace and continuance,' as 'kindness,' 'help,' 'generosity,' 'welcome,' 'promise,' 'pardon' and 'gift.' . . . It is 'permanent thanks.'" As if these were terms too daring and altogether not fit, or safe, for him to handle, Mr. Gilman looks about for *some* password the author might be familiar with: what about "penis"? No, the author gives it as "horn." He's not one of "us."

Instead of discussing the novel in terms of its fictional aims and achievements, which are considerable, Mr. Gilman is all the while elaborately tiptoeing away from its subject. A novel about family be-longs with "apostrophes to elk," unfit for "all displaced persons" who are only "looking for their outlines against the backdrop of ruins."

I don't, myself, see *how* any novelist, applying himself to any sub-ject at all—and I thought choice of subject, like choice of home ad-dress, was free—could benefit by cutting off any source of wisdom that he was heir to, or that he knew of at all—or *why* he should. Yet his reviewer, proclaiming himself thus crippled in feeling and cut off from some primary sources of understanding, is here swearing it's bet-ter that way. So did the Fox Without a Tail offer his suggestion to improve the rest of his tribe.

But if Mr. Gilman, self-generating up there in the prevailing winds, thought he was here delivering the body of the Southern novel a *coup de grace*, he has plain missed—by not knowing the nature of its vital-ity. He has kept himself meticulously removed from the *life* of this book and so has escaped the discovery that its territory is interior to greater extent than it is exterior. He sees it, from off, as "largely bereft of dramatic incident, intellectual complication, or any sense of full destiny." But seen in its own terms, this long, complicated, evolving novel has embraced a theme no less than the continuity of human experience.

I can't help suspecting that Mr. Gilman's trouble might have been that some deep nerve was touched. He says at the last that he came to find the novel wearing him down. With all of its being "archaic," it seemed to possess, and to wield, some strange power. But he's plainly not ready yet to recognize this power for what it is, the passionate working of a gifted and highly individual imagination.

When the catchwords it's secured by are taken away and the review is deflated of its nonsense, it remains a pretty shabby article, I think, to fly in the face of such a novel. I hope its hostile gyrations will not distract more investigative readers from finding out for themselves what an experience—rich and earthy, and also quite sufficiently mysterious (Gilman's report that the novel is "entirely without symbolic dimension" is to my mind perverse)—is waiting for them in *The Surface of Earth*. It is a novel for all readers to whom human relationships are of first importance and lasting significance, readers who are able to accept the reality of other people, living or dead, who have spoken and acted and dreamed out of their own lifetimes, to ask for and to give and to receive and to generate, as they can, affirmation and love.

New York Times Book Review, 20 July 1975, pages 24–25. Gilman replies that Welty has misread his review "thoroughly and perversely," page 25.

Introduction, *Inaugural Papers of Governor William F. Winter*

Every Mississippian who has at heart our state's arts and letters must have felt a charge of hope with the election of Honorable William Winter as our next governor. He has shown all along, in his public capacity, a genuine concern for our cultural, intellectual, and artistic life. Now, on the eve of his inauguration, he has set this symposium, with the theme of "Mississippi and the Nation, 1980," to which he has invited representatives of our number to take part. He has made it clear that he not only intends to support the furthering of arts and letters in our state, but has marked them out as a significant force in the state's future.

As a Mississippi writer, I warmly respond to this. I believe with my whole heart that our writers in their best work have a communication to make that can travel into the future and across the state line.

It's the nature of their work that writers make stories intended to reflect the life they see around them. Stories are efforts to understand, efforts to see human life clearly, and then to keep on and see as far as possible into it, to interpret it, and then communicate it through a sustained act of the imagination.

All art reflects us in our time, in our place. Fiction wrests out of life some inner truth about ourselves in our society. It achieves its moral power when it faithfully reveals us to ourselves, shows us our society in its full and larger context.

Rich in writers, Mississippi is rich in resources for the writer. Our primary resource is the place itself. Place is where the writer has his roots. In his experience, out of which he learns to write, and will always write, place provides the base of reference. In his work it frames his initial point of view. I think the sense of place is as essential to good and honest writing as a logical mind. Our critical powers spring up from the study of place and the growth of experience within it. Place never stops informing us, for it is forever astir, alive, changing, reflecting, like the mind of man itself.

Mississippi bred us, its writers, and brought us up. It has nourished us, though there've been times when for some of our number that nourishment was bitter. And whatever our differences and divergences, we have all known ourselves to have a shared identity. Mississippi artists and craftsmen, a bunch of individuals if there ever was one, possess a character as Mississippians that is unmistakeable. It comes out strongly in our art.

Visiting the remarkable exhibition of Mississippi folk art of four centuries, in the halls of this museum, I was struck by how the work of these ancestors or predecessors of ours here in Mississippi—Indian, white, African, Chinese—itinerants, slaves, storekeepers, mothers of families, farmers, visionaries—had in all its variety its own local story to tell. Folk artists are untaught, self-taught, and what they have made shows the ingenuity of our people in finding ways to hand, in times that were often hard and hostile, to satisfy their needs for self-expression.

The museums, the libraries, the Department of Archives and History, the auditoriums and theatres, the halls of our colleges—all give evidence that Mississippi is alive with the creative impulse. I remember that when Greenville was a town of 20,000, seventeen living citizens there were published authors. (I apologize to Greenville if my memory's got that figure too low.)

Mississippi writing comes out of a background of great density of experience. Our history is long and strenuous, complicated, its fate at times uncertain. Heroism and shame have lightened or darkened pages of it. It is filled with extremes—some of it is tragic, some of it ugly beyond bearing. But in order to be good writers, we need to face and encompass all we are—no human action is too good or too bad to forego being understood. We must not disown any part of our heritage, just as we must not claim for truth some grandeur that is not there.

I don't think it can be said, whatever we've lived through in the centuries in Mississippi, that there've failed to emerge from our ranks historians, poets, dramatists, novelists who have helped us see ourselves—as we were, as we are. You couldn't have kept these writers from their responsibility, their fierce desire, to show forth human truth.

As to what the writers of the 1980s will do, who is to say? Life is changing rapidly here as it is changing everywhere. The writer, as always, will find new paths and new ways for himself, his own vision of what we are. In the future, as ever, the writer must keep writing out of what that writer knows—and there'll be more to know in 1980. And if Mississippi's novelist to come portrays his native countryman of the 1980s, which I think nobody else can do, and which I believe he must do, then whatever new form it takes, his work, carried out honestly and well, will make its own connection with the world.

Regardless of how fast society around us changes, what remains, at any time, is a relationship in progress between ourselves and the world. Our subject remains humankind, and we are a part of it. When we write about our people as we know them in our here and now, if our work is worth doing, we are writing about everybody. Our work will connect our lives with other lives.

"Only connect." Those are the words of a novelist. "No man is an island" is the wisdom of a poet. "No man is an island" is a spiritual truth, and we apprehend it spiritually. In the sight of God, and also in the sight of his fellow man, no man is an island. And this is the very truest assumption of art. No man is an island, and no woman is, and no child, and no race is an island, and no state is. Mississippi is no island.

We have, within the memory of most people here today, consciously and voluntarily joined the world. To make an artist's response to our new governor, who has brought us hope:—in all our lasting—I think everlasting—identity as Mississippians, and in the full awareness and strength of that integrity, we assume, with you and with your leadership, our place in the nation as 1980 begins. I believe your governorship will produce a climate in which the intellect can freely flourish, in which the arts can flower.

The voice of the singer travels outward. When Leontyne Price lifts her voice in *The Star Spangled Banner* at the Inauguration tomorrow, she herself will be the living and proudly hailed connection between Mississippi and the whole of the nation.

Edited by Charlotte Capers. Jackson: Mississippi Department of Archives and History, 1980, pages 21–24.

Prologue, Inauguration of
Governor Raymond Mabus

We citizens of the State of Mississippi have voted and brought to office a good Governor—and we know it. It was for good cause that the Inauguration festivities were splendid and varied; the great crowds of us that joined in—in person at the Capital City and in attendance throughout the state by way of television—were just a single measure of our pride.

We had a good basis for our pride. I think it was clear that our jubilation—during those stirring days and nights of festivities which this book records—rose out of a wonderful change in the public spirit. It expressed the conviction, and the gratification it brought, that we'd placed the right man in our highest office at the right time in our history. Our cheers were a long shout of welcome.

We rejoiced in the Mabus victory as a victory in which we believed we richly shared. So does the Governor believe it; and on Inauguration Day he stood before us and rehearsed to us what this meant; his part or our part; and this expressed—because it defined—that welcome change of spirit too. The Governor's address to us, clear-minded, firm-spoken, direct, practical—and, for all those reasons, eloquent—is based on the fullness of that double responsibility.

Back of Governor Mabus as he spoke, we were warmly aware of the solid tradition of an earlier good Governor whom he had served in his day, William Winter. It's a background that has added its own contribution to Governor Mabus' fine knowledge of the history of our State and to his highly developed sensitivity to our needs.

Most clearly and importantly, we know Governor Mabus to be familiar with the whole variety of us. We've learned that his vision of government takes in the whole Mississippi spectrum of needs, plans, ambitions, hopes—and the emergencies inherent in those, the measures that most ask for priority. We have seen him set Education at the head of all the rest.

He brought the fact into sharpest, clearest focus throughout his campaign. The gates of education must open still wider—to their widest, so that all of us can learn to know, learn of how much there *is* to know, and discover what it forthwith means to the way we live: each citizen of our State, by pressing on with a good education, could learn what education could make of him. Governor Mabus himself stands as a prime example of this today. Our education will determine our future and produce the leaders of it. Our greatest potential is the new Governor's greatest concern.

In his stirring address, quietly delivered, we felt more strongly than ever the force of a mind that would continue to be counted on and heard from: active, open, and tirelessly informing itself. From a man of this stability, this straightforwardness of speech, we can expect the balance and reason we need in approaching our problems.

It strikes me that we Mississippi citizens from far and wide, in all our variety, alike value Ray Mabus and Julie Mabus for the safest of all reasons: they belong to the family of *serious human beings*. They have put their whole good minds, their whole good hearts, into the work they see together lying ahead in the next four years.

That is also why, when we saw him come forward to take the oath of office, this young Governor, a man in his prime, alive to his world—*our* world—one of our own, we knew him to be, at the same time, able and equipped to move and take part in today's increasingly wider world as well, and to bring us within that perimeter, where we belong.

Printed as "Prologue: One Measure of Our Pride" in *Our Time Has Come: Mississippi Embraces Its Future*, Inauguration of Governor Raymond Mabus, 12 January 1988. Jackson, Mississippi: Oakdale Press, 1988, pages 1–2.

VIII. MORE STORIES

A Sketching Trip

"Violence! Violence!"

Delia Farrar, driving along slowly in deep country with afternoon lunch, water-color pad, and fruit jar of water packed in beside her, suddenly felt a smile on her lips. A memory, uncalled-up, was perfect—she could not doubt it, and yet she had scarcely listened to it at the time. Just at the gates of this old spot, Fergusson's Wells, Mississippi, from both sides of the lane at once, little black ragamuffins had once run out holding fists of wild violets at the carriage windows, and what they were crying was "Violence! Violence!" Those calls were urgent as bird cries, and passing by she was almost listening for them now, as if those little boys, like some midsummer creatures, always came assaulting here, though twenty years might have gone by since the last vacationer had ridden away.

She had come here once as a child, with her mother, and that was twenty years ago. If she had ever since thought of Fergusson's Wells it was as a closed place; and it was not only with the idleness of complete faith in her own past and childhood, but with a further idleness—an undisturbed belief that the greatest happiness had quite naturally occurred here, some magnificent festivity, a spectacle of beauty.

Only a wall of trees could be seen from the road. She stopped her car. Why not this place? She would look it over; she might work out a quick sketch or two. She got out with all her paraphernalia, which was in a flat straw basket. Beyond the gate, to her right, was a field with elm trees—the pasture—and so deeply recognized to her in its pattern of intense afternoon, the horizon-curve against blue air, the grass in tree shade and cloud shade, the bright dark of the night sky, almost, with a Milky Way of clover through it, that she wondered with a moment's absurd anticipation what had kept her from returning long before this. Her home was only twenty miles away. That one summer's buggy ride had made it remote. Under her feet were wild strawberries and mint dense as a small forest. She opened the iron gate—touched it and it swung back—and walked into the almost hidden cinder drive.

The sky was violet and silky, like one of those big plums. It was a day you could touch. It was texture she had always wanted—she was excited, a little, going under the fragrant trees—and hoped so much to learn; and surely, texture she had felt as a child at Fergusson's Wells— then she had first put out her hand and touched what was around her—an outer world. *At the time* she knew it—that was the remarkable thing. She knew this was discovery; she had reached with her full reach, put out adoring hands and touched the world. In her painting, she had never shown this joy—were you ever able?—a joy that had no premonition or thinking back, that had neither pity nor calculation or other thought of herself—only a touching of the outward pulse, the awareness of a tender surface underneath which flowed and trembled and pressed life itself. It was as if this pulse became the green of leaves, the roundness of fruit, the rise and fall of a hill, when she began to paint, and could have become—anything.

She walked on through the old park, crowded now with young wild cherries, overgrown with honeysuckle and woodbine, and vines of passionflower stretched like nets and wires across the cinders, setting those curious fringed and crushable flowers, with their little towers, under foot. There stood a well—Number 3—its little round upper structure lacy as a doily and eaten like lace now; and another, head-high in ribbon grass. There had been twelve, all numbered on little green iron flags atop—you drank only from the one that suited your complaint. Her mother had been pregnant in the hot summer. What of the Wells waters now, the "benefits no one should do without"? She came to the turn, and there was the house.

It was a dilapidation, that old affair. It was faded like an old photograph, and elaborate as a ship. After the columns, then cupolas, lattices, lightning rods, and weathervanes formed over it like barnacles—they in turn edged and twined all around with ribbon grass and moonvine; clear around, the chinaberry trees dropped their little flowers, and in front of it the double-tree spread, a weeping willow struck by lightning and held together by a wheel of slatted seat. All details were clear but the whole faded, with the fading of all things with summer lives and of something being, in that very moment, forgotten. Now the enormous veranda seemed tilted, about to sink, like a waterlogged boat in a dead-quiet bayou. Delia approached, and put out her hand, and the warm white column shed flakes like snow.

She hesitated there on the steps and a soft breeze came up behind her and then circled round her skirt. The other summer ran out to meet her like an old bird dog that remembers you before you remember him. And she could see the Wells as it was then, when she and her mother had come for the month of June, for the benefits no one should be without—her mother to go circumspectly to her room and let Delia run wild. The long slick gallery tilted slightly from the door toward the steps then, as a welcome, reflecting vaguely like a dim pool, among ferns, the great slow-turning blades of the fan in the ceiling. The rockers rocked gayly and competitively as chopping sailboats, where fat summer dresses spread. The flaky steps bordered with warm pots came shallowly down, and fern fronds reached for legs walking up.

2

The owner had been Mrs. Fergusson—or no, Mr. Fergusson (people corrected you) would be the owner. But his wife, spreading her hands, palm up, welcomed everybody.

"Who's that?" Delia pulled her mother's skirt, sharply at the sight.

"Why, that's Mrs. Fergusson," said her mother, as if she had asked a rude and reproachable thing.

Mrs. Fergusson's reddish-gold hair was shaped on her head like the paper in a Christmas bell. Her brows were thin and perfect, and over them were tiny holes in the skin as though she had been pricked with the thorns of roses. And Mrs. Fergusson's hand would go to her breast of dotted swiss bertha until she seemed to have been pricked, pricked, pricked, forever through her life. What tender eyelids she had! They were like the wings of sweet-sucking insects that flickered; the pulse would move in them when she thought. In the swing, moving only gently, with crossed ankles, she sat giving off in sighs the odor of almonds—of Bird Eggs, those almonds covered with milky colors that could be bought at the Century Theatre in Jackson. When she walked, there was a kind of jangling and sliding of scents, like the moving of bead strands over the breast and bracelets down the arm, and floating like the plumes of bird-tails from her hair, and she smelled like all the sweet of the world.

This was what made Delia follow her at first, follow her straight into the house, ahead of her mother, and afterwards all around, drawn slightly inclined forward all the time to smell the air behind her. And it was not from love. It was very strange—Mrs. Fergusson was rather the first person she had not loved. She followed her out of a lack of love, and the more remorselessly—more as she would follow a man selling cotton-candy at the Fair with a paper cone of an evil-looking strawberry-colored froth in each extended hand, just because he was selling it. We don't always follow what we love, Delia thought, as she stood now hesitating on the steps; we follow something followable.

Often Mrs. Fergusson, with a little start, turned and smiled. Up close, her cheeks were like figured satin, creased by weeping on a pillow. "What is it, precious darling?" she would say.

And the sky was the color of a ribbon. All was warm to the touch, all was the temperature of the flesh of a lady's upper arm. The six or eight children would be calling and crying down the wells, "Hello!" with the water barking back at them down below. Number 9 was the deepest. The warm and smelly water itself was drawn up very seldom, it seemed to her. For who could like it? Nobody, Reuben said, and he shook his head over it, for he had to pull it up in stocking-shaped buckets and tote it. At six in the morning he would bang on your door and hand it to you in a tall clay mug, and you poured it in your chamber pot if you did not like it. The pigeons, as if they moved by clockwork, keys in their tails, crossed the grass on their purple feet. All sizes of babies, mixed like a handful of wildflowers, swayed pressed together in a nurse-shaded sandbox. The long chain swings, which young girls sat in on Sunday, moved slowly as pendulums in tall clocks under the big trees. The owls hooted in the woods, and the doves on top of the springhouse roof sobbed all day. An iron bell was rung in the yard for dinner.

Delia mounted the broken steps and walked across the porch. Of the interior, why did she remember such a busy whispering? It was her own; she had found a great deal to whisper to her mother about at the table where it was impolite. Relish dishes and cruets and cake stands were all glass as heavy as iron in the dining room, and the white butter, in tiny butter dishes for each person, had no salt. And salt got hard in small boat-shaped urns with tiny, beaded salt-spoons at each plate that pricked the mouth like diamond rings. There were plates with green ponds and castles in them, and as you ate your watermelon away and left the rim, you could spit all your seeds in the pond. There were napkin rings with faces and masks and flowers raised on them that would burn into the brain.

And after such food! Fingers dripping from the fingerbowls, you were dragged, like a sack, up to your bedroom. Washstands, massive forward-leaning wardrobes, waited round the bed to be hung with a kind of thin, rainbow waterfall of near-sleep. There wallpaper was hot to the touch, tiles on the tinned-over fireplace and hearth were beaded with sweat like the forehead of the room. She climbed up into the bed, under thick drapes of mosquito netting which she thought were beautiful as the skirts of a bride. She could not go to sleep; sometimes she held out one arm and dropped marbles from a great height into a tin cup. Yet sleep through the soft afternoon hung overhead and stirred only a little, like a banana leaf, ribbed and veined with green light. Voices floating on the surfeited air were Negro voices. "You know what Cat does? Cat catches him a mice and he climb on de fence. Cat drop his mice in de garbage can. Cat's smart. I's told *several* people about Cat." That was Reuben's voice.

Delia tried the front door, and it opened. She stood in the hall, in that dark dell. Something was gone—something besides some great, zigzag, marble-topped piece of furniture. The odor of food was gone. And suddenly she thought, "The pavilion too!" and ran back to the door and looked out into the thicketty park—it was gone.

That dance pavilion had crowned the whole place. It actually had a second floor, with a little paintless frame stair running up. It had been open all the way round, edged with narrow benches, like a steamboat there in the park with a piano in it—it had been gray-white and lacy. There was not an inch of the pavilion that did not have some name carved in it. You could read it all day long, even the stair rail was full, and the four sides of the little splintery posts all the way up—just like a nutmeg grater under your hand, and the benches were corrugated under your legs with names and arrowed hearts. Now it had gone.

3

Delia turned and walked gently down the hall and past the staircase, fluted like a pipe organ. She thought she heard something then—a movement—but wasn't it thunder? She remembered, about three

o'clock every cloudless afternoon a storm would come abruptly somewhere near-by, the sky would go black in the west, and at the Wells
somebody would run from room to room, not glancing at a person, and
put down the long rattling windows, and when the round was done,
run back and put them up again. For very likely only little cyclones of
dust would whirl over the lawns and follow, sometimes, the very walks
that went so narrowly from well to well; thunder would sound in the
woods and a rain would fall that could just be seen against the trees.
Reuben would wear a strawberry box over his head.

Then, that threat being over, the guests came out, like four-o'clock
flowers, and just after the four-o'clocks opened. Through the freshened
air, Delia followed Mrs. Fergusson, who turned and said, "Precious
darling, what is it?" And even to her, made a tender, charming gesture
with her hand.

Delia put up her own hand and exchanged a little squeeze most
promptly and eagerly, with, like a dark germ of wariness, a brief disappointment falling each time into her heart—disappointment that
was a kind of excitement. For Mrs. Fergusson, though enchantingly
dressed in pale georgette and her cheeks pinked beyond the imagination, never once transformed herself, even in her voice, by saying
one thing to this person, another thing to another. Everybody, even
Mirrabel, a common brown rabbit around whose neck Mrs. Fergusson
had tied a blue candy ribbon, was "Precious." She was a creature of a
baffling and terrifying sameness. To Delia she was never, for one moment, an allurement—it was a kind of outrage with a promise to it. As
from a germ, a seed inside, she knew that spreading, helpless gesture of
Mrs. Fergusson's palms made her feel not her own fresh chivalry, but
old chivalry, used, stale, ancient—other people's, and especially Mr.
Torrance's, the man who would be standing behind Delia. She would
let her hand be relinquished, and go off in skips.

Under the warm dangle of the weeping willows, the ladies strolled,
their parasols, from moment to moment, more luminous than the blue
sky, and their shining little dogs at their heels. On the wide banis-
ters along the length of the veranda, goldfish bowls sparkled like suns,

and the fish darted and pushed their faces at the promenaders. On the green grass at twilight, the croquet balls moved slow as leviathans through a deep sea.

One of the three dining-room doors at the hall's end stood open, and Delia looked into the dim room. In some draft, light through the floor-length slatted shades lifted and merged its bars in the air, which was like under-water. The room was empty at one end, and all the tables had been pushed together at the other, as though a great hand had come in and cleft the room. There was a creak, then, and the door blew shut behind her. She turned quickly. Nothing was there, but with that sound how dearly it had come back to her!

Mr. Torrance had entered at dinner. He went by, very close to them, going to his table.

When Mr. Torrance spoke ("H'rrum, nice day"), Mrs. Fergusson gave him as radiant a smile as if he had invited her to some charming spot. Like the opening of a summer parasol, the smile spread and played the pinkness and the floweriness of her face. Nothing could ever go beyond this smile; it was the limit of Mrs. Fergusson's face, its whole intent. Its signal replied to the signal of that creak of the door, when Mr. Torrance entered the dining room. That creak of the center door, which was actually like a baby's fretful cry, seemed the special announcement of Mr. Torrance's wonderful, heavy entrance. He came shaking the floor, and was immediately and ruddily reflected in the hundred flushed faces of the cut-glass vinegar cruets and compotes of strawberry preserves which watched him with the compound eye of an insect.

Mr. Torrance was silky-looking with a mouth of silk. He seemed full of the well waters, brimming. He drank out of Number 1. He was weighty as a seal. When he sat alone at his table the room seemed pinned, anchored down; it was his chair that fastened it for keeps to the round world. Food steamed toward him on its little winds. He groaned in joy all to himself, as he drew the napkin over his rolly lap, like a mother covering her good child and wishing it sweet dreams. He was as perfect as wax fruit in his pink-shaded hands and face, and a

pin tried in his cheek, she had imagined, would be likely to make only
a powdery hole—from which the wind of his laughter, though, would
suddenly strike you, and his near, choppy teeth would shoot crumbs
of his laughter like dragon fire at little girls.

Eating, he entered his world and dream. He ate off in a remoteness,
and not until he was finished and had drawn a sigh would he return
from that long perspective back to your presence, seeming to shudder
his plump coat a little like a robin finishing up. Then he simply flew to
your side, fronting and touching you with his breast if you were a lady
near-by, if you were Mrs. Fergusson, and not if you were a sad lady in
black just beside her.

Delia walked around the echoing room in the patchy light. There
was the piano. It was strange to draw a finger through the warm dust
on a soundless piano key; it was like finding dust on a person's eye-
lashes, a person sleeping in the sun. The top of the old maple upright
was propped open by a tennis ball, molded green. There was a wasp
nest inside, against the strings, and the dining room itself was filled
with the awkward swinging motions of wasps, and a dead one drifted
in a breath of air down the keyboard to—C, Ranny Randall's key.
That was what he played *Nola* in.

She remembered Saturday night at Fergusson's Wells, the three-
piece orchestra in the double-decker pavilion, and Ranny Randall, sitting straight as a ruler in a blazer, playing *Nola*. The back of his head
stuck out so far it was like a question mark, very shiny in Stacomb.
The smell of cut grass in the night seemed to rise up sharply, and then
the ladies' floral odors, and they in turn pursued by hoops and wreaths
of men's tobacco smoke. Among the little girls was no scent at all,
only the rapid sound of fans being opened and shut on their hot little
chains that cut the neck. They wound arms and strolled three together
over the park. As they went they discovered under each of the round
well roofs, by each of the wells, a man and lady kissing as if appointed
there. Kissing was all over the park—everywhere, at twelve wells, like
the state of grace, falling over all at the same moment, like a flock of
birds lighting in a tree and all starting to sing.

Outdoors was filled with the leafy glide of moonlight. Her party dress was white, and she would grass-stain it. In the pavilion the dancers danced on two floors in the light of paper lanterns—one would catch fire. Ranny Randall's hands were flying from his striped cuffs like fluttering flags, and his teeth were bared. He could play *Margie*, anything that was asked of him, and he always played in C. The children climbed and hung like monkeys on the pavilion.

Mrs. Fergusson was a dancer. Paper lanterns—she loved them, loved Ranny Randall, loved music, she said. Her face was mother-of-pearl colored, and nearly unreal—for surely every kind of wash and scent and color had covered it again and again, Saturday night. Mrs. Fergusson, even dancing, had farsighted eyes, very soft and wide, the color of forget-me-nots. "Precious darling," she said, bending and kissing Delia where she stood wrapped on a post, watching the dance. Delia kissed her respectfully.

Back at the house, the porch was full of rockers, all occupied, as all the boxes in the stable stayed full of hens—seemingly busy with bright eyes though they were very still. Mr. Torrance might dance in the pavilion and shake it, but when he went by the porch, clearing his throat, the world changed. The way a night breeze in moonlight suddenly shatters the intricate pattern of quiet within the leafy porch and someone will rise and another will say, "Well—good night!" and no more stories will be told that night before any child stretched listening on the steps—that was how Mr. Torrance revolted their world.

4

And, Mr. Fergusson?

Mr. Fergusson always came last—now even to the memory. He was a poky man. And soon, always, he was out of sight again. There was just the X of his suspenders disappearing through a door; you only saw his back. He would put his head in again, and say, "Excuse me." He would take himself off in an old black planter's hat and sit in a shed, making something. He had one good eye and one that had had sand rubbed in it, a lesson to children in summer. Off at a little distance, with perhaps one little boy following him, he could be seen carrying things from one point to another across the park, across the back yard—ladders, lengths of chain, buckets and demijohns, a purpling flour-sack of figs. Perhaps he did the work. For the Negroes were Mrs. Fergusson's, and wore white coats. He was the one that early in the still morning went snapping off the Cape jessamines (that was what woke her up, and made her mother flutter her eyelids) and put them in dishes on the tables and tubs in the doors, where they glowed in the dark rooms and halls as if they marked a trail.

And hadn't there been a happening of some kind, one night? Delia ate a plum. She had not meant to eat her lunch in here, but she had brought out some plums and pinched the cheesecake, and at last she spread everything on a paper on a dusty table. She thought she heard a noise in a room close by, like the flat of a hand on the wall. Tramps did not bang away—it might be the jump of a rat. She might have left then and missed everything, but she finished her lunch, and as she was walking out past the parlor the sun came through a tear in a blind and lighted a little square picture on the wall, and halted her.

Oh, heaven! What was it? A painting by a lady. It hung tilting at her, over the parlor mantel. She walked toward the red and blue thing, varnished mirror-bright, at first seeing only its seashells of landscape-clouds on the top shelf of sky. Surely this had not hung here in the old days. But it had. The wallpaper faded from it. And it represented— she shivered all at once—the near-by haunted house that looked down from the hill, in its pristine, untouched state—a virgin of a house with every brick clean as a breastpin. The green had not lasted, leaving the cedars on either side a faded kingfisher blue.

Delia studied the bad little oil with the interest which the complete lack of imagination always serenely asks for, like a beggar-child. The painting offered, whether or no, a version of a beautiful 1810 or so house, its Georgian design tempered by the Spanish—with wings connected by loggias, which were drawn tight as wires here. And the fanlights—why, they were true fans! She could hardly believe the dainty little ribbed affairs, how the hand had trembled to set them just so over the doors, above and below. The proportions were fantastic, somehow cupped in and stricken, and instead of spaciousness—Delia squinted—the house gave off an influence like a bird cage. Little people studded the galleries, the garden, and the orchard, holding hands to and three together—a house party, an entertainment for some General.

She felt strangely vindictive toward this painting. But it was indeed the haunted house she knew and remembered now. It was right for its picture to hang in the Wells, over a mantel, like a parent portrait. The Wells, filled as it had been with light, airy light, was always the shadow of that older place on the hill. Her eyes narrowed and she searched the corner of the bad picture. It was signed "Mews," in a calling card script.

She turned her back on the painting and stood lost, thinking of the haunted house as it was the day she saw it—sun-drenched, light-drenched, a bird flying about the grayed wooden cornice which was carved with the Greek key. Looking at her memory like a picture of her own, she saw a halfway ruin of a very plain, beautiful, surely rather small Georgian house, the red of a rose. There remained of it then the central structure and one wing. The roof over the loggias, fallen to the ground, lay leaning against the house, softened, like a coverlet, wrinkling over the hidden steps, and sea-blue. Nothing gave a sign of the galleries except a naked brightness in the brick. One wing was gone except for a shell of front wall and the chimney at the end, and the other wing was intact, square, its chimney tall in the air.

Who had taken them there—all the children picnicking?

Old-maid half-sister of Mr. Fergusson—Miss Mews replied her memory succinctly.

The painter! Painter and storyteller. She had been a storyteller that day, and all the time it was she, Miss Mews, who had stood there, the lady in black, dark as a bare bough beside the fruity Mrs. Fergusson every evening. Delia was remembering the picnic now, whoever the storyteller had been that easy day when they all ran holding hands, popping the whip, seeming barely to listen. She had hold of the hand of a boy in an Indian suit, and the stickiness of little black cherries cemented them all together, the playing children who were going to disobey that storyteller and perhaps trip her up at the right moment.

5

Oh, that day! It was like this—yet inexpressibly a different day; so that you would always know—even then—that no two days can ever be like each other as two fruits from the same tree are twins, since night comes between. They went in leaf hats—nasturtium, sycamore, and fig, pinned with rose thorns, the boys' hats down over their eyebrows. Under their concerted rush, the claybanks rose, and shimmered wistaria-colored, warm, hard, and burning with sand to the skin; and one of them took off his sandals and left them on a purple cliff, to be found in case they never returned. Up there was a field where the sun was hot as a spasm and made anyone sneeze just to go in it; the space in front of the eyes was always filled with a gyration of gnats and cottonwood fuzz.

In the bright distance was a solitary cabin, its roof a Joseph's coat of wood and tin bits, its chimney rose-red. A pale and undulating fence, silvery in the hollows, closed it in, and when they came to it they played on the pales with a stick and it sounded like the most distant music; nobody came out. Walking ahead of them the cows went with their tails streaming silver in the light like the wake of a boat. Giant thistles shone, taller than children. Like even brighter islands in this brightness were the wide, circular mounds of Cherokee roses, and they touched at them, boat-like, one by one. Beyond the field they went single-file through a shaggy ravine and up a cedar-grown hill, pulling their way by roots, on all fours, and from the place where they all fell over and laughed, the Confederate Cemetery could be seen gleaming miles away like a honeycomb in the distant light.

Then Miss Mews silenced them. They were fingering the rusty ro-settes of a barbed-wire fence, holding the wires for each other and for Miss Mews, who was of course scratched. Then they were in a body on the other side looking up. Delia stood feeling alone, looking and divining something, she could not tell what, in that warm ruin on the blue air, that firm print of a house on the earth against a blue sky which broke through and descended upon it. She stood in deep bliss with her hand moving upon the trunk of a cedar tree, with its purple-green above her dense like the breast of a bird.

But it had a story. Miss Mews would tell it. "This haunted house is Mrs. Fergusson's ancestors' home." And all the time Miss Mews was telling them, telling them, the children were running off and dart-ing away. Was this running the excitement of beauty, after all—and more than the breaking of authority? And what would her story, tell-ing what people *did*, have come to without the weight of that rose-red brick in the hand, its reach of color into the eyes—the sudden sight, licking like fire at the feet, of the snake moving in the empty well—the mockingbirds drunk on cherries careening over the rooftop—the taste of the plaster, that white, thin-as-silk plaster that was vaguely sweet on the tongue? (Had they even eaten of the place?) What if the chimney's wasp had not stung anybody? He stung Billy in the Indian suit who screamed like an idiot and ran around Miss Mews with her black skirt clutched in his hands and wound her like a Maypole in the middle of all she said—so that she told more. And little Carbuncle Fergusson—the Fergussons had had a son! His real carbuncle had come and gone the summer before; only the name was left. He had no sense, except that he could always play Casino with his little dirty cards with the red parrots on them, out in the big road, each play burying itself in a puff of dust. He stood in front of Miss Mews and listened too, like a bird, perhaps for whispers and sounds underfoot.

Walking around the haunted house, you saw the structure all laid bare—it was no mystery as in other houses. She could see, with the walls half away, exactly how all the rooms were, exactly how the house had been made—what rooms opened off other rooms, which connected and which had never connected, where the fireplaces were, what the windows all looked out on. The anatomy of the story Miss Mews thought so much of was well explained.

Here the lady lived, there her husband. The rooms connected, the fires burned back to back. This was the window through which he climbed, the lover to meet the wife. It was there the husband had come in by the door, just in time. ("Here's the window he jumped out of and hung by his hands!" Billy jumped and hung by his hands on that warm and flaking ledge.) Hush, said Miss Mews, it ended with a duel! Of course, through the room there, so bare now, across the sun-soaked hall, through there, down there, the husband did chase his wife. The room where she ran and he killed her, where he put his hands around her neck (here LeRoy took hold of Minnie Belle), was the top room, on the left. The wife had run up instead of down, further into the house instead of out. She could not escape.

That was where she said . . . what? Oh, Delia could not think now what the lady had said; and how had anyone ever known, except Miss Mews, what she said? The stairs were swaying like a spider web under the children's feet. But down that stair and out and here to the well (where the snake ran out! "Run, Miss Mews! It's poison!") he had stamped carrying her and thrown her down the well. Miss Mews paused. (Down which of his twelve wells would Mr. Fergusson throw his wife if he could? Twelve choices for a thing not done yet.) Down, down, dead, with her hair floating up in a long yellow twist and covering the top of the water, said Miss Mews—"She had always been proud of her hair." And the lightning came and printed her picture on the windowpane, saying Look for me! The story ended with a duel over her, both men wounded to death, and all dead.

Miss Mews had marched them to the window and they had seen the lightning-picture, but restlessly, since they believed it enough already.

Even the small, gap-toothed Fergusson could run over the house and go where all that had happened in the time it could take to tell it, and look out the window like an imp in a bottle, and show a laughing face through the lightning's ragged little profile with the long bent neck like a flower stalk. For that was all the story.

"Is that all?" Delia herself asked.

Miss Mews nodded, and at that nod the children sprang up wild and scattered as if for good on running feet. They ran and ran. They covered all that haunted ground with fast and dust-flying feet, circling, catching each other and letting go; they chased, called, collided, flung up and down the dark ravine and trod on the crowded spears of iris. They broke every little blood-red rose and sucked them in their mouths or hung them in their hair. They swung on the sucker-thick orchard trees which had borne the summers that no one had counted, unless it were only Miss Mews, and last they found the cherries, the little wild ones, and ate all they could hold, until Carbuncle cried. Miss Mews, all silent, waited, for all must calm down in the end. She was the iron fountain black in the sun, and all this was still *her* sad story. Far off, down and beyond the hill, someone was singing, though—the kind of song that comes from a young girl who has to go by herself through a field and becomes in love with flowers and clouds, and forgets herself entirely. Delia heard it and fell over in the grass and lay still, tipsy, her lap full.

They went home another way. Little cabins, the colors of twilight clouds, lay along the different fields. They came to an empty school in the country. A remote and yet clandestine look it had. The leaves rustled, rustled, like flight after flight of birds going through. On every window there was still pasted a paper jonquil with side leaf. "This is *my* school," Miss Mews said. They all looked at her carefully, then standing together and turning their eyes to her. She was suddenly shy. She was all in black, and she had *moles*. Her face was nippled with moles. Their parents had all gladly entrusted them to her for the day. How was it grown people always had respect for such outrageous persons?

She marched them home. And in the hall at Fergusson's Wells—deserted, of course, for they were all dining—she had said in a loud, teacher's voice, "I gave them a lesson in history! Which *all* would do well to heed."

And Delia smiled. For suddenly, just here, in the parlor, where they had all been ushered to put their wildflowers by the pressing-book, loomed Mr. Torrance, with his lips pursed for a kiss. His mouth was like an agate, that pride of boys in spring. He was leaning over just ready to give it to Mrs. Fergusson—strike Mrs. Fergusson's little glassy mouth with it, with that hard, thumping release an agate would get under the thumb of a frowning boy. What would have happened? Would Mrs. Fergusson, struck with the agate kiss, have flung back and scattered everything in Fergusson's Wells apart with a rainbow light? Not yet. Mr. Torrance, with almost a push of his eyebrows at her face, let her go. Almost like a beetle he wielded her on ahead of him out of the parlor, with his eyebrows forking and driving her before him, reserving her for future lairs. While she, a morsel, all inviting and caught, seemed to be making little dazzling motions, the rings on both her hands twinkling phosphorescently in the hall gloom. She was laughing.

6

So it was that night that Mr. Torrance did magician tricks. It was in the dining room. The ladies got it up after supper.

First Mr. Torrance had done some tricks with cards—the thickened old cards with the parrots on them that lay on the porch all day. As a magician, he bestowed his smile for the first time over the entire dining room. Then—

"I should like to borrow a hat," said Mr. Torrance. His eyelids drooped and closed for a moment. It was as if he put on a mask and watched them through little holes. The dining room became magical. The ladies, who had got this up to let Mr. Torrance see what he could do, waited. For only Mr. Fergusson wore a hat in his own house.

"Mr. Fergusson?" said Mr. Torrance, opening his eyes. He held out one pear-shaped hand, and lifted the other with the wand in it.

"Your hat, perhaps, Mr. Fergusson?" he said.

Hat? Hat? . . . the room echoed. As if the echo turned it into a dark ravine where people moved and climbed by lantern light, and held a conclave, the deep and twinkling dining room waited in that moment for Mr. Fergusson to walk through the eyeing watchers and give up his hat to Mr. Torrance.

Mr. Fergusson rose—he was at the back, of course, Miss Mews beside him—and he looked no better than he ever had. He walked through the room, the wand with which Mr. Torrance beckoned seeming to draw him by the coatless shoulders and pull him, and his horny hand was clamped over his hat as if a wind were blowing. Never had Mr. Fergusson, or his hat either, looked so disheveled, so "common," ladies said—would he ever get there? It was as if the wind he was mistaken about had truly blown and buffeted and got him confused.

On the little stage, where Mr. Torrance held his wand ready, Mr. Fergusson came and stepped up. What would he do? Whatever else he might have done, with time, he took off his hat and gave it to Mr. Torrance. Then he turned and looked back.

They all looked right at his head. The emerged and naked head of Mr. Fergusson shone under the grand center dining-room light. Exposed, bald as they had known all the time it would be, his head glowed like a small, single light itself, a chilly light; and Mr. Fergusson turned from side to side a moment, silently—like the Biloxi Lighthouse light when the sun goes down, sweeping over the people enjoying themselves. He reached a point of gaze and stood still—his good eye glistened. He was looking over their heads, stony and single-eyed, like a lighthouse, at his wife. He was standing up there because of her, be-cause of them too—a sea of pleasure, swelling and wild. Who would dare look at Mrs. Fergusson, who was caught now in his glare and beam? What if her arms went up over her head! Suppose her hair rushed up over her ears as she sank! Still no one would look. Delia strove against the strictness in her neck—she looked. Back and forth, so quickly it hid her face as well as a curtain, Mrs. Fergusson was waving her special little fan, made of feathers.

"Thank you." Mr. Torrance balled his lips. He showed the hat, and knowingly waved his wand back and forth over the dreadful thing that had covered Mr. Fergusson's head. While they looked, while Mr. Fergusson, his attention rapped at, looked, there was a flicker of live motion, and Mr. Torrance pulled a rabbit out of the hat by the ears. It was Mirrabel.

There was just a moment of silence—then a sigh. Was it terror—satiety—disappointment? Mirrabel was very well known. Then—led by the ladies—applause. Pursed lips smiled at pursed lips.

With a lissome bow Mr. Torrance offered Mr. Fergusson's hat back to him, rabbit inside.

"He wouldn't take it *back!*" someone—quite an indignant old lady—was saying.

Mr. Fergusson's horny hand drew back. Then bald as a tombstone he was rocking down the aisle cleared for him between the knees drawn up, and it was known all over the room that he would never touch that hat again. Mr. Fergusson left the dining room, leaving the door open, left Mr. Torrance with his hat, with Mirrabel in it, darting her well-known round sideways glances out at everything. Mr. Torrance then had to set the loaded hat down on a little wobbly table of some kind.

Immediately flicking his cuffs for a new trick, "You see, I have nothing up my sleeves," he said.

"So of course he has," Delia thought without rancor, but feeling at one with the audience and with the world at that moment.

Then there was a noise from behind. It was the teasing noise of the door. Mr. Fergusson was back, standing there where Mr. Torrance used to stand and eye the room. His hat was once more awesomely missed from his head, as if its absence would expose him afresh every time, like the lifted veil of a nun. He brought his little rabbit gun up to his shoulder and to his chin like a completion of his face, and pointed it straight into the room.

In the corner of the eye a flowery plate seemed to tip, bow, and fall off the rail first, and then even before it touched the floor came the crashing of everything. The room shook like a forest of china.

Delia stood up and pressed forward from her helpless mother, burrowing as she went against the hot silky backs of ladies. In a moment some hand was going to stop her, but while she could she wanted to see. It had not turned out the way she had thought, at all.

Beneath arches and barriers of ladies' arms she could see. Mr. Torrance stood reared in a pose of sorrow on his stage, with his jaw hung widely down; he was looking like Samson's lion. He reared there for a moment erect with his paws in the pulled-back sleeves held apart in the air. Then he tenderly clasped himself and descended; ladies hips and skirts bulged and hid his fall.

Crying softly, struggling in some feminine grasp, Delia heard it on all sides—the breaking, the shattering and echoing—it was the imminent closing of the Wells, the end of vacation, of her own adventure, she heard—all and each gave out its fragile, summerlike, falling crystal sound. Then a lady named Miss Delta Random fainted, and then one after the other, as if they were weak, three ladies more lay pale across the chests of the shouting, pinioned men. And poor Miss Mews, Miss Adella Mews, went down on her knees as she did to go under the barbed-wire fence, and crawled under the table.

Delia could see Mrs. Fergusson plainly, for she was not crowded by the other ladies but rather framed by them, as always. She rose up from her chair, her feather fan slid down under her pointed satin shoe, and she went toward the front.

"Let me through," Mrs. Fergusson begged the baracade of men.

But they would not.

Delia was picked up and carried out crying, as Mrs. Fergusson would expect of her, but kicking her legs. Mr. Fergusson was still standing at the door, looking on, rubbing a little spot over his eye.

The incident had never been mentioned again. They left in the morning; the only one who stayed was an old lady—she might never be going home. She made her own beads out of some sweet pastes, in milky blue or pink colors, each bead a little lopsided, and there was always a dinner plate of them, not quite hard, in a window. She would string them with small jet and silver beads in between.

The Fergusson's Wells carriage had borne them all smoothly away and the little colored boys with their wilted fistfuls of flowers ran out and pleaded, "Violence! Violence!" beside the rolling wheels. Delia had hung herself half out of the carriage and stretched her arms back toward Fergusson's Wells and cried, "Mirrabel!" It was mostly in delight.

7

There was a sound directly behind her—the complaint of the door.

Delia turned and saw Mr. Fergusson walk in—faded, grayed in his face and hands and in his clothes as if by moonlight, but no ghost. That was a human and remembered walk, the hitched, dawdling walk of the unwelcome. He went past her.

She begged his pardon, began to explain herself, but he did not appear to listen to her. When he saw her, he showed her a scrap of paper he held in his hand. On it something had been written with a wetted pencil. "Three turns to the left, 3 to the right, and you ther."

"Give me a hint, Reuben," said Mr. Fergusson with a sigh. "I want you to tell me if I'm warm."

There stood Reuben in the shadow, no faintest gleam of light about him, shrunken, smaller and older, watchful in a different way now. Change was on him, but no impairment, as if a cat grew old and turned blackbird.

"You's warm, but you's lost," said Reuben.

"My son and old Reuben got 'em up a game, got 'em up a little game with me," said Mr. Fergusson, smoothing out the note on his palm. "My son in Memphis and old Reuben here. They have an understanding! (*Listen* at Reuben.) To keep me from finding it too early in the day, old Reuben, he hides it from me, and then he leaves me a little note here, a little note there. Telling me what turns to take, and up or down. I think he learned to write just for the purpose!—make me run myself ragged. My son sends it, by the case, and Reuben hides it. There'll be another note to go today, before I get hold of it. End of day'll most likely find me in the attic, up in the dark, reaching for it. But I'll find it." He fingered some little button he wore in his coat, which of course he had found too.

"Mrs. Fergusson—" she said, and stopped, astonished at herself at the mention of the name.

"She—Mrs. Fergusson, she went off with him, you know," he said presently. His voice was flat in idleness after telling how he hunted.

"With—who?"

"Torrance. Mrs. Fergusson went off with Torrance the end of that summer. They live about forty miles from here."

"I thought—he was dead—that you—"

"Why, everybody knew it," he said wonderingly. "We had to close the Wells." He proved it for her with a gesture around the room.

"I thought you shot him and killed him," she said, and suddenly she was ready to accuse him. "I thought he was dead."

"No, Torrances are hard to kill," he said matter-of-factly. His eyes shone a little. Was it the weak teasing tears of laughter that shone in them? But he did not laugh. "I thought she'd sweep me off my feet," he said. "I *still* thought she'd do it, one day. Up till the very minute I fired that load of rabbit shot I thought she might." He looked closely at Delia—that spark in his eye was pride.

How could you ever tell the ones who wanted to be swept off their feet in the world—those who were just going to taste the lotus, but hadn't yet? She remembered how he had gone forward to give up his hat that night seeming to putter, almost, along the way—Mr. Fergusson had been such a putterer.

He said solemnly, politely now, "My son's 'way up in the world in Memphis. He's successful and all. He seldom gets down but he sends me cases of Bourbon regular, right on the dot. I don't eat much," he said fastidiously. He called out, "Reuben, Reuben, come out on the porch with the fan. You'll have to fan me and this young lady a while, till she has to go. *You* know it's as hot a day as God ever sent us." He guided Delia to the front porch, to one of the long benches which whispered with little leaves and the petals of blown roses. They sat down. She knew all at once how grandly he lived, in what anticipation.

"For just a little," she said.

Reuben moved near and, lifting both arms gently and wide, fanned them with two palmettos, attending them in the darkening of the day like a mother bird.

But she only stayed long enough to be polite. When she said "Good-bye," Mr. Fergusson's hand reached for hers in the twilight of the porch.

"Good-bye, Reuben."

"You's grown," said Reuben.

Outdoors, the light was still good. The western sky was clear and the sun would be going down whole, just in the direction of the haunted house, where she now was going.

Why, it was only a few steps away. She followed a dirt path up a gentle hill, and could see a solitary chimney. In its distance it stood rose-red among cedars, infinitely still in the woods, almost a tree itself. Somehow she knew that that chimney was all she would find.

She went through the ravine, where it was almost dark, and up the old drive, full of rain-valleys and partly gone, and came to the place, to the chimney.

It was so perfect that for a moment she was imagining the house not as a ruin they had ravaged—children, and poor frightened teacher, and now of course the Negroes stealing the bricks and firewood—but as the original. (And Miss Mews had done only this.) How could I? she thought, opening her eyes, standing subdued and humble before the one red column.

She sat down at a little distance and made a sketch. As she worked, noises set up all around, chirpings, singings, clickings, dronings, the swell of the locusts, and a female cardinal sat on the chimney top sending out noises like the clicking of castanets; after a little, she sang.

Delia made three sketches, and none pleased her. The sun went lower. Small clouds were floating seed-like now in the transparent west, as if a pomegranate had burst open.

She stood up and gazed awhile at the color of the bricks intensified with the deepening light. The badness of her work went out of her. The chimney itself, in its beauty, in its presence, as long as it stood there, was enough. Enough, she thought, for all the error applied to that place, all misconceptions, for all that went astray in sight of it, better than a dream. Not the house as it had once stood, but something before that, some exuberance of its inception, seemed hovering about it. She had felt it as a child; all the children had felt it. Smoothed, worn by them all, it rose taller than any happenings or any times that forever beset the beauty itself of life. It was no part of shelter now, it was the survivor of shelter, an entity, glowing, erect, and a fiery color, the ancient color of a phoenix.

Gathering her paraphernalia, she went down—the ravine track, the path, then the carriage drive. She could see her car in the road beyond the gate. All of a sudden there was a breath of stir in the bushes where blackberries grew up tall over everything.

Her heart leaped when she saw him—a little boy, brown-haired. Dappled like grass in the last sun, he lay in the curve of the embankment with his scratched, ruddy legs straddled upwards and his toes curled in the clover, silent while his eyes followed her. She opened the gate and came out, carrying her three wet paintings; he was eating berries from his cupped hands, his lips stained purple and gently parted.

Atlantic, June 1945, pages 62–70. "The Sketching Trip" was included in the *O. Henry Memorial Award Prize Stories of 1946.*

Hello and Good-Bye

This morning, when I saw in the paper that some Beauties had gathered in my town in a contest for a Queen—the prize a trip—and had their logical picture on page three, something made me look along the line for a little soft face I saw once, but if it was there I couldn't find it. Not strange—this was several years ago, and the little soft country face belonged to a girl who was a Queen already the day I was taking her picture.

"Are you ready?" I remember asking. I was down on my stomach in the clover on the Capitol grounds, sighting up, and the Queen looked down scared and called me "Ma'am." I wouldn't have asked most Beauty Queens that, chances are.

The Hostess was the other Beauty, and she wouldn't have been caught dead asked that. "This other photographer, in Washington, D.C.," she said from her more advanced pose at the Queen's side, "when he was just before taking it, he would say 'Give.'"

"All right, give," I said. This was Jackson, Mississippi, and taking publicity pictures was a new part-time job I had.

I remember how, at the word, the Queen swallowed and first drew her hands behind her back and then brought them together in front. Black satin is what she wore. Slowly her purse, which she held pressed to her under her arm, where it trembled like a bride's bouquet, slid down her side and sank out of the picture.

"Never mind," I wanted to say. But they were posing with hats, purses, suitcases, and everything, in front of the State Capitol, saying Good-bye, Jackson! Hello, New York! The purse was retrieved, and they posed again, smiling into the sun.

It was a hot summer afternoon. When she held a pose, the Queen would gradually roll her eyes right up, like Little Eva dying. After the click, I heard Mr. Whoever-it-was on the side lines give a sound in his cheek, so somebody, at least, thought we had got it at the right minute. He was from the Sponsors—a middle-aged VFW taking time off after lunch.

"I bet the cannon's where we're headed next." The Hostess had the dreamiest voice, but she did every bit of the volunteering for us all.

We started on again across the Capitol grounds—the Hostess, a buoyant girl, dressed *pour le sport* in a pink pleated skirt, in front; the Queen trying to keep up; the gentleman next, carrying along the suitcases, which were bona fide; and the photographer at the tail end, counting up the film. We looked like a chase that wasn't very serious.

Once the Hostess stopped in her tracks, and we all stopped behind her one after the other. "Of *course* the *magnolias* aren't blooming!" she said in deepened tones, sounding like Tallulah Bankhead. Then on again.

The Hostess, sure enough, went straight down a terrace and up a little mound, to the cannon; she flung herself upon it and held there tilted, gay seemingly by contact, a smile lighting her up on the dot. The Queen had a harder time, her skirt not being pleated, but we got a picture and were off again, same procession. "Did you get the flag in? That should have been showing right behind my hat," the Hostess yelled beck at me over her shoulder. Her hat never showed either, behind so much hair.

Once I made a suggestion; there was some old ship's figurehead in the bushes, a chesty figure, Columbia or some such patriotic lady, coming with upraised arms out of a big starry shield. Plenty of times I had climbed on that as a child, and it had been recently shined up by a WPA project. The girls stared at Columbia. The only thing to do was to take hands under the lady's blessing, and the Hostess, rightly, bore it with short patience. The lady in the figurehead looked ready to brain them both, and made a third party.

"The front steps of the Capitol is a mighty sure thing," said the Hostess. We trailed over there. That was the best place, except for so many little boys coming home from school just then and making monkey faces at us. We took several poses.

"Wait till these are released," the Hostess said. "I'd like to see the American Legion's face then."

"Why?" I asked her. Our conversation through the view-finder was like one over the telephone.

"The American Legion is going to be so sick. They thought they were going to get me to be in their old parade again, in Chicago, but they were too late. Too late!"

"Put your weight on one foot, honey," I said softly to the Queen. When the Queen listened to the Hostess, she sank back on both heels.

"Nobody can just wait till the last minute and expect to get a girl involved in a *trip!*" cried the Hostess, with a little ripple somewhere.

"Are you ready?"

2

The Queen's head fell just as I made the exposure, but she didn't know it, and I hadn't the heart to tell her. She was so tired, and so hot in silk "traveling" clothes in August. The Hostess, though, could have endured even black satin, little Spartan that she was. When they smiled they looked alike, two little young, brown-haired 4-H Club girls, looking forward to the Mississippi State Fair. The Queen had so patently won her first Beauty Contest for this—her friends had *told* her she could win it—and had stepped incredulous out of New Hebron or Monticello or Carthage, or somewhere, with the cheers of some consolidated schoolhouse behind her; but she just hadn't known she was *this* pretty, that it would cause so much to happen. It affected her like grief, homesickness.

The Hostess began to wave at me, gracefully. She was probably a Delta child.

"How do you like waving pictures? Waving right *at* them. I like them because they're sort of soft. You know—soft." She stood on the top step and waved softly at me and then softly at the Sponsor, whose name was something like Mr. Murray.

"Say, that's O.K.," said Mr. Murray.

"All right, wave."

"Of course I could be coming down the steps *and* waving. You too." The Hostess turned to the Queen and jabbed her arm. She seemed to feel that she must arouse the Queen whenever she wanted to speak to her. "Right beside me, waving."

"Whatever you say," said the Queen. Her short upper lip trembled. She was probably three years younger than the Hostess. She shifted her purse to her other arm, then put it back. Again I wanted to take it away from her, but it was obviously her proudest new purchase for the trip, and could not be set down. It was patent leather, about the size of a toy drum, and reflected the light like steel.

"Would you like to let Mr. Murray hold your purse while I take the waving one?" I asked.

She cried out. "Oh, no'm, I'll just hold onto it." She was about to tell me it had that great big long ticket in it, but she just held her breath.

"All right, put your weight on one foot," I said, climbing onto a buttress. The whole building was as hot as a boiled egg in the shell.

"Wait! Let's decide what we're going to be looking at," said the Hostess. She inspected the city. "Look at the Robert E. Lee Hotel."

"Where is it?" asked the Queen nervously, still with her weight on both sturdy legs.

"I forget you've never been to Jackson," sighed the Hostess. If she had heard of it, she would have said, "One forgets." "Right yonder to the right. To the *right*—not the Baptist Church. Now don't take your eyes off it, and don't bat 'em, either."

"I was through once but we didn't stop," said the Queen, staring unflinchingly at the Robert E. Lee.

"Give?" asked the Hostess, pursing her lips.

"Sure," I said.

"Give," said the Hostess, nudging the Queen, who lifted her arm and smiled over at the hotel, although tears from the sun in her eyes streamed down her cheeks. She tottered a little, and I thought the Hostess knew it by some sense, although she was standing in front.

"Well, that's that," said Mr. Murray. "Isn't it?" He was red in the face, and most of the afternoon he had kept shaking his coat sleeve, as if something inside tickled his arm.

"We haven't got one by the Soldiers' Monument," I said, pointing, and we started off. To my surprise, the Hostess waited and put her arm around my waist and gave me her full smile—it expressed confidence—all the way there. Then I saw Mr. Murray had paired off with the Queen. Just in front of us, the Sponsor was helping hold the handle of the Queen's purse, with it swinging between them, and the Queen's eyes riveted upon it.

"Have you either one ever been to New York?" I asked, to break a dead silence.

"No'm," said the Queen over her shoulder.

"Never any farther than Washington, I haven't," the Hostess was saying meditatively. "Been everywhere but. Just never got around to old New York, till now."

"I never been anywhere but to the Coast," said the Queen flatly, with another backward glance. The Mississippi Gulf Coast, she meant.

"Oh, this time last year," laughed the Hostess. "Just this time last year. Fixing to go to California. Will I ever forget it! I was Miss Know-Your-Native-State-Better: white satin shorts. Now I look like an old maid." She stuck up the toe of her shoe and made a face of disgust. "I hope you all release pictures of me with clothes on to the out-of-state papers. It's her is the one in the bathing suit this time."

She gave a long vindictive look into the back of Mr. Murray, but he did not turn around. He and the Queen reached the monument, and she drew in her purse, like a fishline, and got it back to herself.

"Well, the American Legion is going to die, anyway," said the Hostess, and dashing at the monument sprang into place. She pinched the Queen. "Wake up!—You all beat their time," she explained to Mr. Murray. "The VFW beat the American Legion's time."

"Well, fine," said Mr. Murray.

3

The Hostess ran her eye up the monument with an almost posses-sive air. It was of oversized wounded soldiers being aided by towering women, and around it ran words: Our Wives—Our Mothers—Our Daughters—Our Sisters. "The American Legion got me here one time, they sure did. That was before I put on this weight. I put on nine pounds."

The Hostess posed the Queen through her own system of jabs; with the side of her hand she flicked the Queen behind her knee to make her bend the right leg. Then she relaxed and posed herself, left hand on hip and eyes directed upon the Jackson Infirmary.

"How's my East?" she asked, giving herself a little flicker, like a bathing bird. "It's looking right at the sun."

"Just give," I said.

"I still like the one on the cannon," declared the Hostess, speaking the instant the exposure was over. "I think that had something."

"On the cannon we got to sit down," agreed the Queen.

"Oh, I don't mean so much legs, but just sort of the idea," said the Hostess. "The *cannon*—" Again she made her gesture to denote the abstract.

"Oh, I'm so hungry!" gasped the Queen, and looked right at me.

I just stood there. "We both are," the other child said, turning to me too, but she had the sanctimonious manner of a devotee that reminded me somehow of middle-aged or old women at funerals. "Hungry, and exhausted, and tired.—I bet our eyes aren't any more *shining*!"

"I haven't had a thing to eat all day," gasped the Queen. A tear flew like a bullet out of her eye. "I *couldn't* eat."

"She's excited," said the Hostess.

"Let's stop and get some food," I said.

"Sure, sure," said Mr. Murray, shaking his sleeve.

"We really ought to have one with him telling us good-bye and wishing us luck in New York City," said the Hostess severely, running a wet finger over each eyebrow. "I mean after all, he wore his coat, and he's here, and he'll be gone in the morning. Giving us the trip. Shaking hands, just shaking hands and smiling, not waving. Our Sponsor."

"Can you wait for one more?" I asked the Queen.

She said, "Yes'm."

Mr. Murray said calmly, "You want my hat on or off?" He looked stiffly at everybody, and lifted his hat and set it back on his head, then lifted it again. He seemed a nice man, but had thought all along he might have to do this. "Is this to suit you?" he said directly to the Queen, as if she were the fitting one to decide.

"Oh, yes, sir, it's all right with me, either way," she said.

"Maybe it ought to be off, but I think it *looks* better on," said the Hostess. "More—you know." She spread her hand on the air, and Mr. Murray glanced sharply at it. Then he carefully adjusted the brim at a slight tilt, loosened his shoulders a minute, and swung his arm in the wilted white sleeve, shaking hands a few times with the air.

"We're certainly going to write you a letter from New York," said the Hostess to Mr. Murray, tête-à-tête without warning, smiling softly at him while I worried with my camera.

"Yeah, tell me all about it," said Mr. Murray, loosening his arm.

"You mean that long a letter?" She widened her eyes.

"Sure, yeah," he laughed.

"We'll leave out the things we think you all won't care to hear about," she said. Then with an abrupt little frown she turned on the Queen and shoved her into place beside her and a little to the back.

"Watch where you throw your weight," she said, pinching her. "Wake up. Now. Let's look *just beyond* Mr. Murray."

"Which hand you want me to wave?" asked the Queen.

"You don't wave," said the Hostess with patience. "You're through waving. This is just a quiet good-bye, with Mr. Murray and the suitcases, and you're looking just a little past him."

"One of you take his hand now," I said. "Watch out for the suitcase, Mr. Murray, don't step back. Closer, everybody, or I'll never get it all in."

"Do you mean 'Contact'?" smiled the Hostess.

"Contact," I said. "And thanks. That's all."

"I can't wait, can you?" said the Hostess, whirling.

"It won't be very long now," the Queen responded, sitting down all at once in a stone urn planted with petunias, at the corner of the monument—just her size.

"When I was Miss Winter Resort, I waved from a palm tree— maybe you saw it." The Hostess circled the Queen, waving, and then stopped and looked down on her. The Queen seemed to sink a little deeper, her round legs spilled out in a childish way.

"No, I don't believe," she said, with a blank look in her eyes.

"I was right high up," the Hostess said. "Of course there was another girl with me in the tree, to wave toward the other side. We wore white bathing suits. This time I have to be—you know. Discreet. A chaperone, ha-ha."

The Queen gave something between a smile and a yawn. "My mamma wouldn't have let me come if she'd thought there wasn't a real chaperone," she said gently, and went on in a voice of collapse, "My papa said I'd get lost sure in New York and they'd have to hunt me."

"Listen, we're going to have us a good time," said the Hostess, just as softly. "And I mean good. Little Amy's careful, but she's going to have fun, hear?" She was bending over the Queen, and directing at her a very serious look.

"Oh, I know it," protested the Queen from the urn. Tears suddenly gathered motion on her cheek and she gazed past the Hostess and at the skyline of Jackson, with dilated eyes.

The Hostess gripped her wrist and pulled her up and then down out of the urn.

"We're going to have us a good time before we get old and die," said the Hostess between her teeth.

The little soft-faced Queen accorded that the least response it might ever have gotten anywhere. She said, "Well." She knew it was not enough, and swallowed, and nodded her head one time, and the Hostess let go her wrist with a slowness that held us all hypnotized.

Then Mr. Murray made the clicking sound in his cheek, and we all went off together and had a sandwich in the Robert E. Lee Hotel.

Atlantic, July 1947, pages 37–40.

IX. LOOKING BACK

Looking Back at the First Story

In June 1936, *Manuscript* (Volume III, Number 3) published "Death of a Traveling Salesman," giving me my first appearance in print. *Manuscript* was one of the "little" magazines of that day, and was longer-lived than most. The editors, I had reason to know, were rare: John Rood and Mary Lawhead, husband and wife, printed their magazine at their own press, the Lawhead Press, in Athens, Ohio; they were friendly, enthusiastic, promptly responding editors with a practical dedication toward the discovery of young, unknown writers. In the issue that brought out my story, Mr. Rood characteristically wrote in his editor's note about it, "It seems that all best things come unannounced."

The disbelief that was mixed with my gratitude at the story's acceptance was justified, for "Death of a Traveling Salesman" was also my first submitted story anywhere. Before now, no one had read it. I had asked my friend Hubert Creekmore, an already published poet who lived up the street from me, to suggest where I might try sending out my story, but had not risked showing it to him first. It was easier to take, to expect, a rejection from the unknown than from family or friends. And since I was in my own mind a serious writer, I wanted from the first to be a professional.

If it had surprised me to have my story accepted, it shocked me to see it for the first time in print. In public print, your story looks back at you; for the first rime, it is beyond your reach. Too late now for you to change it, try to make it better! In print, it has the upper hand. It is fair to say it is now in a position to expose you in all your lacks and failures. "Death of a Traveling Salesman," now forty-three years old, almost twice as old as I was when I wrote it, is here to meet me again and scrutinize me anew from a reappearance in these pages. I see it afresh, and in doing so I recognize it as a member of the general family of my work, not lacking in earmarks good and bad. I find it still packs a challenge for its author, for which I respect it.

"Death of a Traveling Salesman" belongs to the family of all my stories in that its origin, its generative force, comes out of real life. A neighbor of ours in Jackson in the 1930s, Mr. Archie Johnson, traveled the state for the Highway Department, inspecting and buying up land for the right of way, and when he came back to town on weekends he would have some tales to tell. Mississippi roads in those Depression days were not numerous and were poorly kept up, all but unmarked. In remoter parts, to reach a householder not easily accessible by car, he would have to get out and walk. There was a fair likelihood of a stranger's finding the gravel or dirt road he was trying to reach some-where on had simply petered out. Getting lost would have been easy: probably Archie Johnson couldn't have got entirely lost, but my imaginary R. J. Bowman could; and besides, Bowman had had the flu to weaken him the further for his defeat.

Mr. Johnson (long and happily married, a jolly talker) was not R. J. Bowman, but it was Mr. Johnson whose tales, and whose traveling life, made me imagine this story. He had an account of which I remembered this one vivid thing: the remark made by the wife of a farmer he'd gone to see on his business: "He's gone to borry some fire." That remark didn't leave me, has never left me; to think of my own story to this day is to hear those reported words. I could not have made up "He's gone to borry some fire," but, beginner though I was as a writer, I think now I began truly, for I knew that for a story when I heard it.

Those words count and signify because they pertain to the lives in those ill-provided times in a poor, remote part of Mississippi. They were true to life, they were the truth of that life. In subsequence of that, but only in subsequence of that, they had an overtone: they suggested life, of a fallen, larger kind, referred with simplicity to being in touch with it, free to "borry" from it. Not the myth, but that *remark* was the seed of the story; all the rest—characters, plot, the design of the whole—stemmed all but instantaneously from hearing it spoken.

By instinct—I think it not accident—I had found early the story approach most natural to me. The journey of errand or search (for some form of the secret of life) was of course in itself nothing new: that motif may have *never* been new. It was to underlie many stories I wrote after "Death of a Traveling Salesman," from "A Worn Path" and "The Net" to "A Still Moment" and "The Hitch-Hikers," however different they all are. It is the extended motif for the collection of later stories in *The Bride of the Innisfallen*.

While my characters and their movements and the feelings that drive them rise most often from present, ordinary life, this motif, or plot in its essence, must have started its work on my imagination with the myths and fairy tales I steeped myself in as a young reader. A course through which my storytelling imagination could readily and delightedly flow had been laid down deep in my consciousness, or deeper than consciousness, where myth's real home lies in us all. Jason, Theseus, Odysseus, and all those kings' sons, all those who went forth seeking, from Dick Whittington to Don Quixote, bent upon errand, rescue, fulfillment of promise or prophecy or destiny or curse: by the time I was writing stories of my own, I drew on them as casually as I drew on the daily newspaper or the remarks of neighbors. In the connected stories I wrote called *The Golden Apples*, myth enters daily life openly, almost visibly. I see no reason why it shouldn't.

"Death of a Traveling Salesman" is not alone from my others in the appearance of a mythological figure passing through—in this case, on the run. My good angel told me that the symbolic needs to be indigenous to the story. Prometheus was in my mind almost at the instant I heard Mr. Johnson tell about the farmer borrowing fire; but Rafe in the story retains his own identity and builds upon it, running with the brand in a pair of tongs, and brings in his borrowed fire in front of all present and in front of us, and puts it to use on the hearth. I didn't say Rafe was "*like* Prometheus"—I let it be, for its moment, shown, which was a hopeful sign in a new writer.

So this first story attaches itself to the family of my work in that it taught me, in the writing, how to write it. At least I learned that I was *going* to learn that procedure is an essence of what its writer knows to be truth of feeling, that this truth is something that can be reached only from the inside. It has to be first hand. The characters and what they do are invented, or invent themselves, to carry this truth out.

As my work would continue to be, "Salesman" was visual in texture; but I had not taught myself in time for the first story to see in the specific detail and selectively. This landscape is general, and set down in it, the "unpainted cabin" appears made-up, invented, though incompletely—I was shy of its interior. I regret that literary broad-brimmed hat in which Bowman sees himself in the wavy hotel mirror as "something of a bullfighter." Bowman would not have known what a bullfighter looked like, and neither would I except from books; he wouldn't have dreamed of himself as fighting bulls.

I allowed myself to write "stream" instead of "creek," making it audible, although all water that runs in Mississippi is slow, brown, and quiet—nothing makes a noise but the big Mississippi itself. Bowman hears the stream running, it means a great deal to him. Clearly I was trying to suggest that he'd come near, now, to the stream of life, and so betrayed it by giving it a poetic name and an unnatural sound ("soft, continuous, insinuating") for the territory. It doesn't justify its use that *I* had heard a stream: what I used here was borrowed from my grandmother's mountain home in West Virginia. *It* was a stream, its running sound could be heard in the night and in the day too, it had been to me as a child a source of mesmerization. But moving it to the red-clay hills of Mississippi shows I had not learned to present a setting in ways that were accurate beyond question. The white speck of the man's shirt moving homeward in the dusk is from the same far mountains, but it traveled. It's fundamental to learn too, down to the least physical detail, what will transfer over from real life and what will not.

It was in the course of preparing these remarks, and thanks to the editors of *The Georgia Review*, that I was brought up with the fact that "Death of a Traveling Salesman" as it appeared in 1941 in my first book, *A Curtain of Green*, had undergone changes since its original publication in *Manuscript*. I had been working from the book version, not remembering at first that I'd changed anything. When I sent the book publisher the typed-up collection in 1940, the manuscript was lost in the mail, and never did turn up. Not having copies of my own, I made a new manuscript by typing from the various magazine copies. It is almost impossible to type over your own words without changing as you go, and evidently I yielded to various temptations in typing "Salesman."

Rafe's name became Sonny in the book version. I had got sensitive to the importance of proper names, and this change is justified: "Sonny" is omnipresent in boys' names in Mississippi and is not dropped just because the boys grow up and marry; "Sonny" helped make the relationship of the man and woman one that Bowman could mistake at the beginning; and at the same time it harked back to the fire-bringer.

But all my changes were not for the better, and indeed serve to show me the traps I was to fall in later on as well. For instance, after the line "... He had known several, no, many fine women in his territory," not knowing enough not to bring them in at all, I exposed myself in the book by elaborating: "Women? He could only remember little rooms within little rooms, like a nest of Chinese paper boxes, and if he thought of one woman he saw the worn loneliness that the furniture of that room seemed built of." The addition may be made up for in the subtraction, from the concluding paragraphs, of the "blackhaired girl on McKee Street"—she is not in the book version. I had trouble both times in introducing an element of the salesman's life that very likely did belong in the story; but I never got it right, and did better with the mule which comes directly on scene and looks in through a window.

In writing "Death of a Traveling Salesman" I faced the serious hazard of imagining myself inside characters whom I had no way of really knowing: all my characters were experienced in ways I was not. But this wasn't a hazard as I saw it—it was the charm, the lure, the magnet. I never doubted, then or now, that imagining yourself into other people's lives is exactly what writing fiction is. I had no hesitation then, only eagerness, in trying to convey a middle-aged traveling salesman deprived of the fulfillment of self-knowledge, of the ability to love; a hill-country farmer and moonshiner; a woman in the prime of a fruitful marriage. I rushed in, to show the weight of a pregnant woman's arm as she lifts it to point to her husband coming; to show a man as he is dying and show it as the explosive revelation of what it was he wanted all his life. I had to know how to do such things, and knew I had to know. I drove my imagination to put me inside these characters on a premise I accepted, then as now, that the emotions, in which all of us are alike involved for life, differ more in degree than in kind. Imagining yourself inside the skin, body, heart, and mind of any other person is the primary feat, but also the absolute necessity. Whether the other person is man or woman, old or young, black or white, whether it's a person at the point of coming into the fullness of life or of leaving life without it, makes only a secondary challenge.

Georgia Review, Winter 1979, pages 751–55.

Welty contributed this note to *Manuscript* to accompany "Death of a Traveling Salesman": "I'm already twenty-six years old, was born in Jackson, Miss., went to school in Mississippi, Wisconsin, and New York City; studied painting and advertising. Now I am back in Jackson, living with my family. It would be interesting if I had been in jail or trodden grapes like other young writers. I didn't even suffer early in life, except from my father's being from Ohio—a Yankee. Just now I am in

New York while a one-man show of my photographs goes on at the Lugene Gallery
here. The pictures are from a collection of three hundred unposed studies I made
of Mississippi Negroes. I did the job out of pure interest, but it broke me, so I hope
a publisher here will buy them. . . . In Mississippi there is a lot still to be written.
When I had taken these photographs for a while I lost interest in writing stories
that took place in Paris, although I admit they concerned things that could not have
happened anywhere. In this one year I seem to have got my bearings. Now to sound
them out."

A Word on the Photographs for
Twenty Photographs

The Lucky Snapshot has not been accidental, even though an amateur has made it. His own eye has seen first, has chosen, what the eye of the camera is to take in, and directed the instant for the film to register it. The photographer learns the possibilities of his tool—what depth or intensity of focus will reward him, what advantage can be taken of light and shadow—but beyond this, it is essential for him to be sensitive to the speed, not simply of the camera's shutter, but of the moment in time.

Among all living creatures, only human beings seem to have the knowledge that the moment is passing, and the acute wish to hold that moment. In the most unpretentious snapshot lies the wish to clasp fleeting life. Framing a few square inches of space for the fraction of a second, the photographer may capture—rescue from oblivion—fellow human beings caught in the act of living. He is devoted to the human quality of transience. Here lies whatever value his picture-taking has.

So no photograph is without its subjective implications; the eye of
the camera is recording what the eye of the photographer is discover-
ing. In the eye of the beholder arrested by pleasure or recognition, the
photograph becomes subjective too; it speaks in its way of the joys and
sorrows, the humiliations and the pride, of the human predicament.

By recording what passes, the photographer offers the illusion of
not letting it go. These pictures represent such efforts. They are among
hundreds made by me in the late 1930s and early '40s in the State of
Mississippi. If a value persists in them, it is because life, whatever it
meant, had to mean, in those poor times, speaks for itself in the unchanging language of movement and gesture, and looks undefeatedly
back at the camera's eye.

From a pamphlet "Eudora Welty" included with the portfolio *Twenty Photographs*
arranged by Stuart Wright, Winston-Salem: Palaemon Press, 1980, page 3.

Foreword, *The Optimist's Daughter*

The Optimist's Daughter takes place in a courthouse town in Mississippi, and the time is recent. Mount Salus is imaginary but not untypical—a modest but long-established small town. Its ways appear on the surface as easygoing, while in fact they are fairly tenacious. People like Judge McKelva and his cronies, and their wives—his own wife Becky being the exception—acknowledge in their lives the familiar social pattern while not denying its limitations; in fact they enjoy its limitations, while Judge McKelva—the optimist—has devotedly taken on its responsibilities. The generation following his, appraises and relishes its absurdities. His daughter Laurel's set have never stopped referring to themselves as "the bridesmaids"—a term they make both ironic and possessive, harking back to Laurel's wedding that's now so long ago, Laurel now being a widow.

I wanted to show the stability of Mount Salus society so that the outsiders could best be seen against it. In Mount Salus, outsiders not only make the exception—they, and especially they, generate situation;

some of what they generate lives after them. They cannot help but question the accepted order of things; they disappoint local expectations; they tend to throw earlier, long-accepted relationships into a different light and subject emotions to a harder test. There are three outsiders in *The Optimist's Daughter*, two living and one dead.

Becky, now dead, the Judge's first wife and Laurel's mother, was in her lifetime not a social outsider but a maverick: married into Mount Salus, she has never pretended to give up West Virginia—"up home." A passionate and passionately individual woman, she has fearlessly trusted to what she saw and found out for herself in order to know what is true and not true. Then her vision fails. She is further trapped by a stroke. Trust in others, in the world, in love, fails her. She is in exile from her second home where she lies helpless, as well as from her first. Before she dies, everything fails her but her passion.

Fay is an outsider as Becky's successor, and socially she never will fit in, in Mount Salus. Self-conscious, combative, unable so far to tell the truth, even to herself, unequal to crisis, and then (she has a lot of vitality) not grateful for pitying help—*that* can cause affront!—she in effect refuses to become a part of the local society. Laurel, with the marriage connection to confront, is disturbed more seriously by a deeper flaw: the lack of feeling on Fay's part for what she is going through and what others are going through.

Laurel is not *apparently* an outsider—she's only been away, living and working in Chicago. But she has removed herself to a certain inward distance—a reticence guards her, a standing-off, and she is slow to make known her feelings. And back home, the parental generation, while welcoming her now with all the sympathy in the world, take care to let her know they think she should never have left in the first place. Look who her father went and married and brought to live in this house. And now see what happened to him. . . .

This framework, set by time and place and the events of the Judge's death and funeral, I found both circumscribing and freeing to what I wanted to show: the progression of human relationships. Their tensions act as the directing force; and the plot of the novel tests the movement and pull, with and against, the power and strength of kinship.

Kinship brings Laurel home from her established life in Chicago at the first signal of trouble, and keeps her there until the whole story of her family life has been resolved, has become well enough understood to leave behind her. Kinship magnetized Becky back to the mountains of her original home every summer of her married life. Kinship drags the protesting Chisoms from Texas to stand by Fay on the occasion of her husband's funeral—just as it brought the Dalzells in from the country to camp out in the waiting room of the New Orleans hospital while Mr. Dalzell in intensive care was dying. Kinship, universally in the South, still acts as a summons, as unquestioned as it is inevitable.

Kinship runs all through the novel—not only blood-relationship but the kinships of feeling—and kinships of not-feeling, as we see in Fay's big family. Neither blood-kinship nor the relationship of marriage proves, in the course of the novel, to be tie enough to ensure loving-kindness. An affinity that is neither is sometimes more merciful: on the day of the funeral, the unspoken attachment Miss Adele Courtland has long cherished for the Judge makes itself as strongly felt in the room as Fay's throwing herself upon his coffined body in protest to his having left her a widow; and Fay as the widow identifies herself to Laurel as one of "the great, interrelated family of those who never know the meaning of what has happened to them."

While I was writing *The Optimist's Daughter*, I was living with the fact that the story was very close to me—not in its literal circumstance, but in its concern, its subject, its weight of meaning for me as a person. The time I began it (while I was also finishing *Losing Battles*, a novel of a very different kind) was soon after the long illnesses of my mother and my brother had ended in the deaths of them both in the same week. Part of the universal experience of personal loss is the urgent wish to find a way back through the exercise of memory and the acceptance of the responsibilities of feeling and understanding, to apprehend, absorb, and save some essence of the life that is just over. The imaginary Laurel, through the dramatic circumstances of the story I invented, presses her way back, as far as she can seek it out, into the life of the marriage of father and mother, and its outcome, in the long run coming finally abreast with her own survival, and to terms with her own life.

Though the story was not "like" my own, it was *intimate* with my own—a closer affinity. Writing it involved my deepest feelings, their translation into the events of the story was demanding of my ability as no other novel, so far, has been. It taught me, all the way, as writing always manages to do. *The Optimist's Daughter* may be teaching me still, since I find it difficult, even after the lapse of time, to write a foreword to it.

I am certainly not Laurel, although she moves through feelings and apprehensions, surmises and despairs of mine—I could not otherwise have known enough to invent her, much less try to involve the reader in her life. A writer cannot describe an unfelt emotion. I was the child visiting her grandmother in West Virginia. I share with Laurel the loss of a parent in my middle age—nearly all of us share that. The character of Laurel comes out of it, it is her source.

Laurel's father, Judge McKelva, is altogether remote from mine, who was born in Ohio, became a Southern businessman, and died young when I was barely grown. (His vision was untroubled.) Becky McKelva has in common with my mother the West Virginia background and the trouble with vision. Drawn as she needed to be drawn for *The Optimist's Daughter*, she does not represent a portrait of my mother, nor was she intended to. All the same, there are in Becky qualities I came to know through knowing my mother—qualities that are at the heart of *The Optimist's Daughter*. It is also true that here and there in particles and bits and in deeper reverberations sometimes, my mother is diffused over other characters I've written about—very differing characters—in other books; she is part of Ellen in *Delta Wedding*, and a rather large part of Miss Julia Mortimer of *Losing Battles*; there's a shadow of her in Miss Marcia Pope of the short story "The Demonstrators."

My habit as a fiction writer is not to write autobiographically except in the most important respect: the feelings are true; and to me, human relationships furnish the truth of fiction as they furnish the truth in life. Invented characters are better made to convey, to carry out, to bring into the open and reveal these feelings than am I, writing in my own person, though I might be a part of them all.

Because of its nearness to me, I allowed a period of time to go by in between *The Optimist's Daughter*'s first appearance—in *The New Yorker*, which ran it in a single issue—and its final preparation for book publication. I revised it then, not noticeably in expansion of scene, not at all in mood or purpose, but in degree of intensity: the passage of time had perhaps this result, that the intensity shows more openly.

This had been its due, for *The Optimist's Daughter* is a novel concerned with vision. Vision is central in all that transpires, its presence and its absence; and intensity is one of vision's properties.

"Our eye," as Dr. Courtland so colloquially and so rightly calls it—we do all share as a community in what we see and can't see—is the actual physical door from the outside world to the inner. When Becky's vision is taken away, she doubts the very fundamentals of existence, and her heart dies of distrust, and in distrust. When Judge McKelva is found to have a detached retina, and when Laurel, the daughterly nurse both times, sees her mother's suffering through her father's suffering through her own, her own vision is acutely affected by memory, retrospect, recall. Laurel is "our eye" for the novel.

Laurel, the optimist's daughter, knows to her deeps that she has come home to learn now what has lain underneath what she has seen, or partly seen, before. She becomes, in the stormy night in the bereaved home, like her mother going in the raft down the icy river to stand by her own father in his ordeal. Laurel rides through her night in the house on a raft with them both—father and mother—and with herself as their child. It is in a way the same river—a river that has run through all the periods of discovery in her life: the river that runs below the mountain in West Virginia, with its sounding shoals; the river made known by its lit-up bridge the night of her father's death when the blind comes down in his New Orleans hospital room; the rivers coming together at Cairo seen from the train bridge above it by Laurel and Phil on their honeymoon—the confluence itself. I meant the river for more than visible landscape, and I meant it for more than symbolic value: its presence is there as the presence of experience itself, ever moving and powerful and deep-running, however seldom in view. It is the past pouring into the present, the old into the new, and it is real, dangerous, mysterious, changing, converging, life in its own right.

Laurel reaches the point of believing that it can never be, really, too late to begin to understand what has happened to you. When this understanding does break its barriers, it begins to reach back through all the years it has taken to arrive at the present; it is an essence that irradiates past experience as well as what can come next. Clarity is born, or restored, in the mind's eye. By the time she's ready to return to her own life, she sees, from her moving car, the lifted arms of schoolchildren she's leaving behind, waving good-bye to her.

Printed as "A special message to subscribers from Eudora Welty" in *The Optimist's Daughter*, fourth edition, limited, signed. Franklin Center, Pennsylvania: The Franklin Library, 1980, pages ivx–xv. *The Optimist's Daughter*, 1972, won the Pulitzer Prize.

Afterword, *Morgana*

The seven short stories that make up the book *The Golden Apples*, of which "June Recital" was the first, were written during the middle or closing years of the 1940s in Jackson. All but one happen in and around an imaginary small town in the Yazoo-Mississippi Delta called Morgana—the kind that is a world to itself. The stories are connecting. They are about human relationships in their beginnings and changes among the characters in their different times, all within the frame of Morgana. The exception, "Music from Spain," happening to one Morgana character who gets himself all the way to San Francisco (it was written in San Francisco) makes its own comment on what the spell of place can do, the way it may contribute to our fates.

In writing my stories, I've always been indebted to place—most often the South. It has informed me and nourished my imagination in endless ways, but in "June Recital" I became indebted to place in a very specific respect: to an actual street location in my town.

Our family house and the Music Building of Belhaven College stood directly across the street from each other. Drifting out through the open windows of the practice rooms opposite and, floating across Pinehurst Street, in through the open windows of my upstairs room where I sat at the typewriter working, came the clear, searching, repeating sounds of piano practice. Its sound traveled unimpeded: that was a year when air conditioning had not arrived to shut us away from each other, and the traffic on our residential street hadn't yet revved up to come between us. The pupils—I never saw them once—were few in number; they played in their turn, never conflicting. On their warm, young, patient or impatient fingers they practiced alone.

Though I was as constant in my work as the students were, subconsciously I must have been listening to them, following them, for some time. I realized that each practice session reached me as a solitary outpouring. And longings so expressed, so insistent, so repeated, called up still more longings *un*expressed. I began to hear, in what kept coming across the street into the room where I typed, the recurring dreams of youth, inescapable, never to be renounced, only naming themselves over and over again.

Certain pupils were working up show-pieces—the *Warsaw Concerto* as well as "Country Gardens." But it was the tender, insistent *"Für Elise"* that tugged at me, continued in my ears even when it wasn't being played; and I stopped my typing. *"Für Elise"* penetrated into my own life and found me a story to tell. It gave me "June Recital" and its perpetrator, Virgie Rainey. At the same time, another source, older, had been tapped—my memory.

Little girls when I was growing up in Jackson took piano lessons almost as a matter of course. It was inevitable (only if you were a girl, however) that you should "take"; your family was cheerfully prepared to sacrifice, if need be, so that you should not go without a piano in the home and weekly lessons from a teacher. So of course there were dozens of teachers in Jackson. None of them, as far as I knew or ever heard of, were in the least like Miss Eckhart, the other leading character in "June Recital." None of the teachers were German, to start with.

And when I gave Miss Eckhart her key line, "Virgie Rainey, *danke schoen*," I had never heard German spoken. I'd only heard music-teaching spoken.

My own teacher, like most of the others, I presume, was a deep-dyed Jacksonian. Though she dipped her pen in ink and wrote "Practice!" on my sheet music with a "P" that looked like a cat with a long tail, and though she did occasionally rap my erring fingers with a fly swatter, and though she had a metronome, she bore no other resemblance, inner or outer, to Miss Eckhart. She was not (so far as a child was aware) troubled by passionate feelings.

But was she a recital giver! Of course. Indeed, she was a formidable recital giver, terrifying us all through the month of June. But by the nature of their calling, all piano teachers of the young are recital givers, and all recitals are probably variations of the same anguished pattern—almost a ritual of summer—on which I freely drew for my story.

So where did Miss Eckhart, who did have passionate feelings, and who had no predecessor in my real life, come from? She was invented whole, for the purposes of "June Recital." She was not simply a teacher, she was the bringer of the entirely new dimension, that of art, to the life of Morgana, Mississippi. (And don't we all know some heroic figure like that?) She came able to perceive the natural artist in her best pupil, Virgie Rainey, to challenge her to pursue her gift, to call her to account when she rebelled, to encourage and to love her. This potent character tries and tries again, challenging, demonstrating, providing a terrifying example, suffering and demanding, on behalf of Virgie's own gift which Virgie in her carelessness and wastefulness throws away.

Miss Eckhart had, and discharged, passionate feelings. She had no real-life predecessors, and her force was unqualified, quite unsheathed, and, in its form of love, repudiated. She was one of the characters in *The Golden Apples*—perhaps the pre-emptive one—that sprang from deep within my own imagination. Perhaps all the more because she had no real-life counterpart, her force was allotted its full range. There were only children to feel that and reject it.

Both "June Recital" and "Moon Lake" are about the young. "Moon Lake" had its inception in a two-week period when for the first time in my life I was away from home without my family. I was nine years old, in a summer when groups of Jackson children went in relays across Pearl River to a camp in bosky Rankin County. It was called, I think, Camp McLaurin. We lived by a lake and slept in tents under the supervision of local young ladies attached, if I'm not now mistaken, to the Jackson Y.W.C.A. They wore middy blouses and put up their hair in puffs over the ears. One wore an Indian head-band, one played a ukulele, and they all smelled of citronella.

I finally learned how to drink water from a spring, but it just served to wring my heart with homesickness for Jackson water. Everything made me homesick, and homesickness made me tormentedly sensitive to, and startled by, everything new in the life around me. This included the fact that a matching contingent of orphans from one of the Jackson orphanages shared the two weeks with children who'd come off and left their homes and families behind, like me. They seemed to stick very close to us, but they kept mum. They didn't care to answer your first question or to ask you one back. I credited them with being homesick for their orphanage, here in the woods that smelled mockingly like Christmas trees, with red clay banks to run up and down, hot as fever to the bare feet, here by the muddy lake into which, if you looked too hard before putting your toes in, you could see the turning shadows of snakes. When we sat cross-legged around the campfire after dark and sang "There's a Long, Long Trail a-Winding into the Land of My Dreams," which we knew was a song our doughboys sang when they were "Over There," as I sang I cried. It was my only chance. After "lights out" in our tents, when we had said our prayers, we were supposed to go to sleep; but it was possible to look out where the flap in the tent was pulled back. Then, like Nina in "Moon Lake," and with her fearful rapture, I saw the whole mysterious night.

At camp that summer, nothing ever really happened in real life. But in the story, what has its beginning in nameless apprehension, and then steals up through surmise, finally takes center stage: there is the shock of a happening. While all the campers stand witness, it threatens to expose for them the secrets of the world, of life and death, in spite of a ring of chaperones. Childhood, ready or not, is jolted forward into adolescence.

"Moon Lake's" characters and events rose out of the story as the story rose out of my childhood. The invention of Easter—scornful, fearless orphan Easter—and the events of her near-drowning and the gawky ritual of rescue—were the outcome. Though the real-life situation made it possible, indeed all but called for it to happen, the plot was entirely invented. The characters too were all made up toward that end, though memory helped, and every female character probably—inevitably—had parts of me.

I have to amend the claim of inventing everybody. My brother Edward was in fact a Boy Scout, who, one summer, acted as life guard and was beleaguered in a small camp for girls; but that was in a later year, in another camp, in another part of Mississippi. I brought him, along with his bugle, to "Moon Lake," where I needed Loch. Like Loch exactly, I remembered, when Edward was at a stage where he could hardly endure the presence of girls, he lived surrounded by them, more or less at their mercy. Whatever happened at that camp, he was on hand, dwelling in boredom and disgust, but, as a Boy Scout, *prepared*. For Loch at Moon Lake I didn't change Edward a bit; he was perfect as he was. But as far as he ever mentioned, he was never called on to perform artificial respiration on anybody.

Some stories bring their writer a greater surprise of joy in the doing than others, equally absorbing or demanding, manage to bring. In the writing of *The Golden Apples*, "June Recital" and "Moon Lake" were for me so blessed.

And now they have been blessed again, from a modern source. The spirited, sensitive, wonderfully congenial black and white illustrations Mildred Nungester Wolfe has made for this book have brought to the two stories a rich additional life of their own.

In *Morgana: Two Stories from* The Golden Apples, Jackson: University Press of Mississippi, 1988, pages 147–51.

My Introduction to
Katherine Anne Porter

When in 1937 Robert Penn Warren, Cleanth Brooks, and Albert Erskine, editors of the *Southern Review*, had decided to use two of my stories, the significance of that acceptance was not lost on me. They had thought my work good enough to take a chance on, to encourage. Still I had not been prepared for a letter out of the blue from Katherine Anne Porter after the stories appeared. She was not an editor, but a *writer*, a writer of short stories; she was out in the world, at Baton Rouge:

> 961 America Street
> Baton Rouge, Louisiana
> October 25, 1938

> Dear Miss Welty:
> Ford Madox Ford has been given control of the fiction department of the Dial Press, and asked me to help him look about for candidates

for publication. I thought of you first, with your admirable short stories. It seems to me that if you have no other plans, and have a book length collection of stories, it would be an excellent idea to write to Ford, giving him some notion of your manuscript. He will then no doubt ask to see it.

Also, if you like, I would be glad to name you as candidate for a Guggenheim Fellowship for next year—rather, for application in the fall of 1939 and 1940 Fellowship. I have already named a candidate for this year. This is done by request of the Secretary of the Foundation who looks constantly for likely candidates, and naturally is no sort of engagement or promise. But if you should care to apply, I should at once write a letter about you to Mr. Moe.

I take this liberty because of my admiration for your very fine work.

Katherine Anne Porter

◆ ◆ ◆

I seized on the belief Miss Porter offered me; she was the writer of short stories I revered. Her letter was an act of faith, and I was able to recognize this. It also foretold something about her lifelong habit of mind: there was no mistaking the seriousness of her meaning; there never must be, with her, as all learned sooner or later about K.A.P. She spoke truth as she saw it about the written word, about the writing of the written word, the act itself.

She was to give encouragement to me from that time on in the ways that always applied to the serious meaning of a young writer's work—and life; as indeed she gave encouragement to many young writers.

Thus I'd sent along my stories to Ford Madox Ford, who turned out to think well enough of them to try to place them in England up until the time of his death not very long afterward. I'd applied for the Guggenheim in 1940 with Katherine Anne's blessing. It wasn't awarded on that first application. But it was the existence of Katherine Anne Porter's hopes for me themselves, successful and unsuccessful alike, that filled me with gratitude.

However I had been able to express this to her, she wrote back:

> 1050 Government Street
> Baton Rouge, Louisiana
> March 7, 1940

Dear Eudora:

Please remember that my recommendation of your work costs me nothing; that it gives me pleasure, and is the best proof I can offer of my faith in your talent and hopes for the future. It is no doubt one of the marks of your seriousness of character and intention that you take obligation for any little help offered or received; in this case, let me assure you, a purely imaginary, self-assumed sense of obligation. Try not to remember it; I would much prefer your friendship, in the most unburdensome meaning of that word. And it would really disturb me if you felt in my debt for such a small thing as a word of praise from me.

I am still hoping that your luck will be good this year. Enough for the present, for if this year is good, the others can take care of themselves ...[1]

> Katherine Anne

And even if this year turns out *not* so good, that is no sign at all that the coming ones shall be unlucky!

◆ ◆ ◆

In September 1940, as I was travelling to Vermont, she invited me to stop off at Yaddo, the artists' colony where she was spending a time working. She wrote to me afterwards:

Yaddo, Saratoga Springs
New York, September 18
1940

Dear Eudora:

It was simply lovely having you here even for such a little while, and I wish you could come back now, for I'm moved upstairs to a much pleasanter place and there are bedrooms all over the house, unoccupied . . .

Diarmuid Russell[2] wrote me, and I wrote him and he wrote me again and I just answered, so you see we are getting on splendidly. He gave me some advice which I followed and it worked; and he is a most secure admirer of you and your work, so it is delightful to know you are going to be looked after. He is really in earnest about it; says he finds himself mentally shaking his finger at editors about you. I feel serenely conscious that it is all going to end well. Yours will be a war of attrition, as mine was, Eudora. You just go the way you're going and the editors will fall in, in time. And you have all the time in the world, and all the gift you can handle; in fact, you've got a handful, perhaps more than you know.

I have out of a clear sky but not without premeditation, finished two short stories—whales, about eight thousand words each. One to S.R., one to Harper's Bazaar, as usual. I think I was working on the first when you were here. Well, there are two now. "Season of Fear" and "The Leaning Tower." That makes enough floating around for a collection, and I'm going to get out another book of short stories, willy-nilly; they can take it or leave it. We have *got* to beat down this conspiracy against collections of short stories . . . It's a long war, but we will win.

Katherine Anne

♦ ♦ ♦

By 1941, Diarmuid Russell after two years' unremitting work had succeeded in placing all my stories in magazines, which had made them acceptable as a collection to a publisher who would risk a book of short stories. And now, John Woodburn of Doubleday, Doran in New York had by his long and patient work persuaded his house to publish it. The book was given a title, *A Curtain of Green*. To cap this, he had invited and persuaded Katherine Anne Porter to write an Introduction to it. She added to this wonderful news by writing to me:

February 19, 1941—Olivet
[Olivet College, Michigan]

Dearest Eudora:

All the news about you is good news and makes me happy for you, and for myself, because nothing is better than to see you getting off so bravely.

I write with pencil because I am in bed with a crick in the neck which seems to be my way of having a cold, and all my paper, pens, etc., are on the other side of this blizzard-swept campus in my office. A splendid letter from Diarmuid full of rejoicing about you and the new baby.³ Please tell him in your next I have his letter and will write when I am better able.

Meantime—Send the collection *with* "The Robber Bridegroom"⁴ et al to Yaddo. I will do what I can to have it included— Above all, tell me *when, where* the preface should be sent; deadlines are my snare—But I will make it.

I know well already what I think of your work, but reading all the stories will give pointers.

No more for the moment. Albert Erskine will be delighted with this news. Meantime my love and good wishes, may all your good beginnings bring you to a happy end!

Katherine Anne

And soon after:

Yaddo, Saratoga Sprigs
New York, May 2, 1941

Dear Eudora:

Elizabeth Ames tells me you have been invited here for early June, and I hope you like the place and can stay a long time if you want . . . It will be lovely to see you. Mrs. Ames had said something about inviting you before the regular season, but I heard no more of it.

Your letter was useful and I am keeping it with my notes for the preface, just for the tone. We'll talk all that over when you get here . . .

Nothing more just now, I am at the last gasp of that novel, and must finish now before I do anything else. But after, I shall be free; and meantime I scribble down something else about your work as it comes to me, so the notes are piling up nicely against the day . . .

I got the deed to South Farm, today. So it is really mine, and the work is beginning on it almost at once . . . The end of the summer should see me in it. But believe me, this novel is the foundation of this whole thing, and it must go soon . . . I've written it so often, really, it is high time to let go, now!

Waiting to see you, with my love,

Katherine Anne

I showed your collection to Glenway Wescott, and he was pretty well bowled over. I said, "My money is on her nose for the next race," and he said, "Mine, too. She is marvelous." So your audience grows. He is a good friend to have—never will let his friends hear the last of you . . .

+ + +

I arrived at Saratoga Springs as one in a dream.

Yaddo was in the old, rural, comfortably settled part of New York State west of Albany, near the town of Saratoga Springs. The estate was private and well guarded, though its gardens were, at that inno-cent time, open to the public. The Mansion faced you head-on as you approached it through forest trees; it was huge, elaborately construct-ed: it looked made by impulse for eternity, out of the rock on which it stood. The artists came for their summer at Yaddo solely by invi-tation. Elizabeth Ames gave her life to being its director—a woman of Quaker-like calm and decisiveness; she was beautiful and to some extent deaf. She stood ready for crises.

The artists—painters, composers, writers, sculptors—lived in the reaches of the Mansion, and beyond their rooms they were given stu-dios to suit their particular needs; these stood hidden away among the old forest trees, at various calculated degrees of remoteness. Artists ate their lunch alone; it arrived in a tin box left silently outside their doors at noon.

Katherine Anne and I were enviably installed in the "farmhouse," a small frame building a distance away from the Mansion on its hill across the road. We shared the farmhouse with only two others, con-genial both—a Canadian composer and an Armenian-American etch-er, who *did* work all day in their respective studios.

Upstairs, across the hall from Katherine Anne's combined bed-room and studio, was my bedroom. My studio was downstairs in the farmhouse kitchen. On the outside of the studio door was a sign tacked up: "SILENCE. WRITER AT WORK WITHIN." My immediate work consisted of reading the proofs of my forthcoming book, and that was over quickly. Already, though, my editor John Woodburn, in New York, had begun to write me little bulletins, instructing me to remind Katherine Anne about the Introduction: "And kid, you keep after her! She promised to write it *now*! Remind her we've got a dead-line."

And I knew I couldn't do that.

In the early evening of each long summer's day, Katherine Anne—with her spring-heeled step, catching up her long skirts—and I set out in single file walking the woodland path up to the great stone Mansion for dinner. This was the only hour of the twenty-four when all the guests came out and showed themselves. They had supposedly been solitary all day behind their studio doors, working.

Within the Mansion, the atmosphere, even the hour, seemed changed; it was hushed, moody, and somehow public. The great room we entered spread out like a stage set for a grand opera on which the curtain might at any moment go up. An overture was in the making: an interior fountain close to us was murmuring, and offstage somewhere an organ began to growl; it was possible that one of the resident poets was still at work, thinking something through.

I began to feel apprehensive that we were all expected to *perform* here, that the assigned soloists and the combined chorus were *us*. The great hall was appointed with throne chairs, divans, velvet stools (one also noticed a sleigh), with candelabra, wine glasses, wine.

If I supposed our opera would be one about the arts, or artists, something like *La Bohème*, I wasn't on the right track. This was 1941. The company was in great part European. Elizabeth Ames had come to the aid of many artists who no longer had homes and were seeking refuge and a place to carry on their work. Our evening was indeed operatic, but it wasn't about the arts; it was about politics. Katherine Anne rose to the occasion—her clear voice would enter as if on cue with cries of *"Au contraire!"* One end of the great room gave onto the coming night; the window was a great tall frame holding the Yaddo moon, and I watched it climbing. Out there beyond and below the stone balustrade, the garden descended, with its statues of the Graces rising from the beds like another chorus. I could smell, without seeing it, the summer stock, the nicotiana. They made me think of home. That first night, I knew for certain only what the *garden* was doing.

From New York, John Woodburn, who was my champion, who had staked so much in bringing out this first book by an unknown, young, Southern, female, short-story writer, wrote to me nearly every day. "How far along is she? How's the Introduction coming?" "Keep after her, kid! Tell her one more time about the deadline!" "Get it out of her, baby."

Was she writing it indeed? If I heard from across the hall her little Olivetti typewriter start up, or still more, if I heard it stop, I felt like an eavesdropper. I let myself out of the house and walked down the road to Saratoga Springs.

It was lovely to arrive there, too, in the bright Northern summer morning. Lining either side of the main street, the great hotels stood facing each other under the meeting boughs of lofty elms, the United States Hotel and all its sisterhood: their red faces, their black iron columns across the front, twisted like Venetian barge poles, and the figures of black, turbaned, Oriental slaves mounted at the top of the steps with an arm crooked up to hold branching lamps with clusters of globes made for gaslight.

The length of the street was strung overhead with banners and flags bidding Welcome. Along the sidewalks I moved with a wonderful crowd of perambulators here for the waters, the races, the sights and parades: invalids, sporting people, sightseers, families stalled in circles on the sidewalk in a chorus of argument over what to do next. I visited the racetrack where the horses were working out, and the busy public halls where the waters were being dispensed.

By the time I walked home to Yaddo, I might be carrying onions, soup bones, maybe a fresh stalk of celery or bunch of carrots to Katherine Anne, who liked to keep the soup pot going on her little stove, as well as her windup gramophone going, and sometimes now her Olivetti going.

I knew it was to be a wonderfully happy and carefree summer for me—if only I didn't have Katherine Anne's awful deadline hanging over my head: the unmentionable.

Outside our farmhouse sat a brand new Studebaker car—it was Katherine Anne's. She had not quite learned to drive it yet. But I could drive it, and she said she had something to show me: we would take the day off from work!

It was a little distance off, in deep country: the house her letter had told me about securing the deed for. She confided that she was actually now in the very process of restoring it. She had christened it "South Hill." She would finish it, make it all her own, move into it, settle down and *write*. It became a part of nearly every day to jump into the Studebaker and drive out to South Hill.

She could count on a Mr. Somebody who came to see to everything. So a yellow-coned cement mixer churned away among the trees, and at times drowned out the birdsong, and the carpenters who stripped the upstairs walls now down to the laths found little feminine slippers that K.A.P. identified as being a hundred years old, and further came on—roused up—bees in the walls too, which had been at work storing honey there for, she estimated, the same length of time. K.A.P. and I stretched out on the long sweet meadow grass in another part of the shade. At peace, we puffed on our cigarettes, and I listened to her tell the way she had discovered Joyce for herself: somehow a copy of *Ulysses* had been carried into this country and ended up on a second-hand bookstall in Galveston, Texas; Katherine Anne had walked by and just picked it up.

When the spirit moved us, we would jump into the Studebaker and ride all the way to Albany and there find six wonderful French antique dining-room chairs, or cinch a roll of ruby-red carpeting, perfect for the stairs when they were made ready to climb (at present we were crawling up a plank to reach the upstairs). All were now entrusted to storage. It was the clearest thing to K.A.P. that everything we engaged in all day long was South Hill in the making. There was supporting magic attached to finding treasures that would take their rightful place in it. There popped into my head the lovely little French virginal that Katherine Anne had showed to me, the very first thing, on the day when I'd come on her invitation to see her for the first time; it was in her new house in Baton Rouge. Where was the virginal now? I wondered, but did not ask. It must be in storage somewhere.

We sank into the luxury of talking books as easily as we sank into the long, sweet meadow grass; we had all day and a picnic lunch. We listened to the birdsong and the carpenters at work. Katherine Anne would often be laughing out loud.

But if it was hard for me, being there night and day with my very presence putting Katherine Anne on the spot, did I think of how hard it was for Katherine Anne? I am certain beyond a doubt that *I* could not have written the first line about anybody who was, at the time, staying in the house with me three steps away across the hall. And if that person knew about my purpose, and was waiting on me daily to set down the words on paper? And if at the same time that person had turned out to be a friend? I'm afraid the possibility never occurred to me that I *could* conclude my stay at Yaddo before my invitation was up.

Then the day came when she tapped at my door and came in holding out to me a whole sheaf of typewritten pages. "You may read this," she said, "if you would like." It was what she'd been working on, the first seventy-five pages of *No Safe Harbor*—her novel (which of course was to become, in the end, *Ship of Fools*). In allowing me to read it, and at its beginning, she had made me a gift of her clear confidence in me. As far as I was concerned, the Introduction she was going to write for me had been conveyed to me by way of a blessing. If its significance was to relate to her literary trust in me, I had already received it.

The novel was years later on to appear in the finality of print, but what I had been living across the hall from was the immediacy, the presence, and something of the terror, of its pages coming into being one by one. I'd *heard* the living words coming through her fingers and out of her skin. I don't think I was ever again as stirred, and as captivated, to hold a fresh manuscript in my hands and realize what I held.

The summer was deepening, and with it the pleasures of Yaddo. By then, friendships had ripened among the set of artists, informality had caught up with formality, and picnics sneaked into the lazy noons. Katherine Anne made onion soup for her friends. That could take all day, and as we all agreed, it was worth every minute of it. There was music in the evening at the Mansion, but music was *always* to be heard at our farmhouse. The gramophone would be kept wound up and playing. K.A.P. kept stacks of French records, from Piaf back to Gluck, back to madrigals. In the performance of the opera *Orphée*, when the moment arrived that I listened for—Cerberus barking—a live little dog filled the role.

There was everything going on at once those days. Some way or another, the little Olivetti was seizing its chances, too. From across our hall, I heard it very well—its insistencies, its halts, and again its resuming, the long runs as if this runner could not now stop for breath. And we didn't leave out driving nearly every day to visit South Hill—what else was the Studebaker for?

At South Hill Katherine Anne and I sat in the meadow downhill from what was going on, and watched the building slowly come to pass before our eyes. For the plain, century-old house (looking something like an ark) that she was making her own, the elation, the intensity, the triumph, the impatience of her vision of it took hold of her afresh every day. It made me aware that the planner was profoundly a story writer.

As I look back now, I believe she was putting the house together like a story in her head, restoring to it its history—a story that had as much to do with her past as it had to do with her future. It was a work-in-progress she was highly conscious of, and scrupulously attentive to, a self-assignment she was meeting, an autobiographical deadline.

"How far along *is* the Introduction?" wrote John Woodburn to me. How hard this was on John too, and how well I knew it! He adored Katherine Anne. He had travelled up to Yaddo to ask her in person if she would write the Introduction; they'd celebrated the agreement in Saratoga Springs in the grandeur of the United States Hotel; and he was a sensitive man. *He* couldn't ask her a word about it now, either. But I could hear the groan in his words to me: "Get it out of her *now*, kid! Do you want our book *postponed?*"

It was postponed. The day the Introduction was due came and went, and at Yaddo I had never mentioned it to Katherine Anne. But I had *been* there. And I still was there—the live-in visitor from Porlock. I think now, in this long retrospect, that she made a daily brave attempt to forget about the interfering deadline for the moment at hand,

and that what I was actually doing there was helping her forget it. At any rate, *this* was a success. And though I would not have known it at the time, this Introduction was undoubtedly only one of the things Katherine Anne was being pressed to do. She was constitutionally a besieged woman.

I'd begun to realize that the summer was of a kind not unexpected by Katherine Anne. Her whole writing life was one of interruptions, and interruptions of the interruptions. I was to learn that writers do generally live that way, and not entirely without their own collusion. No help ever comes, unless in the form of still another interruption.

The one thing that was uninterrupted in her life was her seriousness of intent. And when I look back, I seem to see her surrounded entirely by papers, by pages or galley sheets, by her work—"Old Mortality," "The Leaning Tower," and, on that blue typewriter paper, stretches of the novel. It seemed then that she was always writing. *Writing*—its conception—was ever-present to her. At Yaddo, at South Hill equally; writing was the future of her house, the *intention* of her house. And writing was—yes, even for her—very hard to do.

To me it came as no shock that writing itself, the act, might always be hard. The better the writer, the harder writing knew how to be. In fact, the harder Katherine Anne's work was for her, the more exhilarated, liberated my own spirits were accordingly. What I felt able to understand for myself was that writing well was for the writer worth whatever it took. The difficulty that accompanies you is less like the dark than like a trusted lantern to see your way by. I hoped proudly for myself that acknowledging and valuing the role of difficulty in writing well would remain always with me. Katherine Anne was helping me to recognize living with difficulty as a form of passion.

Certainly I was slower in learning to know Katherine Anne than I believed I was in the summer at Yaddo. Our friendship had shown me day after day the enchanting brightness she could shed around her, but it was later, through letters she wrote when we were no longer in the same place, laughing, that I became to any degree aware of the dark, its other side, which she lived with on its own terms in equally close commune. I wondered in retrospect if hers hadn't been the sort of exultation that can arise—must arise—out of some equally intense sadness, wondered if, as South Hill was taking shape before her eyes, there wasn't also something else in the course of being left behind. She was combatting unhappiness, even desolation, I now think, through that whole summer and for times longer than that, and bravely.

John Woodburn sent me the last of his bulletins in August, to Jackson where I'd returned: "Baby: Here is the Introduction, unproofread, which I finally got out of Katherine Anne by distilling her. There was no other way...."

In the end, of course, she had written her magnificent Introduction "very quickly," she told me. And all her generosity, her penetration, serenely informs it, doing everything in her power for the book and for its author, as she'd intended to do all the time.

It is time itself—there was never any use denying—that is forever the enemy. I learned in those early days that K.A.P. would always take on any enemy—and time in particular—with a deep measure of respect. The price of writing that Introduction had to have been the postponement of something else. As well we know, *Ship of Fools* suffered many another postponement to follow this, the one she assumed that summer for introducing *A Curtain of Green*.

Katherine Anne wrote to me:

Yaddo, Saratoga Springs, New York
August 27, 1941

Dear Eudora:

I go on missing you quite steadily, the whole place changed when you went, though the activities kept on. I got to Albany by bus, not too dull, and at good hours, but there was a grim air of business about the trips, no more pleasant escapade in the morning air, no unexpected finding of Hindu wool rugs, no fun, in a word. My eyes managed to give me the worst upset in my nerves of anything I have known in my life. I was almost reduced to a state of pure terror, night and day, for the better part of a week. My efforts to conceal my state made it worse; I wished to collapse, to tell my troubles, to call upon God for help. I cannot be blind, that is the one thing I would make no attempt to face . . .

. . . Far from being part of the pressure, your preface is gone, accepted, perhaps set up in galleys by now. I came home with my goggles on fine afternoons, sat down and batted out that opus in two evenings' very pleasant work, mailed it special delivery and received some very kind and pleasant words of rejoicing from John Broadside; so have that off your mind as it is off ours . . . . Now of course I think of some other things I might have said to good effect, I wish I had gone a little more into certain stories, such as A Memory, Old Mr. Marblehall, and so on. But I can do it later when I write about your work again in another place. For certainly I expect to do so.

. . . I am being moved from North Farm to the Mansion for the month of September, since a new set are going to be settled here. This weekend must be spent packing, sending half my things to storage, taking mss. and music with me, and all. But I shall make quick work of it and work there as well as I can. South Hill is going faster, all at once, the plastering is begun, I should think that is a good sign. Every time I see it, I am pleased with it, it really is my house and just the one I wanted. And some day we will cook our supper on a charcoal grill in that terrace fireplace, maybe with snow outside, and the fire shining through the windows on it . . .

. . . To work, to work. It has always been later than I thought, but now it is later than ever . . . still I expect to make the deadline this time, the fourth for the novel . . . it just rolls along, I don't worry about it any more; there is this about all that space, it allows such a long line of continuity, and time for cumulative effect; and I always did know what I wanted to say in this book, my mind hasn't changed, and how could I write anything that didn't belong there? I trust myself, at last.

You trust yourself, too, darling. You are as good as there is in your time, and you have a long way to go and to grow, I can't see the end of it, thank God . . .

With my love,
K.A.

I missed her too, and a long life of correspondence started between us, easygoing and as the spirit moved us—about reading, recipes, anxieties and aspirations, garden seeds and gossip. She'd never let me thank her for the Guggenheim, or Yaddo, or possibly even the Introduction, in any proper way. But *she* was a born thanker, for any miscellaneous trifle that might come in the mail from me, wanting to make her laugh:

> Yaddo, Saratoga Springs, New York
> October 7, 1941

> Dear Eudora:
>   The sugar cane arrived in the most mysterious style, fascinating to think about: in one very short piece with the address tag on it, and a long stalk simply accompanying it, with not even a piece of string on it, unaddressed, un-everything, independent, unattached, there was nothing to stop it from going on to some destination it might have liked better, or turning in its tracks and bolting back to Mississippi again. But no, it stuck to its companion, and came in as it were under its own steam. And how good it tastes: I am still occasionally sitting down with a sharp knife and stripping off a section and gnawing away at it. My father told me once that when he was a little boy, strange and new to Texas, he and his slightly elder brother ran away to Louisiana because they were so homesick for the sight and taste of sugar cane. I put that in a story once. I know better now just how they felt, though . . .

> Katherine Anne

◆ ◆ ◆

Doubleday was giving a party for *A Curtain of Green* in November, in New York, and of course Katherine Anne's presence was called for. "I take for granted in some strange way that I am to be in New York for your party, it doesn't seem possible that I should miss it," Katherine Anne wrote from Yaddo on October 19. But on November 5, a telegram followed to tell me in New York, where I'd already arrived:

Dear Eudora, be happy and gay at your coming out party and remember me just enough to console me a little for not being there. All the good luck and reward in the world to you. You deserve everything. I hope to see you there or here before you go home. With my love, Katherine Anne.

She continued to work on restoring South Hill, and finally a letter arrived, dated August 28, 1942, on handsome letter paper only slightly different a shade of blue from her familiar typing paper, imprinted with SOUTH HILL, R.D. 3, Ballston Spa, New York. It reads in part:

Dear Eudora:

   This is the very first letter on the very first page of the letter paper, and this is the first day I have been here by myself. You can hardly imagine the confusion of household gear piled up here and there, but this nice south east room upstairs is in a bare and lovely order, with my table set up and the work-lamp ready, and when I look out I see the maples and the front meadow on my left and the corner of the sun room and part of the east meadow on the right.

   . . . I must get settled in before the winter closes around us. Now you can think of me as here: Caroline Slade came this morning with a big, flat basket of vegetables from her garden, beautiful as a bouquet, every little carrot and tomato and celery head all washed and polished, and I put the parsley and some celery leaves in a bottle of sauterne vinegar at once, thinking you cannot begin too early with such things.

   . . . Here all is weeds and unkemptedness, but the rosa regosa and white lilacs I planted in April are flourishing, it was a lucky rainy summer for I had to leave them to their fate almost at once. They didn't mind at all. They will be strong and fine for transplanting in the spring. They started as little dry sticks and are now green full little bushes. And so other things may go as well too . . .

♦ ♦ ♦

For a few months her letters continued to be full of pleasure and happiness and invitations. But when winter arrived and closed her in, she grew too cold, and her old enemy pneumonia caught up with her and defeated her. South Hill, like some earlier dreams, but a dream completed this time, had to be put behind her.

By December 28, 1946, she was writing to me from Santa Monica, California. "I live within six blocks of the Pacific," she says. "Sometimes at midnight I hear that desperate creature beating its brains out on the beach, but musically. At last I have some of my books and music; this little place is like a birdcage, open and round, and I have sat here on the edge of my chair for a year, thinking any minute I may find a house of my own . . . I bought a little mountain top in the Mojave desert, after selling South Hill to the Willisons—did you read his *Saints and Strangers?* a fine piece of historical writing . . . I feel well. The novel is not finished, but I think now I have my road cleared a little, there is always so much to be done about other things, other people. But it does really seem that maybe I have reached the end of that, too."

Georgia Review, Spring/Summer 1990, pages 13–27. Notes to the text are Welty's.

1. The use of an ellipsis in K.A.P.'s letters, when the letters appear in their entirety, is her own. When I quote segments of her letters in passing, I have indicated by ellipsis that the quote is an excerpt.

2. My literary agent in New York in the newly formed firm of Russell & Volkening. Katherine Anne was considering his offer to act as her agent. But she preferred in the end acting on her own.

3. His and Rose Russell's second child, William.

4. This short novel was later published separately by Doubleday.

Acceptance Speech for the National Book Foundation's Medal for Distinguished Contribution to American Letters

When I was about nine years old, a newspaper advertisement appeared in the Memphis *Commercial Appeal* inviting children to write a jingle and win a prize, in praise of a product named Jackie Mackie Pine Oil. It must have been a household lubricant, for use on sewing machines and squeaky hinges and the like. Whatever it was, an invitation was all I needed: I responded.

In my jingle, Jackie Mackie worked a spell. I turned him into a magician. My instinct was right, in one respect. A jingle, as well as a poem, a story, does involve magic. My jingle won first prize, and my mother said she wasn't surprised. Jackie Mackie sent me a check for $25. The time was that of World War I. I remember because my prize was converted into a War Bond, helping to defeat Kaiser Bill.

But all writers here will understand the important thing I was finding out: the joy of sending something you had written out into the world. You discover that somebody—not your mother—at the other end will actually read it. Whatever happens to it, this written word that goes forth from you now exists. It has a life of its own.

I loved from the first, as a child, the act itself of writing. The act could not be separated from the story. They spring up, grew, and came along, together. Each story became, for the time being, my teacher. So what serious writer could ever come to the end without starting another, starting anew?

The editors and the publishers, and the literary agents who have entirely made it possible for my work to appear, for my work to continue, I shall think of out of the clearest of vision and with love. Some of them are present here tonight. Those who are no longer in the world are present to me in spirit.

My father and my mother, my two brothers, would have been expecting it of me to make a better speech than I am making, to express their pride and my gratitude in this moment, all in one. That too supports me.

It is for all these people that I practice my art.

Yes, I regard writing as an art, an art of communication. We each in our own way will keep on with, and practice as well as we can, what it can keep teaching us to do. There are more stories to write—always more.

To the National Book Foundation I would like to say that your wonderful prize tonight is wonderful too in not being an end in itself. It can encourage an eighty-two-year-old. It's now on to the next story. In the prospect of work emerging—or for that especially—I now most deeply thank you.

20 November 1991, www.nationalbook.org/nbaacceptspeech_ewelty.html.

Index

CPSIA information can be obtained
at www.ICGtesting.com
Printed in the USA
FFHW021840121218
49851702-54407FF

9 781496 821072